Bad Bill Dahlen

ALSO BY LYLE SPATZ
AND FROM MCFARLAND

Yankees Coming, Yankees Going: New York Yankees
Player Transactions, 1903 Through 1999 (2000)

New York Yankee Openers: An Opening Day History
of Baseball's Most Famous Team, 1903–1996 (1997)

Bad Bill Dahlen

The Rollicking Life and Times of an Early Baseball Star

LYLE SPATZ

McFarland & Company, Inc., Publishers

Jefferson, North Carolina, and London

LIBRARY OF CONGRESS CATALOGUING-IN-PUBLICATION DATA

Spatz, Lyle, 1937–
    Bad Bill Dahlen : the rollicking life and times of an
early baseball star / Lyle Spatz.
      p.   cm.
    Includes bibliographical references and index.

    ISBN 0-7864-1978-4 (softcover : 50# alkaline paper) ∞

    1. Dahlen, Bill, b. 1870.   2. Baseball players—United States—
Biography. I. Title.
GV865.D25S63   2004
796.357'092—dc22   2004015875

British Library cataloguing data are available

On the cover: Background ©2004 Wood River Gallery. Foreground
Dahlen as a member of the Brooklyn Superbas, one of baseball's
unrecognized great teams

Manufactured in the United States of America

McFarland & Company, Inc., Publishers
  Box 611, Jefferson, North Carolina 28640
   www.mcfarlandpub.com

For my sons, Dana and Glenn,
who have brought me continuous joy
from the moments they were born

"If Dahlen had devoted his entire time to baseball, he'd have been the greatest infielder of all time."
— Hall of Fame shortstop Hugh Jennings

Acknowledgments

While dreading omitting anyone, I would like to thank the following people for their kind assistance in my getting this book written. Bob Moyer, of Fort Plain, New York, was at Cooperstown for the first Hall of Fame induction ceremony in 1939. Along with the late Bob Diefendorf, he has devoted years in trying to get Bill Dahlen elected to the Hall. Bob was a source of much local information, as was Sandy Cronkhite, the historian for the Village of Fort Plain. Also from the Mohawk Valley is Mat Rapacz, a reporter for the *Little Falls Evening Times*. Mat had done his own research on Bill Dahlen's career, which he generously shared with me. Chicago baseball historian Ed Hartig helped me immeasurably with his knowledge of all things related to the Chicago team of the 1890s. David Vincent, keeper of the Society for American Baseball Research's (SABR) Home Run Log, supplied me with all the details of Dahlen's 84 career home runs. David Smith, founder and president of *Retrosheet*, seemed to have every piece of information I asked for, which was a lot.

Members of SABR, as always, were ever ready to assist where needed. I have already mentioned Ed Hartig, Dave Vincent, and Dave Smith, but there were others who helped in one way or another. They include Mark Armour, Ellen Canepari, Bill Deane, Joe Dittmar, Eric Enders, Bob McConnell, Peter Morris, Pete Palmer, Bob Schaefer, and Dick Thompson. Thanks also to Paul Wendt and Tom Simon, chairmen of SABR's Nineteenth Century Committee and Deadball Era Committee, the two time periods that encompassed Dahlen's career. I could always rely on members of both committees to supply answers to my most trivial questions.

All season and career statistics come from the seventh edition of *Total Baseball*.

Table of Contents

Acknowledgements   vii

Introduction   1

One — From Nelliston to Chicago   3

Two — The Best Young Player in the Game   8

Three — A Record-Breaking Hitting Streak   23

Four — "A Disorderly Element," but Another
          Marvelous Season   34

Five — The Captain Becomes Expendable   47

Six — A Trade to Brooklyn Brings a Championship   60

Seven — One of the Great Teams of All Time   74

Eight — The American League Comes Calling   93

Nine — "It Has Always Been My Ambition to Play in
          New York City"   110

Ten — The Most Hated Team in Baseball   124

Eleven — From "Bad Bill" to "Bill the Wizard"   136

Twelve — The Giants Fade, and So Does Dahlen   149

Thirteen — Banished to Boston   160

Fourteen — Managing the Dodgers   170

Fifteen — Building a Contender — for Someone Else   184

Sixteen — The End of the Line   199

Seventeen — From Nelliston to Cooperstown   206 x **Table of Contents**

Appendix A: Bill Dahlen and His Hall of Fame Contemporaries   209

Appendix B: Bill Dahlen and Hall of Fame Shortstops   212

Appendix C: Bill Dahlen's Lifetime Batting Statistics   217

Appendix D: Bill Dahlen's Lifetime Fielding Statistics   219

Notes   221

Selected Bibliography   232

Index   235

Introduction

Baseball historians will always designate one ex-major leaguer as "the best ballplayer not in the Hall of Fame." The term, as it is used, does not apply to those who have recently retired. It is for those who have been out of the game for years, but just have not received their due. Their cause is most often championed by their fans, certain members of the media, and those that played with and against them. Many recent inductees, men like Richie Ashburn, Orlando Cepeda, Nellie Fox, Bill Mazeroski, and Tony Perez, were all at one time or another thought, at least by their supporters, to be "the best ballplayer not in the Hall of Fame." However, for many historians whose study of the game takes them beyond the year of their own birth, that title for years has belonged to Bill Dahlen.

It is common knowledge that after their careers are over the reputations of some players grow while others decline, and still others just seem to get lost in the shuffle. Somehow, Bill Dahlen has gotten lost in the shuffle. The mention of his name, even to the most erudite of baseball scholars, brings either blank stares, or, occasionally, a faint glimmer of name recognition. Thus, the intention of this book is to familiarize current generations with Dahlen's career and his accomplishments and to provide them with the information necessary to decide his Hall of Fame worthiness.

Dahlen was a major presence in baseball for almost a quarter-century, during a period of enormous growth for the national game. He began his big league career as the National League's outstanding rookie with Cap Anson's 1891 Chicago Colts. His debut took place just one year after major league baseball had survived its most divisive season ever, with the established National League and American Association triumphing over the upstart Players League. His career continued through 1913, when he managed the Brooklyn Dodgers in their first season at Ebbets Field. By then the American Association was long gone, and the American League had risen up to gain equal status with the Nationals.

1

When Dahlen's active career ended, in 1909, he had played in more games (2,444) than anyone in major league history.[1] He also stood second in walks and in total plate appearances, and in the top 10 in runs batted in, extra base hits, singles, and stolen bases. Additionally, he ranked 11th in runs, hits, doubles, and total bases, and 13th in triples and home runs.

And, it is important to remember, Dahlen achieved these lofty offensive rankings while playing shortstop, a position traditionally more valued for its defense.[2] Most everyone above him on those lists were outfielders and first basemen, positions where the principal contributions were expected to come on offense. Dahlen, of course, ranked much higher among those who were primarily shortstops, a group that included future Hall-of-Famers Honus Wagner, George Davis, Hugh Jennings, and Bobby Wallace. Among these contemporaries, he was first in games played, runs, home runs, and walks, second in runs batted in, hits, triples, total bases, and extra base hits, and third in doubles and stolen bases.

Defensively, among the shortstops of his day, Dahlen was the leader in putouts, assists, successful chances accepted, and double plays. And amazingly, considering that he played in an era of rocky infields and mitten-sized gloves, only one shortstop from any era — Rabbit Maranville — has exceeded Dahlen's total putouts, and just two — Ozzie Smith and Luis Aparico — have topped him in total assists. Roger Peckinpaugh broke his record for most career double plays in 1925, while Maranville passed him in career putouts in 1930 and in career games at shortstop in 1931. Dahlen's mark for total assists, the one exceeded by Aparicio, lasted for 61 years.

Dahlen was "a cat on his feet, a sure fielder, and one of the quickest thinking players of his day" wrote the *Reach Guide* for 1924 in looking back on his career 15 years after he had played his final game.[3] "He was always a step ahead of the opposition, and usually he thought too quickly even for his partners at second and third base. There never was a ballplayer with a keener intuition than Dahlen nor one more capable of carrying out his intuitions."

Are Dahlen's rankings indicative of a career worthy of Hall of Fame recognition? Is Bill Dahlen the best shortstop not in the Hall of Fame, the best player of his era not in the Hall of Fame, or perhaps the best overall player of any era not in the Hall of Fame? Is he one, two, or all three of the above, or does he not belong at all? I hope over the course of this book to recount Dahlen's career, the good and the bad, and make the case for why I think he belongs in Cooperstown.

ONE

From Nelliston to Chicago

The small Montgomery County village of Nelliston sits on the east side of the Mohawk River, situated almost directly in the center of New York state. For a time in the late 17th century, what is now Nelliston had been the capital of the Mohawk Indian nation. Directly across the river is Fort Plain, a larger village, with whom Nelliston's history has forever been entwined. The first white people to settle in the area were mostly from a minor German state called the Palatinate, described as "a lovely land of forests and vineyards, towering peaks, romantic castles and rich corn plains on the banks of the Rhine."[1] The Palatines left in response to the political turmoil that enveloped much of Europe in the late 17th and early 18th centuries. They made their way down the Rhine to Holland, later to England, and as early as 1710 began to establish settlements in America. Those settlements were mainly along the Hudson River in the British colony of New York. Within several years, many Palatine families moved west, remaining in the New York colony but settling in and around the Mohawk Valley. Among the early settlers in Nelliston was the Nellis family, for whom they named the village of Nelliston.

Germany also provided the next great wave of immigration to the area, which came in the mid-19th century. Two ingredients fueled that exodus: four consecutive years of bad harvests and the revolutions of 1848 that swept most of the European continent. German historian Veit Valentin estimates the number of those who emigrated from Germany between 1849 and 1854 at 1.1 million, approximately 2.5 percent of the population.[2] Most went to America, with a large number from southern Germany settling in the Mohawk Valley. German families continued to arrive in Nelliston throughout the second half of the nineteenth century. So many arrived in that era that German became the language used in most of the homes and churches.

Daniel Dahlen, born in the Palatinate in March 1832, was one of those who came in the 1850s. A popular man, trusted by his neighbors, he won election as Nelliston's second president in 1881, a position comparable to a current-day mayor. Dahlen eventually became the most prominent of the Germans who migrated to that area of New York. He was a master mason, remembered by locals for having "built most of the brick blocks in (nearby) Canajoharie and Fort Plain."[3] Dahlen Street, named in his honor and still in use today, was opened in August 1885, two weeks before his death on September 2.

Daniel Dahlen married twice, both times to the daughters of men who had been earlier immigrants. Coincidentally, the two men were now next-door neighbors. Elizabeth Swartz, the daughter of Christian Swartz, bore Daniel a daughter before passing away at an early age. In December 1868, he married Rosina Shellhorne, the daughter of John Shellhorne. Daniel and Rosina had five children. Two, Daniel G. and Frank, died young, but three boys grew to manhood: Daniel Jr., Harry, and William.[4]

William Frederick "Bill" Dahlen was born at his parents' home (on what would later become Dahlen Street) in Nelliston on January 5, 1870. Young Bill was a self-proclaimed "live wire" and practical joker as a boy, although many of his neighbors, along with the workmen and merchants of Nelliston, would have thought a pest (or perhaps worse) was a better description. Certainly one group of men who worked for Bill's father did not appreciate a "joke" he played on them one night.

As a contract mason, Daniel Dahlen often had up to a dozen men in his employ, some of whom he boarded at the Dahlen household. Cattle hair, used to make wall plaster more adhesive and blanketlike, was an important ingredient in building houses in those days. Bill thought it would be great fun to place several strands of this cattle hair between the sheets of the beds slept in by the six masons then boarding. His prank led to a night of mysterious itching by the masons, which in turn led to a trip to the woodshed by Bill and his father. The result of that visit, Bill later remembered, required his "eating his meals standing for the next few days."[5]

Another session in the woodshed came after a prank with potentially far more serious consequences than a night of itching. Nelliston was a one-store town in Bill's youth, a grocery store that had as its centerpiece a long glass case filled with candy. Conrad Shellhorne, Bill's uncle on his mother's side, owned the store. Although recognized by the villagers as reputable and honest, Shellhorne, whom almost everyone called "Coon," also had a reputation for "frugality" and grouchiness. So while the candy he sold made regular customers of Nelliston's youngsters, his appearance and demeanor — he was fat, had a beard, and spoke with a thick German accent — made him a natural target for those same youngsters. The boys, and especially Bill, were a constant source of irritation to him. One day, Bill and another boy decided to use the large plate glass window at the front of Coon's store as a way to "put a scare" into the grouchy grocer. The window was Shellhorne's pride and joy. A rarity for Montgomery County back then, he had installed it at great expense. A self-published local history describes young Bill's participation in the "prank."

> One night after obtaining a lot of worthless glass and a shot gun, he and a confederate engaged in a fake quarrel in front of Coon's store, and when it was the loudest and had gained attention inside the store, Bang! went the shotgun and to the sidewalk went the worthless glass. Coon's first thought of horror had to do with that fine glass front, and with a groan he fell helpless to the floor. A physician was summoned and a case of apoplexy was side-tracked. Subsequent investigation revealed to Coon that the much-loved glass was intact, a desirable condition that convinced Dahlen's father that the worst thing due to the mischievous lad was more woodshed calisthenics.[6]

As a youngster, Bill attended the Nelliston school, a brick building completed the year before he was born. Beyond making mischief, he loved playing baseball, which he started doing on the Nelliston sandlots at age 10. Dahlen later recalled that the first ball he played with was made of yarn with a covering supplied by the village harness maker. In 1887, at age 17, he enrolled in the Clinton Liberal Institute, a coeducational boarding school in Fort Plain. It was his baseball ability that got him there. Clinton paid his tuition in return for his serving as a pitcher and occasional second baseman for the school's baseball team.

Founded under the auspices of the Universalist Church in Clinton, New York, the school had relocated to Fort Plain in 1879, where most of the population, including Bill, was Lutheran. The CLI overlooked the town, occupying nine and one-half acres of landscaped grounds atop Seminary Hill, also known as Institute Hill. Future president Grover Cleveland had graduated from the Clinton Liberal Institute, as did Simon Lake, the inventor of the modern-day submarine. Clara Barton, the first president of the American Red Cross, also attended for a year in 1851.

Terry Collins, a retired history teacher, a trustee of the Fort Plain Museum and the author of the only published history of the Clinton Liberal Institute, believes the CLI was a cross between a high school and a junior college. "They had courses that ranged from sub-high school to a four-year college program," he wrote. "Students ranged, as I understand it, from about twelve up to their early twenties."[7]

Clinton was in a Mohawk Valley area prep school league, one that included teams from Utica, Rome, and Little Falls. Dahlen played three years of baseball there before signing late in the 1889 season to play for a semipro club in Cobbleskill, New York, for $40 a month. Though primarily a pitcher at Clinton, he became a second baseman at Cobbleskill. "I could always hit, and they wanted me in the game every day," Dahlen would recall more than half a century later.[8] The next year, Cobbleskill entered the New York State League, and 20–year-old second baseman Bill Dahlen was a professional baseball player. When Cobbleskill folded very late in the 1890 season, Dahlen joined the Albany team of that league. He appeared for Albany in its final game, playing second base and batting fourth. His combined batting average for the two clubs was .343, the New York State League's second best. Dahlen also finished second among second basemen in fielding average, while his 137 hits and 18 triples were league highs.

Although Albany manager Thomas York had signed Dahlen to a contract for 1891, others had watched and been impressed with his play at Cobbleskill. Dahlen's outstanding season had attracted the attention of Joe Battin, an umpire in the league and a former major league third baseman. Battin had played with Cap Anson on the 1873–74 Philadelphia Athletics of the old National Association. He recommended Dahlen to his former teammate, now the manager and star first baseman of the National League's Chicago White Stockings, who immediately signed him.[9] York, claiming that Dahlen belonged to him, protested the signing vigorously, but unsuccessfully. National League president Nicholas Young ruled that because the Albany club was not part of the national agreement it had no legal claim to retain Dahlen, and that he was free to sign with Chicago.

Not yet 21 years old and every inch a product of small-town America, Dahlen was on his way to America's second largest city.[10] Yet if his own campaign of self-promotion had succeeded, he would have been joining the Philadelphia Athletics of the soon-to-be abolished American Association, rather than what was already one of baseball's most celebrated teams. In 1896, when Dahlen was a five-year veteran and an established star, Washington Senators president J. Earle Wagner told of receiving a letter from this brash young infielder in the summer of 1890. Wagner was associated with the Philadelphia Quakers of the Players League that year, but would move to the Athletics when that league folded, and then to Washington when they got absorbed into the National League in 1892.

In his letter, Dahlen was offering his services to the Quakers at the bargain price of just $75 a month. Wagner, however, was not interested, saying he would never sign a player without having first seen him play. "The purchase of a young ballplayer is as big a risk as buying an untried two-year-old race horse. And players, like race horses, have their good and bad years," he said.[11]

Actually, a third team had almost entered the bidding for Dahlen's services in 1891. Sam Crane, a weak-hitting second baseman, was finishing a well-traveled, if extremely mediocre, career with Jim Mutrie's New York Giants in 1890. Crane, who had also managed briefly, would go on to a long and distinguished career writing baseball, primarily for William Randolph Hearst's *New York Journal*. Years later, he would recall being so excited after seeing Dahlen play second base for Cobbleskill that he tried to get manager Mutrie to sign him for the Giants.

But baseball was in turmoil in 1890, and no team more so than the Giants. The two existing major leagues, the National League and the already weakened American Association, were in a fight for survival. Teams in both those leagues were losing their biggest stars to the Players League, a breakaway league started by the Brotherhood of Professional Baseball Players, the game's first players union. For the 1890 season, the Players League had positioned teams in eight big league cities, challenging the teams already there for fan support and fan dollars. The biggest battle was, of course, in the biggest city, New York. If they could win the battle there, the Brotherhood believed, they could crush the National League.

So while all teams suffered defections, the Giants, the defending world champions, suffered the most. Gone were Buck Ewing, Roger Connor, Tim Keefe, Cannonball Crane, Jim O'Rourke, George Gore, and Danny Richardson, all of whom had contributed to that 1889 championship team. The war with the Players League so depleted Giants owner John Day of funds that the National League had been forced to bail him out. Whether it was because their attention was focused on the ongoing struggle for New York supremacy or because they lacked the money, Day and Mutrie passed on Crane's recommendation. Both would be long gone from the Giants when Dahlen eventually joined the New Yorkers in 1904.

TWO

The Best Young Player in the Game

The Chicago club that Bill Dahlen joined in 1891 was a charter member of the National League of Professional Baseball Clubs, which had been established at a meeting in New York's Grand Central Hotel on February 2, 1876. William Hulbert, a Chicagoan who was then president of the Chicago White Stockings of the National Association, was the organizer of the meeting and the driving force of the new league. Founded in 1871, the association was baseball's first "major" league. However, weak organization, failing and shifting franchises, roughneck and unruly players, and betting scandals had plagued it throughout its five-year existence. Along with Hulbert's Chicago team, the other seven original National League franchises represented Boston, Cincinnati, Hartford, Louisville, New York, Philadelphia, and St. Louis.[1]

With an offer to raise his salary by $500 and allocate 25 percent of the gate receipts to him, Hulbert was able to lure Albert G. Spalding from the Boston Red Stockings to his White Stockings. Led by Spalding, one of the game's first great pitchers, Chicago won the pennant that first season. Besides managing the team, Spalding was also on the mound for 47 of its 52 victories. But after a disappointing 1877 season — a fifth-place finish in a six-team league — Spalding gave up the managerial reins, choosing instead to remain in the front office. He also began to devote more of his time to his growing sporting goods business. Hartford manager Bob Ferguson was brought in to take Spalding's place, but he lasted just one season. When the team could do no better than split their 60 decisions in 1878, Spalding named his first baseman, Cap Anson, to lead the White Stockings in 1879.

Under Anson, one of the great batsmen of all time, the club embarked

8

on a dozen years of great success. They won consecutive pennants in 1880, 1881, and 1882, and again in 1885 and 1886. Three other times they finished second. One second-place finish came in the tumultuous 1890 season, when they trailed pennant-winning Brooklyn by just six games, a very creditable showing for a team badly depleted by defections to the Players League.

Anson had lost most of his best players for the 1890 season. Gone were outfielders Jimmy Ryan, George Van Haltren, and Hugh Duffy; infielders Fred Pfeffer and Ned Williamson; catcher Duke Farrell; and pitchers Ad Gumbert, John Tener, and Frank Dwyer. Now that the Players League had collapsed after just one season, several of his key players were returning. Chief among them were center fielder Ryan, one of the league's top players, although he had never gotten along well with Anson; Pfeffer, a speedy second baseman who had batted fifth behind Anson for five seasons; and Gumbert, a 28-game winner for Chicago in 1889 who had won 23 for Boston's Brotherhood champions in 1890.

Adding these proven veterans to the young holdovers from the '90 team, plus the addition of promising newcomer Bill Dahlen, had Chicago fans predicting a pennant for their Colts in 1891.[2] Dahlen, rated as a coming star by all who had seen him, was one of two rookies trying to make this year's team. The other was Louis Graff, a catcher. Graff had caught one game for Syracuse of the American Association in 1890, which, as it turned out, would be the sum of his big league career.

Anson was a demanding leader, loved by the Chicago fans but hardly adored by his own players. He drove them relentlessly while using bed checks, fines, and Pinkerton detectives to keep them in line. Possessed of a loud, booming voice, he used it to intimidate both umpires and young players. A major innovator of the "spring training" concept, he demanded that his players report when ordered. This year he had made the unusual choice of conducting the training sessions in Denver. As his critics had warned might happen, wintry weather plagued the club throughout its stay. The *Chicago Tribune* suggested that the Colts would do well to break even against their first two regular-season opponents, Pittsburgh and Cincinnati, both of whom had trained in the South. After breaking camp, the team played its way across the Midwest, concluding the trip with a 10–3 win at Fort Wayne. The next day, April 22, Dahlen made his big league debut as Chicago opened the season at Pittsburgh's Exposition Park.

When the Pittsburgh team, newly named the Pirates, arrived home, a letter from a group of fans was waiting for manager Ned Hanlon. The letter asked that Hanlon choose veteran pitcher Jim Galvin to start the opener. Galvin had pitched for the club from 1887 through 1889 and for their predecessor, the Pittsburgh Alleghenies of the American Association, before that. After spending the 1890 season with the city's entry in the now defunct Players League, he was returning to the National League.

Whether or not that letter exerted any influence on Hanlon is unknown, and unlikely; nevertheless, he did choose Galvin as his opening-day pitcher. Anson countered with Bill Hutchison, who was in the midst of what would be a 13-consecutive-game win streak against the Pirates. A graduate of Yale, Hutchison had led the National League with 42 wins in 1890. He would lead again this season, with 44 wins, and tie Cleveland's Cy Young for the lead with 36 in 1892.[3]

For his debut, Dahlen batted third and played third base, serving as a replacement for sore-armed Tom Burns. Chicago jumped ahead early, building a 5–0 lead, but squandered the advantage and had to score a ninth-inning run to send the game into extra innings. Dahlen opened the 10th with a long triple, his second hit of the game, and eventually scored the winning run in the Colts' 7–6 victory.

The rookie's hitting and fielding made a very favorable impression on Joe Murphy of the *Chicago Tribune*. "Young Dahlen played the base well today and made two hits," he said. "He is one of the most promising players that have ever shown in this country. He has speed, a cool head, and a splendid movement."[4] High praise for a rookie, yet when Dahlen was caught napping on the base paths against Pittsburgh two days later, the same reporter took note of his inexperience. "The team will be stronger when Tom Burns is back at third," wrote Murphy. "Dahlen is a most promising youngster, but he has much to learn, and while fast on the bases has little or no judgment."[5]

Young Bill Dahlen as he looked when he joined Cap Anson's 1891 Chicago Orphans.

Bill started his career in sensational fashion. He had nine hits in 18 at-bats as the Colts took three of four from Pittsburgh. He continued his hot hitting at Cincinnati, going three for eight in the first two games of the series. One of his hits was his first major league home run, which came off the Reds' Jesse Duryea. Billy Rhines held him hitless for the first time in the season's seventh game, but he homered again the next day, off Tony Mullane, and followed with five hits in eight at-bats against Pittsburgh.

The 21-year-old Dahlen's spectacular entrance into the National League did not go unnoticed. Barely three weeks into the season, the *Sporting News* was praising the rookie's excellent all-around play, calling him another "great catch" for Anson. "Dahlen, his new man," the paper said, "makes home runs [he had already slugged three] and phenomenal plays with charming regularity."[6] Later, in noting how well he was hitting, the paper said his rookie year could rival that of Bug Holliday in 1889. As a rookie with Cincinnati of the American Association that year, Holliday and Philadelphia's Harry Stovey had set the league record for home runs. Both were now in the National League: Holliday was with Cincinnati while Stovey was the leading slugger for the Boston Beaneaters.

On the morning of June 1, the Colts, at 20–11, were in first place, three and one-half games ahead of Pittsburgh. Meanwhile, Dahlen continued to impress almost all who saw him. After he homered in a 5–3 win at Boston, the reporter for the *Chicago InterOcean* called him "Anson's shrub" that was picked up somewhere on the plains, getting Dahlen's small-town origins correct, if mistakenly placing him in the wrong part of the country.[7] Like his colleague at the *Tribune*, he too was quick to criticize the rookie's lack of judgment. His game account of a 5–2 loss at Brooklyn in early June included comments such as "a stupid play by Dahlen" and "Dahlen seemed to be half asleep all day."[8]

Dahlen had been a major leaguer for less than two months, yet two Chicago writers were already praising his physical skills on the one hand while questioning his mental or emotional ones on the other. That dichotomy between his ability and his attitude, real or imagined, would be a recurring theme in the press throughout Bill's career. Not until he was nearing the end of his playing days did anyone question his day-to-day proficiency at batting, fielding, throwing, or running; yet, writers in every city he played in would at various times question his judgment, and more seriously, his dedication to the game.

A 14–6 drubbing by the Beaneaters on June 11 dropped Chicago into a first-place tie with the Giants as they headed to New York for a four-game series. The Giants won all four, concluding the sweep with an Amos Rusie shutout. In that 5–0 loss, Dahlen displayed his penchant for making both great defensive plays and poor or misguided ones in the same game. After making a spectacular catch of a foul fly, he threw wildly in an attempt for a double play, allowing the two runners on base to advance. He was also regularly chalking up errors, as was shortstop Jimmy Cooney, who played alongside him. For both men, many of those errors came on low throws to first base that Anson was no longer agile enough to dig out of the dirt.

After a loss the next day to Cleveland, the Colts fell to third, behind Boston, which thanks to a nine-game winning streak, was now second to New York. Then Anson's men started winning again, alternating with the Giants for the lead, while the Beaneaters remained within striking distance. Eventually, the Giants dropped out of the race, leaving Chicago and Boston to battle for the pennant. The Colts pulled ahead, but Boston used an 18-game winning streak to stage a sensational come-from-behind stretch run and win the pennant. However, it was a streak that was very suspect, and a pennant so tainted that it generated unprecedented resentment and controversy.

Chicago had run off a couple of midsummer win-streaks of their own. As July turned to August, the team had a seven-gamer which they followed with an 11-gamer in late August. The seven-game streak had come on the road, with three wins at Cleveland and four at Cincinnati, separated by an off day on July 29. That off day just happened to be the first day the trotters would be running at Cleveland's Glenville Race Track. Rather than traveling to Cincinnati after that final game against the Spiders, a group of Colts players wanted to remain in Cleveland and attend the races. That morning, a delegation made up of Pfeffer, Gumbert, Cooney, and outfielder Walt Wilmot approached Anson in the hotel lobby and made their appeal. After initially denying the request, Anson changed his mind that afternoon. The club would stay over, he said, but only if they won today's game. To make a win more likely, he chose Gumbert as his pitcher. According to Leonard Washburne of the *Inter Ocean*, Gumbert was a man who "would rather see a pacing race than eat."[9] Gumbert defeated the Spiders 6–3 with racing fans Cooney and Pfeffer contributing to the run scoring and playing flawlessly in the field. Dahlen misplayed a couple of fly balls in left field, but as Washburne said, it was because of the sun and not because the youngster had no wish to go to the races the next day. In fact, Dahlen was rapidly becoming a regular attendee at the Hawthorne and Garfield race tracks in the Chicago area, along with those in other National League cities. It was a habit he would never break.

On August 31, three days after Philadelphia ended the 11-game streak, the Colts and Giants treated Chicago fans to the best pitching duel of the season. Hutchison and Rusie battled to an 11-inning scoreless tie in a game eventually called by darkness. With the death of the Players League, the Colts were splitting this year's home schedule between two sites. Mondays, Wednesdays, and Fridays they played at West Side Park, their home since 1885. Tuesdays, Thursdays, and Saturdays they played at South Side Park, which the Players League's Chicago Pirates had used in 1890.

Chicago's lead was six games when it hosted second-place Boston on September 4. The Colts were so confident of winning the pennant victory that Anson entertained the crowd by wearing a white flowing beard throughout their 5–3 victory. The lead was now seven games, but 10 days later it was down to four and one-half as they prepared to face the Beaneaters in the final series between the two contenders. Wins in the first two games brought the lead back up to six and one-half games, seemingly enough to end any doubt that Anson's team would win the pennant. Reporters at the *Chicago Tribune* certainly were convinced of it. They were telling their readers that "The good captain's men are champions and no mistake."[10]

The scheduled pitchers in the finale of the series made the Boston cause appear even more bleak. For Frank Selee's Beaneaters it was Charles "Kid" Nichols, 0–9 lifetime against Chicago; and for Anson's Colts it was Bill Hutchison, already with eight wins against Boston this season. However, strong pitching by Nichols, together with seven Colts errors led to a Beaneaters victory. The win launched them on an 18-game winning-streak that would not end until the final day of the season. Boston clinched the pennant on October 1, beating Philadelphia 6–1 for their 17th consecutive victory. Meanwhile, Chicago was losing to Cincinnati by the same score.

Boston's 18 wins, 16 at home and two on the road, came at the expense of Philadelphia, Pittsburgh, Brooklyn, and New York, all Eastern teams. That Boston had mounted its streak against its regional neighbors led to a serious postseason accusation by Chicago president James Hart. Hart, appointed to the presidency at season's end by the retiring Albert Spalding, charged that the Eastern teams had conspired to make sure that Boston, not Chicago, won the pennant. He alleged that those Eastern clubs did not want the Colts, a team with the league's lowest payroll, to be its champion. Hart also believed that resentment against Anson still existed for his opposition to the Brotherhood-inspired Players League, many of whose former players were now back in the National League. Adding to the mix was the animosity Giants manager Jim Mutrie still harbored toward Anson over his refusal to play a postponed contest on an open date of the Giants choice.

Hart pointed to several instances during the streak where suspect fielding plays contributed to Boston victories. His charges centered mainly around a five-game series against the Giants that took place at Boston's South End Grounds on September 28–30 and included back-to-back doubleheaders. For this very crucial series, the Giants arrived without their two best pitchers, Rusie and John Ewing. Also absent were first baseman Roger Connor and second baseman Danny Richardson. Additionally, those Giants that did play did so in such a casual manner that *Sporting Life's* comment that "the New York's beat all records for indifferent and rocky playing," was typical of the reaction by the press.

The New York papers, normally fully supportive of the Giants, also voiced their suspicions. Why, they all asked, were Rusie and Ewing used against Chicago, but not against Boston? Under a headline in the September 30 *New York Evening Telegram* that read, *"Are The Giants Trying to Defeat Anson?"* the *Telegram* writer claimed that "Anson's opponents are doing all in their power to prevent him from winning, but it is doubtful if New York is trying to win. This is unfortunate for it will probably leave a stigma on the National game."[11]

The Giants lackadaisical play was so obvious that even the Boston fans booed their performance, and led Anson himself to accuse the Giants of deliberately losing the games. Word was that Boston gamblers had even refused to set odds on the Beaneaters-Giants contests.

On November 11, the league held a hearing at the Fifth Avenue Hotel in New York to consider the charges. Beyond the previous evidence presented, Hart offered two more alleged items of testimony. He claimed that 10 days before the Boston-New York series, umpire Jack McQuaid had told the Chicago players that the Beaneaters would win all five games. And, Hart added, several Cincinnati players had told certain Colts players that the Giants openly stated that they would do whatever was necessary to see that Boston won the pennant.[12]

Despite the seemingly overwhelming evidence to the contrary, owners Arthur Soden of Boston and John Day of New York[13] denied any wrongdoing, and they dismissed all charges. However, to this day both Boston's 18-game winning streak and its 1891 championship remain clouded with suspicion.[14]

For Dahlen, as for all the Chicago players, management, and fans, the season had ended in great disappointment. Yet personally, he had experienced a highly successful rookie year. In midseason, when Burns returned from his injury to take over at third, Anson had moved Bill to left field and later used him at shortstop. Appearing in all but two of Chicago's 137 games, and batting primarily out of the third position, Dahlen batted .260, with 18 doubles, 13 triples, and nine home runs. The nine home runs tied him for fourth highest in the league. Among his home run victims were National League stars Charley Radbourn, Kid Gleason, Tony Mullane, and John Clarkson (twice).

Dahlen also stole 21 bases, scored 114 runs, batted in 79, and led the club in at-bats and runs scored. He set or tied the Colts rookie records for games played, home runs, extra-base hits, and times hit by pitch.[15] The best offensive day of his rookie season came on July 24, against Cincinnati, when he batted in five runs. He also just missed hitting for the cycle, which commonly means lacking one of the extra-base hits, but in his case meant lacking a single.

Years after Dahlen's distinguished rookie season, Hart recalled his humble baseball beginnings. "Dahlen is one of the few now in the league who came blood new from a punky little league and became a good thing at first jump."[16] He ended up not having quite the year that Bug Holliday did in '89; nevertheless, had there been a Rookie of the Year Award in 1891, Dahlen would almost surely have been the unanimous choice.

Moreover, the fans in Chicago loved him, not only for his batting, but also for his outstanding fielding and quick-witted base running. Although he was not exceptionally fast, Dahlen was a scientific base runner. He had the skill that allowed him to take big leads and avoid tags by using a "straddle" or "hook" slide, in which he twisted his body away from the man trying to apply the tag. "When Bill Dahlen slides back into first base to avoid being caught napping, he does a split that any acrobat would be proud to possess," wrote *Sporting Life* many years later.[17]

"The man I found it hardest to touch with the ball as he came down to second from first base was Bill Dahlen," recalled Cubs second baseman Johnny Evers, whose team would stage so many great battles with Dahlen's Giants in the first decade of the 20th century. "Bill always tore straight down the base line, directly at the base, but there was no telling what he would do in the last ten feet of the distance. He had a way of anticipating where the ball would come from the catcher, and he played his slide to a nicety. Coming straight along he suddenly would drop on his hips, to one side or the other, spread his legs and then use the greatest cleverness in pulling out of reach and twisting himself to hook the bag with either foot."[18]

No one had been more unhappy with the way the 1891 season had ended than Cap Anson. Boston's tainted pennant and the league's exoneration of the clubs involved of any wrongdoing had left him bitterly disappointed. He was still grumbling about it when a change in the team's leadership left him with a new crisis to deal with. Albert Spalding had announced that while he would maintain his position as the Colts' major stockholder, he was turning over the presidency of the club to Jim Hart.

Spalding's decision was terrible news for Anson, his onetime teammate and current employee. The two had been together at Chicago since 1876, the first year of the National League. Exactly how much control Hart would have was not yet clear. But it would not be much if the writer of an article that appeared in the *Sporting News* was to be believed. "Of course everyone knows Al Spalding, the owner of the Chicago Club," he wrote. "Al's mouthpiece is Jim Hart, the nominal president of the club. Al pulls the strings and Jim spiels."[19]

Still, Anson's problem remained; he disliked Hart and Hart disliked him. The mutual antipathy between the two men dated from the club's world tour of 1888. Adding to the feud was Hart's belief that Anson was out of touch with the "modern" game. Anson, whose career began in the old National Association way back in 1871, was the only man who had been an active player in every one of the National League's 16 seasons of existence. For his part, Anson distrusted Hart, who he believed was plotting with the players against him.

In all, it was an unsettling time for the Colts and for the entire National League. For one, the controversy surrounding Boston's National League pennant still simmered. Even the rival American Association had taken note of it. At their annual meeting in Chicago, they congratulated all association members for having never taken part in any act of "hippodroming," the term then in use for deliberately losing games. The major event of their gathering, however, was the announcement that they were adding a Chicago franchise to compete with the Colts. But even before they would try to do so at the gate, the new team in town announced their intentions to sign several Colts players. Getting Dahlen was their main goal, but they also had their sights on veteran pitcher Ad Gumbert and second-year catcher Mal Kittridge. Gumbert was Chicago's number two pitcher, ranking behind only Bill Hutchison. Kittridge, one of the youngsters collectively known as "Anson's Colts," had taken over as the team's catcher after Duke Farrell left for the Players League.

Hall of Fame pitcher Jim Galvin was in his final season when he yielded Dahlen's first big league hit.

Still only 22, Kittridge had come close to losing his life the year before on the club's June visit to New York. He was riding with friends in an open carriage across the Brooklyn Bridge, when the horses became frightened at the sight and sound of a cable car. They took off running at full speed, the driver having lost complete control of them. When they reached the Manhattan side of the bridge, the horses were racing along a path that would have taken them directly into a stanchion. Fearing for his life, Kittridge leaped from the carriage. Neither he nor any of his pals were seriously injured, but he came out of the accident with a wrenched knee and lots of scratches and bruises.

Despite all the bluster, Kittridge, Gumbert, and Dahlen would all be back with the Colts in 1892. There would be no Chicago team in the American Association that year; nor, in fact, would there be an American Association. In December 1891, the association's 10-year struggle with the National League, which became a three-way battle with the formation of the Players League in 1890, ended with the Nationals fully triumphant.[20] In actuality, the American Association was not disbanding; it was

Kid Nichols, pictured here pitching for St. Louis in 1905. In 1891, Nichols' first lifetime win against Chicago launched the Boston Beaneaters on an 18-game winning streak and on to a very disputed National League pennant.

merging with the National League. Gone were its weakest teams, with the four adjudged the most viable — Baltimore, Louisville, St. Louis, and Washington — being added to the National League. (The four would finish ninth through 12th in 1892.) Officially, the title of the new combined league was "The National League and American Association of Professional Baseball Clubs," but people more commonly called it, the "Big League" or "The League."

In recognition of its new members, the National League adopted several association innovations. For the first time the league would play games on Sundays in cities that allowed it, and would also give clubs the option to sell alcoholic beverages in their parks. Chicago, for one, jumped at the chance to host Sunday games. Spalding had wanted to do so since watching the 1888 Chicago Maroons of the minor league Western Association drawing big crowds to their Sabbath games.

The owners still had to deal with the problems created by the sheer size of their reconfigured and expanded 12-team league. Fearing the effect on fan interest, and more importantly on attendance, if too many teams were out of the race, they decided to use a split schedule for the 1892 season. Under this scheme there would be two pennant races, with the winners, should there be two different ones, meeting in a championship series.

As he did most every season, Anson predicted a pennant for his Colts. He also made a side bet with Chris von der Ahe, the flamboyant owner of the St. Louis Browns, on which team would finish ahead of the other in the standings. The stakes were a $75 suit of clothes, which Anson collected when the seventh-place Colts finished four slots ahead of the Browns. Betting by owners, managers, and players as to various outcomes was common at the time, and despite some previous scandals, was in the main accepted by the public. Newspapers openly and regularly reported the details of these various wagers.

One club eliminated as a result of the merger was the Milwaukee Brewers,[21] a measure that had a very negative affect on Dahlen's pocketbook. In October 1891, Brewers manager Charlie Cushman had visited Dahlen at the Columbia Hotel in Fort Plain, where he signed him to a contract for the '92 season. According to the *Milwaukee Sentinel*, Dahlen would receive a salary of $3,000, which included a $500 advance.

It also appeared likely then that two other Chicago players, Mal Kittridge and Fred Pfeffer would be leaving to join American Association clubs. In spite of the potential impact on his club, Anson seemed unruffled by the news. "The more of my players they take at the prices they are paying, the sooner they will be in bankruptcy courts," he prophesied.[22]

Meanwhile Brewers fans were very excited about getting the best young player in the league, and Dahlen was ecstatic about getting a salary more than double the $1,400 he would have received from Chicago. However, a problem existed; he had already signed an 1892 contract to play for the Colts. Anxious to have his Colts contract voided, Dahlen claimed that he had been underage when he signed with Anson originally, and therefore his subsequent contracts were illegal. He went as far as to tell President Hart of the Colts that he believed his contract with Chicago was not worth the paper on which it was written. The resulting conversation between Dahlen and Hart went like this, said the *Sporting News*.[23]

HART: "I don't believe you."

DAHLEN: "I know it."

HART: "Well, I have some good legal opinion about it, and I tell you the contract is good."

DAHLEN: "I have legal advice about it too. You see I have a guardian and my guardian has told me I was not of age and that for that reason anything I signed was not binding."

This last Dahlen comment, about his having a guardian, was a new one for Hart and drove him into a frenzy. All the wrangling would be for naught. The demise of the Brewers ended the dispute, allowing the Colts to retain the rights to Dahlen. His salary would be $1,500, with Chicago reimbursing Milwaukee for the $500 advance. The Colts, in turn, deducted that $500 from Dahlen's salary. That meant he would receive only $1,000 the rest of the season, rather than the $2,500 he would have gotten had Milwaukee survived. Based on a story that appeared in the *Sporting News* in February, it was highly unlikely that any of his teammates had any sympathy to waste on young Bill. The paper claimed that Dahlen, about to begin his second year as a big-leaguer, had as a rookie been "the most unpopular player on his team." He had continuously snubbed his veteran teammates, the paper added, and had offended them even more by never paying attention to their advice.

Remembering last season's wintry experience in Denver, Anson chose the warm weather of Hot Springs, Arkansas, to prepare his club for the season. A week before the opener he traded the disgruntled Fred Pfeffer to Louisville for Jimmy Canavan. It was a nice gesture toward his longtime second baseman, allowing him to return to his hometown, where at midseason they named him manager.

Dahlen played some spring games at second base, but he was back at third for the season opener at St. Louis's Sportsman's Park. A capacity crowd, one that included heavyweight champion (and baseball fan) John L. Sullivan and the reigning beauty of the stage, Lillian Russell, saw Chicago win 14–10. Dahlen, batting second, had a terrific afternoon. He had a single, a double, a triple and again came close to hitting for the cycle. He missed when Browns left fielder Cliff Carroll pulled down a long drive that had the looks of an inside-the-park home run when it left the bat.

Dahlen remained the Colts third baseman until July 11, when the club added rookie Jiggs Parrott to the roster. Called by the *Sporting News* the best third baseman in the Western League, Parrott was batting .323 for Minneapolis when the league folded in midseason. Anson quickly signed him and gave him the third-base job, moving Dahlen to shortstop and releasing the weak-hitting Jimmy Cooney. Parrott played a solid third base for Chicago, but he batted just .201 for the season. Yet even that lowly mark was an improvement over Cooney, who was batting .172 when Anson released him. Meanwhile, Canavan, Pfeffer's replacement at second, batted just .166, the lowest one-season mark in major league history by anyone with at least 400 at-bats. Late in the year, rookie outfielder George Decker was playing second, and the Colts were using Canavan as a ticket-taker.

Overall, it was a disappointing season for the Colts. In this one and only year of the split season, Boston won the first half and Cleveland the second. After it had come so close to winning the pennant the year before, Chicago finished eighth and seventh for a combined seventh-place standing. The team did, however, play one memorable game this season, although it was less than memorable for Dahlen. On June 30 at Cincinnati, the Colts and the Reds played a 20-inning, 7–7 tie. The 20 innings set a record for the longest game in National League history, surpassing Providence's 18-inning 1–0 win over Detroit on August 17, 1882. It would also be the longest major league game of the 19th century. Dahlen had just one hit in eight at-bats, and while he handled 14 of 15 chances successfully, it was his fifth-inning error that allowed Cincinnati's seventh run.

The team's lackluster showing was just part of what was a particularly disheartening season for Anson, one filled with setbacks and tragedy. It had started with Hart replacing Spalding. Then, after predicting he would lead the newly expanded league in batting, he put together the worst offensive season of his career. Additionally, his "ginger beer" business failed, but in the worst blow of all, he lost his only son. And despite the Colts' 13-game winning streak in May, by June the *Chicago Times* reported that Anson's poor play had lost him control of the team. It appeared, they wrote, that every player seems to go his own way and does as he pleases, and hinted that the 40-year-old Anson had grown too old for the modern game. Writers in other cities soon joined in, suggesting that he find another first baseman and do his managing from the bench.

Anson angrily denied all the allegations—that he had lost control, that the game had passed him by, or that the Colts needed a new first baseman. Yet there was not much doubt that he no longer had the complete respect of many of his players. Prominent among them was Dahlen. In July, *Sporting Life* described an incident in Philadelphia in which sophomore, and sophomoric, Bill just laughed at Anson after the manager berated him for failing to cover second base on a steal attempt. Yet as so often happened, a newspaper's negative comment on some aspect of Dahlen's attitude would in the same issue contain a comment praising his physical abilities. Elsewhere this issue of *Sporting Life* remarked that he was proving to be as good at shortstop as he was at third base, a position at which he had the league's best fielding percentage. And, in contrast to that lackadaisical approach in the game at Philadelphia, at other times Dahlen would play with an uncontrolled fury. His base path collision with Giants outfielder Mike Tiernan was so violent that many in the press and on the Giants bench called it both deliberate and a dirty play.

There were some high points for the Colts in this generally bleak season, including a 13-game winning streak that sparked a 19–3 record in May. Individually, right fielder Sam Dungan had a fine rookie season, batting .284 although his fielding was below big league standards. Veteran center fielder Jimmy Ryan compiled a 29-game hitting streak in midsummer, and Bill Hutchison accomplished something that no major league pitcher has matched since. His 37 wins were more than half Chicago's total of 70 victories, making it the second consecutive season Hutchison had won more than half his team's

Pitcher Bill Hutchison won more than half of Chicago's total victories in both 1891 and 1892. No major league pitcher has won half his team's games since.

games. As previously stated, no big league pitcher has done this since 1892.

Dahlen followed his outstanding rookie season with an even better one as a sophomore. The move to shortstop allowed him to use his range to greater advantage than was possible at third base. Newspapers in the cities throughout the league were full of praise for his ability to get ground balls hit to either side of him. His best day of the season may have come in a morning-afternoon doubleheader against New York on September 5. He handled seven chances flawlessly in each game, including three excellent plays in the ninth inning of the morning game. At the plate he had two hits in the morning and four in the afternoon.

For the season, he raised his batting average from .260 to .291, while finishing among the league's top 10 in slugging average, total bases, runs, triples, extra base hits, and stolen bases. His 19 triples set a single-season Chicago club record. Sophisticated baseball analysis was still many years in the future, and so how good a year Dahlen had in 1892 was probably not fully recognized or appreciated at the time. Yet *Total Baseball*, using a measure called total player rating (TPR),[24] has since judged him the third-best position player in the league that year, behind current Hall-of-Famers Dan Brouthers of Brooklyn and Bid McPhee of Cincinnati.

Yet as splendid a player as Dahlen was, the friction between Anson and him remained. After the season, St. Louis's von der Ahe claimed that Anson was so peeved at his young star that he was ready to trade him to the Browns in exchange for their shortstop, Jack Glasscock. While there is no doubt that Anson was peeved at Dahlen, he was not stupid. *Sporting Life's* comment on Von der Ahe's statement typified the general reaction among baseball people. They ridiculed the idea that Chicago would trade one of the league's best young players for the 33-year-old Glasscock, claiming Dahlen was four times the player Glasscock was.

A profile of Dahlen that appeared in the highly respected *New York Clipper* reinforced his reputation as one of the game's best players, if not the best. "There certainly are few young players who have gained greater celebrity on the green diamond in the same length of time than has young Dahlen," said the *Clipper*.[25] It added that many knowledgeable observers now considered him the equal of any player in the game, of whatever age.

THREE

A Record-Breaking Hitting Streak

The National League's decision to use a split-season format for 1892 had been a financial failure. Motivated by the expansion to 12 teams, the league had also lengthened the schedule from 140 games to 154 games. Yet despite these actions, total attendance for most teams dipped, with the league's average per-game attendance declining by 18 percent. Chicago and New York had the most precipitous falloffs. The Colts fell from 201,000 in 1891 to 109,000 in 1892, while the Giants slipped from 211,000 to 131,000.

Club owners had begun responding to their mounting losses even as the season was being played, cutting salaries and reducing rosters to 13 players per team. At the league meeting in Chicago in November, they formulated their cost-cutting plans for 1893: a reduction in the schedule to 132 games, a salary cap of $30,000 per team, and a provision that no player could earn more than $2,400 per year.[1]

Predictably, the players responded to the cuts in salary with wholesale griping and threatened holdouts. Actions by the Colts players were typical of those throughout the league. By late October just four men had signed, only one of whom, catcher Pop Schriver, had been around for more than two years. The other early signers were Dahlen, entering his third season, and rookies' Sam Dungan and Jiggs Parrott. Schriver, who had earned $2,400 in 1892, signed to play for $1,600 in 1893. Foremost among the holdouts were Jimmy Ryan, Bill Hutchison, and Mal Kittridge, all of whom had rebelled at cuts similar to those accepted by Schriver. The Chicago newspapers generally supported the cuts, called those players who had already signed sensible, and said it was likely that the three holdouts would be playing elsewhere in '93. Eventually, all three signed with the Colts.

Recognizing that their experiment with the split season had been a big mistake, the league abandoned the format and returned to the traditional style pennant race. "The clubs have this year acknowledged their error in both the double championship and the lengthened season by abolishing both," said the 1893 *Reach Guide*.[2] Believing that lack of offense was another drag on attendance, the owners instituted a revolutionary change to the game's dimensions. They increased the pitching distance from 50 feet to 60 feet six inches, and replaced the pitcher's box with a mound containing a slab. In reality, the increase in distance was only about five feet. In 1892, the pitcher's box had been an area five and one-half feet long by four feet wide, with a distance of 50 feet from the front of the box to home plate. But because in delivering the ball the pitcher had to keep one foot in contact with the back line of the box, the actual pitching distance was 55 feet six inches, rather than the official rule book listing of 50 feet.[3]

As the owners had anticipated, the new rule achieved its dual purpose; by increasing offense, it boosted attendance. The National League's overall batting average soared from .245 in 1892 to .280 in 1893. Hits per game went from 8.8 to 10.4, while runs per game increased from 5.25 per team to 6.70. The owners' assumption that fans preferred 9–8 games to 2–1 games had proved to be true.

Comparable changes in the pitching statistics accompanied the dramatic changes in the batting numbers. The league earned run average rose more than a run and a half, from 3.29 to 4.67, while total strikeouts plummeted from 5,973, all the way down to 3,342. Many pitchers made the transition easily, but it obviously hampered others. For some, the problem was the additional five feet, but even more were hindered by the requirement to keep at least one foot in contact with the slab at all times. Among the most adversely affected was Bill Hutchison of the Colts. He had been the league's leading winner in each of the previous three seasons and its strikeout king in 1892. Yet in 1893 he failed to lead even his own team in either department. Hutchison won only 16 games while losing 24, and his strikeouts dropped from 316 to 80. Willie McGill was the new Colts leader with 17 wins and 91 strikeouts.

During the off-season, newspapers in New York had printed stories saying that the Giants, dissatisfied with their manager, Pat Powers, were discussing replacing him with Anson. It was strictly Hot Stove League talk, and such a move never had a chance. John Montgomery Ward would be the new manager in New York in '93, while "old Anse" would be back for his 14th season as the manager in Chicago. For this year's spring training locale, Anson chose Atlanta, bypassing previously chosen southern sites such as Hot Springs and St. Augustine, Florida. Anson had not cared for either place, particularly St. Augustine, which he felt had too many distractions, chief among them being the ocean.

Because Chicago was the site of the World's Columbian Exposition, the city was the focal point of the nation in the summer of 1893. Though Chicago, and the nation, was suffering severe economic depression and labor unrest, the Columbian Exposition, the last of the 19th century's World's Fairs, was by far the grandest. Held ostensibly as a celebration of Columbus's voyages to the New World 400 years earlier, it was really more a celebration of United States culture and society, and a blueprint for what life would be like in 20th-century America. Before it was over, the fair recorded more than 26 million entries at a time when the US population was just 65 million. Of course, many people visited more than once. Still, the fair afforded entrepreneurs of every type a wonderful opportunity to cash in. Never one to let a chance to make money elude him, Albert Spalding found his own way to increase his growing fortune.

With Sunday baseball now lawful, Spalding wanted his Colts to play games on the Sabbath to take advantage of the large crowds flocking to the city to attend the Exposition. To do so, he had to get around the team's lease for South Side Park, which prevented them from playing on Sunday. Spalding solved the problem by utilizing a park on land that he owned on the city's west side. Beginning with the May 14 game against the Reds, the Colts played all their 1893 Sunday home games at West Side Park.[4]

Even with the reduced schedule, the league's total attendance went up 22 percent in 1893. The most dramatic increases were in Chicago and New York, the two teams that had suffered the biggest declines the year before. Chicago's attendance of 223,500 was more than double its 1892 count. Making the increase even more impressive, the fans were not coming out to see a winning team. The Colts finished ninth, 29 games behind the champion Boston Beaneaters.

It was an unfortunate finish. With the world's spotlight on Chicago, this would have been a wonderful year for the team to end its six-year pennant drought. However, as it quickly became obvious, this was not a very good club. Perhaps 1893's greatest significance to Chicago baseball history is that it was the year that 21-year-old Bill Lange joined the team. Although most modern fans likely have never heard of him, Lange quickly became one of the most popular players in Chicago history. After batting .281 as a rookie, he averaged .339 over the next six seasons, including a .389-mark in 1895. Lange was a complete player, one whom some historians have called the Willie Mays of his day. Much of the evidence we have points to Lange as the best defensive outfielder of the 19th century. The

eminent sportswriter Tim Murnane has included Lange with Ty Cobb and
Joe Jackson in naming his all-time outfield.

Along with being an outstanding hitter and fielder, Lange also holds
the club record for stolen bases, with 84 in 1896. Al Spink, founder of the
Sporting News, remembered Lange as "Ty Cobb enlarged, fully as great in
speed, batting skill and base running." Clark Griffith, a former teammate
and longtime owner of the Washington Senators, agreed, calling Lange
"Ty's equal."[5] Lange was only 28 and in his prime when he left baseball
following the 1899 season. He quit as a way to satisfy his future father-in-
law, who did not want his daughter to marry a professional baseball player.

Like all hitters, Dahlen benefited from 1893's revised pitching arrangements. But even in that year of overall increased offense, his batting average (.301), on-base percentage (.381) and slugging average (.452) were all
well above the league average. Defensively, he played only 88 of his 116
games at shortstop, but when he did play there, he was most impressive.
"Dahlen's work at short field was of the brand that has gold foil wrapped
around it," said the *Brooklyn Daily Eagle* after a Colts series with the Bridegrooms.[6] When not at shortstop, Dahlen took turns at second base and all
three outfield positions.

Just as the Giants had been interested in prying Anson away from

Bill Lange, the Chicago Colts' handsome center fielder, could run, hit,
and field, and is considered by
many to have been the Willie Mays
of his day.

Chicago before the season began, they
were now interested in doing the same
with Dahlen as it was ending. Beginning
in September and continuing into the
early winter, stories appeared in the New
York newspapers detailing the Giants'
desire to acquire Dahlen for the 1894
season. Manager John Montgomery
Ward claimed that all he needed to
round out his team and put them in the
race was a hard-hitting shortstop. No
one fit that description better than
Dahlen.

According to the scenario being
bandied about, Giants executive J. Walter Spalding would influence his older
brother, Albert G., who in turn would
influence President Hart to allow
Dahlen to move to the Giants. New York
supposedly was offering to obtain
Dahlen via a straight sale, or a sale plus

their own shortstop, weak-hitting Shorty Fullmer. Anson said the Giants certainly could have Dahlen via a straight sale. The asking price was $20,000, an exorbitant amount of money given the game's economic climate. In retrospect, this deal never had a chance of being made, no matter what the price. Hart, knowing what a valuable player he had in Dahlen, and surely remembering his disagreeable postseason encounter with the Giants in 1891, responded predictably.

"The New Yorks may want Dahlen, but wanting is not getting. We would not release Dahlen under any circumstances, and as for selling him, the Chicago club is not now in that kind of business. Dahlen is too valuable a man for Chicago to part with."[7]

That value was undeniable. In spite of his 65 errors in '93 and a fielding percentage that was just about at the league average for shortstops, those that saw him day in and day out could not stop praising Dahlen's play. In Anson's estimation, "Dahlen at short was a tower of strength to the team, being as agile as a cat, a sure catch, and an exceptionally strong batter."[8] In giving a preseason assessment of his team, he had said, "At short we have Dahlen, who cannot be beaten."[9] It was an assessment the *Chicago Tribune* fully endorsed, noting early in the '93 season that Dahlen continued to make "phenomenal plays" at shortstop. Once the season started, Anson went as far as to call Dahlen the best infielder in the league. As if to match his exalted status, young Bill was also becoming quite the dandy. *Sporting Life* offered this description, in calling him the neatest dresser on the Colts. "He wears a white puff necktie that looks like a pincushion. He also goes about in a pair of patent leather toothpick shoes."[10]

As always, there were the negative comments to counter any praise regarding Dahlen's performance. In July, the *Chicago Dispatch* wrote that he was getting a reputation as a "dirty ballplayer" after he threw a bat at St. Louis catcher Heinie Peitz. A few weeks earlier in a home game against Brooklyn, umpire Ed Seward had fined him $5 for his profanity in protesting a called strike. Dahlen eventually reached first on an error, but was later thrown out at the plate. His response was to throw a handful of dirt in Seward's eyes.

Couldn't Anson do something about this kind of action, asked the *Dispatch*? Not likely, responded *Sporting Life's* Chicago correspondent, as it was from Anson that Dahlen learned these kinds of actions. Anson, who would do anything to win, taught that credo to his players, and Dahlen was as quick to "turn a trick" as any of them. Then, in a rather telling observation, he suggested that Dahlen's "light is kept under a bushel in Chicago," and that he would be a great player for a winning team.

The charge that Dahlen gave less than a full effort, particularly for a noncontending team, surfaced again in a postseason piece in the *Sporting News*. Dismissing the possibility that he would be traded or sold to the Giants, the paper predicted he would be back in Chicago in 1894 and again be among the team's best players. Then came the proviso. "Dahlen, if he would exert himself would be a wonder. His work last year was sulky and erratic and clearly showed that the little fellow will not try to play ball with a losing team."[11] (At five feet nine inches and 180 pounds, Dahlen could hardly be called a "little man" in his era, yet he was often referred to that way.)

Teammates and fans could accept the fact that Dahlen "played dirty" or even that he was guilty of the "tricks" he was charged with using. They would classify it as going all out to win. What was not acceptable to anyone, however, were those occasional displays of indifference, as typified by his behavior in a late July game against Louisville. Chicago was trailing after eight innings and had the tail end of the order scheduled to bat in the ninth. Dahlen and Ryan, normally the first to depart after a game anyway, thought they would get an even earlier jump today. Assuming they would not bat in the top of the ninth, they headed to the clubhouse and changed into their street clothes. But the Colts rallied and went ahead. Everyone in the park then had to stand around waiting while the two changed back into their uniforms and returned to the game. As was obvious to all, Dahlen and Ryan were foremost among a group of Colts players who were now openly disrespectful and contemptuous of Anson.[12]

Dahlen and his teammates skipped the usual postseason exhibition games this year to spend a week or two taking in the Columbian Exposition. The fair had been a great success in every way, but unfortunately ended on a sad note. On October 23, two nights before it was to close, a deranged man demanding a city job entered the home of 68-year-old Mayor Carter Harrison and shot him dead. Chicago lost a popular mayor, one who had been a prime mover in bringing the fair to his city, while the Colts lost one of their biggest fans.

Much as they do now, baseball owners in 1894 tended to disagree about almost everything, with one exception. The one thing most could agree on, both then and now, was that they should pay their players less money. After a decade of competition between the National League and the American Association for their services, the players were now living with an ugly reality. The National League, again a monopoly, had decreed reduced roster sizes, the abolishment of long-term contracts, and a maximum annual salary of $2,400. Back in place too was the reserve clause, which essentially bound a player to his team as long as it wanted to keep him.

The Colts made an additional cost-cutting move, although they did not advertise it as such. Anson decided to hold spring training at home, because, he said, his team had never won a pennant after traveling in the spring. He asked his players to report to Chicago by April 1. Dahlen, meanwhile, was getting in shape on his own. He had spent the winter in Chicago, but had also managed to put in some time in rural Morrison, Illinois, where he took long walks, hunted, and fished in the Rock River. In late February, he reported that he was in excellent shape and actually weighed three pounds less than he had when the '93 season ended.

A look through the baseball record books confirms that 1894 remains the greatest of all offensive seasons. The increase in the league's

Jimmy Ryan, who with Dahlen was foremost among the Chicago players who were openly disrespectful and contemptuous of manager Anson.

batting average, from .245 in 1892 to .280 in 1893, was just a prelude to the offensive orgy that batters unleashed in 1894. Eight of the 12 clubs batted above .300, as the overall league average skyrocketed to .310. The fourth-place Phillies led the way with a .350 average, followed by the pennant-winning Orioles, who batted .343. Individually, Boston's Hugh Duffy led the league with an astronomical .440 average. Behind Duffy were four members of the Phillies: Tuck Turner, Sam Thompson, Ed Delahanty, and Billy Hamilton, all of whom batted better than .400.

Chicago's team average was .313, led by Anson (.388), Dahlen (.359), and Ryan (.357). Yet their pitching continued to be below average. Clark Griffith, in his first full season in the National League, won 21 games, but the other starters, Bill Hutchison, Willie McGill, and Adonis Terry, won only 26 between them. The Colts were one of only two teams in the league (Washington was the other) whose pitchers did not throw a shutout all season. Training at home had turned out to be no more successful than training elsewhere had been in recent years. The Colts lost their first six games and struggled all season before finishing eighth, 34 games behind Baltimore.[13]

Of course, overall pitching statistics suffered a decline this year. The league's earned run average, which had increased from 3.29 in 1892 to 4.67 in 1893, climbed to 5.32 in '94. An average game saw teams scoring a combined 15 runs on 22 hits. While it would seem obvious that the increased pitching distance had been the cause of the increased offense, not everyone agreed. Jim O'Rourke, a veteran outfielder, who the year before had ended a career that began in the National Association in 1872, said the rule confining the pitchers to a 12-inch by 4-inch slab was more the cause than the extra pitching distance. Baseball historian David Voight agreed, noting that the slab was "robbing pitchers of the deceptive mobility that they had long enjoyed while hurling from the now discarded pitching boxes."[14]

With all the heavy hitting in 1894, Dahlen's sensational numbers can easily get overlooked, but it was a truly marvelous year for him. Along with his .359 batting average, he had a .445 on-base percentage and a .566 slugging average. He finished in the top 10 in slugging and in runs scored, total bases, and extra-base hits. Dahlen's 284 total bases were the most recorded by a shortstop between 1893 and 1900. He also stole 42 bases, and his career-high 15 home runs trailed only Duffy, who had 18, and Duffy's teammate, Bobby Lowe, and Washington's Bill Joyce, both of whom had 17.

Five of Dahlen's home runs came in four consecutive road games, beginning on June 9. Victimized were Jouett Meekin of the Giants, and the Boston trio of Jack Stivetts, Kid Nichols, and Tom Lovett (twice.) Then in the season's final week, Dahlen staged another stunning performance. Over two consecutive games against Philadelphia, he scored nine runs (five on September 20 and four on September 21), tying the still-existing major league record for most runs scored in two consecutive games. Boston's Herman Long and Dahlen's teammate Jimmy Ryan had done it earlier in the season, but no National Leaguer has done it since.[15]

His spectacular numbers aside, the highlight of Dahlen's season was a 42-game hitting streak that ran from June 20 through August 6. More than a century later, it is still the fourth-longest streak in major league history and the longest ever by a National League right-handed batter. Dahlen was batting .270 and had gone hitless in his previous two games at Cleveland when he began the streak with a double off the Spiders' John Clarkson. After a three-game series in Pittsburgh, where he had two, one, and two hits, the Colts returned to Chicago to begin a long homestand. Dahlen had three hits in the first game against Baltimore and then two in each of the next three against the first-place Orioles. The first game of that series is a microcosm of the season for the hard-hitting, weak-pitching Colts. After scoring five runs in the top of the ninth to take a 10–8 lead, Baltimore came back with three in the bottom of the inning to win 11–10.

Dahlen had been playing third base all season, with Charlie Irwin playing shortstop, as he had since coming up the previous September. Then, on the morning of July 7, Anson decided to switch them, returning Dahlen to shortstop, where, with rare exceptions, he would remain for the rest of his career. Anson still had a problem at second base, however. The club had never adequately replaced Fred Pfeffer, who had played on winning teams in Chicago between 1883 and 1891. Pfeffer was still popular in the city and the fans always roundly cheered him whenever the Louisville club played in Chicago.

"I want a good second baseman," Anson said in May. "That position has cost the Chicago club a heap of money. During the past year or two we have tried more than a score of men."[16] This year's entry was Jiggs Parrott, moved there from third base where he had played in 1893. Parrott, however, hardly seemed the solution to Anson's search for "a good second baseman." the *Sporting News* regularly blasted both his batting prowess (he hit .248 in a league that hit .310) and his play in the field, and chastised Anson for continuing to use him. Parrott's poor performance was just one reason the press was criticizing Anson more severely this year than ever before. "Old Anse" was having another outstanding year at the plate, but there were increasing complaints about his handling of the team and its players. As early as May, the *Brooklyn Daily Eagle* was noting the trouble he was having in controlling his players. He had suspended Dahlen for the May 7–9 series at Cleveland for what the Eagle called "disturbing his sleep," and had sent outfielder George Decker home for no apparent reason.[17]

At the time of Dahlen's switch from third to short, his hitting streak stood at 15 straight, and he had raised his average to .329. The streak reached 20 with three hits against Boston on July 11, 30 with two against Pittsburgh on July 23, and 40 with a lone hit against Louisville on August 4. With Cincinnati in town the next day, Dahlen hit in his 41st consecutive game with a single off Frank Dwyer, but it turned out to be a sad day in Chicago.

The summer of 1894 had been drier than usual, and with so many spectators smoking, the wooden ballparks were extremely susceptible to fire. At 5 o'clock on this Sunday afternoon, with a crowd of 10,000 present at West Side Park, a blaze broke out in the grandstand. It was the bottom of the seventh inning, with Chicago ahead, 8–2, and Anson at the plate. A man seeing smoke in the uncovered seats along Lincoln Street yelled "Fire!" Once the approximately 5,000 fans seated in that area became aware of the rapidly spreading flames they started stampeding toward the exits. Eventually, Anson struck out, and after initially paying no attention to what was taking place in the stands, the players became aware of what was happening and began helping the fans make their way through the barbed wire. The *Reach Official Baseball Guide* for 1895 described what happened next.

"Four strands of barbed wire had been placed in front of the grand-stand and the bleachers, to keep the people from crowding out into the field.[18] For a time, escape was cut off in that direction. The stairways proved entirely inadequate to accommodate the hurrying throng, and the fire was making such rapid strides that the crowd turned again to the barbed wire. People wrenched seats from the reserved section and used them to break down the wires. Then a perfect flood of humanity went over into the ballfield. Men and women were trampled underfoot and jumped upon, and several hundred persons received injuries of more or less serious charac-ter. Before they could control the fire, one-half of the grandstand was destroyed and all the 'bleachers' and fifty-cent seats."[19]

Hundreds suffered burns and cuts from the barbed wire, but "that a few dozen were not killed is exceeding wonderfully," said the next day's *Chicago Tribune*.[20] Nevertheless, two nearby hospitals, County and Pres-byterian, were kept busy all afternoon. The fire, which investigators later determined was started by a lit cigar tossed into a pile of rubbish, was one of four in National League parks that year. Baltimore had a preseason fire at Union Park in January, while the ones at Boston's South End Grounds in May, and Philadelphia's Baseball Grounds, the day after the Chicago fire, broke out during games.

Promising that "we will play ball tomorrow where we played today," President Hart hired a contractor who had his crew out at dawn. True to Hart's promise, the Colts played at West Side Park the next day and con-tinued to play games there even as the renovations were taking place.[21] That afternoon, Dahlen had two hits against Cincinnati's Lem Cross, extend-ing the streak to 42 games. He was finally stopped the next day, failing to hit in six at-bats against Reds pitchers Chauncey Fisher and Tom Parrott. It was surely an odd day for the streak to end, as his teammates banged out 17 hits in a 10-inning, 13–11 win.

Although at the time, Dahlen's 42-game hitting streak was the major leagues' longest ever, the baseball world barely noticed it. Not a word about his accomplishment appeared in any of the Chicago newspapers until it ended. Even then, it was just in passing, with no numbers mentioned. "The usually reliable stickman," the *Inter Ocean* said of Dahlen, "failed utterly in six attempts to get a hit."[22]

The day after the Reds stopped him, Dahlen launched a new streak. This one had reached 28 games by September 9 before an illness kept him out of action for the next few days. Connie Lucid of Brooklyn ended the second streak on September 15, the day he returned, by holding him hitless in four tries. Twelve games into that second streak, the *Sporting News* did note that Dahlen had hit safely in all but one of his last 55 games. That string would extend to hitting safely in 70 of 71 games before it ended. Over that amazing stretch, encompassing more than half the season, Dahlen collected 133 hits in 308 at-bats for a .399 average.

Noteworthy as the streak(s) would appear to be, it was so little regarded at the time that the *Reach Baseball Guide* for 1895 did not even list it in its recap of notable events of 1894. In fact, for most "modern" fans front page news of Joe DiMaggio's 56-game hitting streak in the summer of 1941 was likely the first they heard of Bill Dahlen's streak, and perhaps, even, of Bill Dahlen. And yet, because it was not Dahlen's streak that DiMaggio was pursuing, the press made very little mention of his 42-gamer. Bill's pal Willie Keeler had hit in 44 straight for Baltimore just three years later, and it was Keeler's streak that then stood as the major league record.

So, we might ask, just how good a player was 24-year-old Bill Dahlen in 1894? Good enough for *Total Baseball*, using their total player rating system, to consider him the league's outstanding position player that year.[23] The four players behind him were Hamilton, Delahanty, Duffy, and Philadelphia's Lave Cross. Using fielding runs[24] as their measure, *Total Baseball* also rated Dahlen as the top defensive player in the league, a designation that encompasses all positions, not just shortstops.

Yet even in this, his greatest season, there was another exasperating incident involving Dahlen's "attitude." If his midsummer hitting streak had been the highlight of the season, his May defection from the club was the low light. Discouraged by the team's struggling start — they had lost their first six games, and eight of nine, all on the road — a disheartened Dahlen chose to go home after the May 6 game in Cincinnati. The *Sporting News* wrote that by his failure to accompany the club to Cleveland, he was not showing "the proper spirit." Leaving the team when it needed him the most, the paper said, was an indication that his heart was not in the right place. However, a week later the *News* reported that the "youngster" had realized his mistake in deserting the team. In a meeting with Anson, Dahlen was reportedly penitent and anxious to rejoin the club, which he did when it returned from Cleveland. The $50 fine levied on him stood, but Anson hinted that he would return it if Bill behaved himself for the rest of the season.

Whether Dahlen was perfectly behaved, or even well behaved, the rest of the way is doubtful, but what is beyond dispute is his value to the Colts. They were three games above .500 during his two hitting streaks, and 21 games below .500 in all other games.

FOUR

A *"Disorderly Element,"*
but Another
Marvelous Season

President Hart believed that holding spring training at home in 1894 had been part of the cause for the team's overall lack of success. Hart also believed that the players had not been in good enough shape to start the season, or, for that matter, to start several of the previous few seasons. So shortly after the '94 campaign ended, he announced that in the spring of 1895 the Colts would again go south, and that they would go earlier than usual. Then, taking a swipe at Anson, Hart added that he would pick some place in Texas where, he expected, the weather would be better than in Chicago. On March 1, Anson and his players, including Dahlen, boarded an Illinois Central train in Chicago bound for Galveston. Although spring training would last for six weeks, it was not all hard work for the Colts. As they toured Texas, the wives of pitcher Bert Abbey, catcher Mal Kittridge, outfielder Jimmy Ryan, and of course, Anson accompanied them. The unaccompanied Dahlen, meanwhile, picked right up where he had left off the year before, batting better than .450 in the exhibition games.

Opening day at St. Louis was the traditional mix of music, parades, speeches, and baseball, although one most untraditional sight greeted the 12,000 fans at Robison Park. All of the gray-clad Colts took the field clean-shaven, including Anson, whom no one had seen without a mustache in 30 years. The Colts won the game 10–7 behind Clark Griffith, who had emerged as the staff ace. Dahlen's excellent spring did not extend into the early season. A day after going one for six and committing two errors in the opener, he suffered a severe ankle sprain sliding into second base and missed the next three games.

As usual, Anson made bets with other club executives that his Colts would finish higher in the standings than their clubs, and this year's sums were even higher. His wagers were said to total more than $3,000, most of which was with New York's Andrew Freedman, and to a lesser extent, Chris von der Ahe of St. Louis. The press openly reported these wagers, and the fans took them to be an indication of the confidence the various owners had in their teams. Evidently, neither league president Nick Young nor authorities in the various cities saw anything illegal or immoral in the practice. Nor did they see anything wrong with the horse-race betting that so many players were involved with, including Anson. Years later, Dahlen, a fellow horse-player, reminisced about taking advantage of Anson's habit. He did it, he said, not so much to bilk Anson out of some money, but more to just further bedevil the old man.

"When the ticker service was first installed with its chronicle of sporting events, I learned that I could get the winners of the first two races at Hawthorne or Harlem before the ball game started. Fine! After finding how the horses ran, one-two-three, I would stroll over to Anson and ask him what he fancied, say in the second race. If Anson liked the winner there was no bet, but if he picked another horse, I would suggest a small wager, horse against horse. It was three weeks before the old warrior found how he was being fooled. Then he threatened to fine me for the full amount of his losses."[1]

Although Dahlen preferred to bet on horse races rather than on baseball, he was just as confident as Anson about the team's prospects this season. Bill contended that if former second baseman Fred Pfeffer, gone from the team for four years, were still a member, the Colts would win in a walk.[2] But even without Pfeffer, he believed the 1895 Colts were better than the 1891 edition. And, he said with a reference to that season's controversial finish, the 1891 team had "won the pennant honestly."[3]

An early surge that kept Chicago up among the leaders must have made Anson regret not betting even more money on its eventual finish. On May 10, after crushing Boston 14–1 to stretch the winning streak to seven, the Colts sat in second place, one game behind Pittsburgh. Because of their winning ways and high standing, the team was drawing large crowds. Even the city's elite were attending games, as a Colts baseball game at West Side Park had now become a fashionable place to be seen.

With Chicago in the thick of the race, more than 10,000 fans turned out Sunday, June 23, for a game against the Cleveland Spiders. Sunday baseball was now well entrenched in the city, but there still remained groups of religious zealots that opposed it. One such group was the Sunday Observance League, led by the Reverend G. W. Clark. Based on

Clark's complaint, police arrested the entire Colts team that afternoon, charging them with "aiding and abetting the forming of a noisy crowd on a Sunday." The "arrests" came as no surprise to those involved. Everyone knew in advance that the actors in this little morality play recognized their roles and would go through the prescribed routine. After President Hart posted a bond, allowing the game to take place, the Colts, behind Griffith, sent the crowd of "sinners" home happy with a 13–4 win.[4]

This peaceful Sabbath encounter was in sharp contrast to the violent skirmish that had taken place during the Colts' 8–2 win the previous afternoon. That confrontation, as confrontations so often did, centered around Dahlen. In the sixth inning, Bill was on first when pitcher Phil Knell threw over in a pickoff attempt. First baseman George Tebeau had the bag blocked, so when Dahlen slid back into the base, he caught Tebeau with his spikes. Tebeau, thinking it was a deliberate attempt to spike him, retaliated by kicking Dahlen, who was still on the ground. Bill then got to his feet and threw a right-hand punch at Tebeau that connected and knocked him to the ground.

Both Anson and Spiders manager Patsy Tebeau, George's younger brother, converged on umpire Jim Galvin to plead their respective cases. Galvin eventually calmed everyone down and play resumed, but not for long. Knell threw over to first again, and Dahlen slid back again, this time with spikes high. Patsy Tebeau rushed back onto the field, but before he could get very far, Galvin stepped in and ejected him.

Umpire Galvin was the same Jim Galvin who had won 361 games in a big league career that had ended just three years earlier. (He was also the Pirates' pitcher Dahlen had faced in his major league debut.) This was his first year as a National League umpire, and while he had handled this situation well, he would not last the season. League president Nick Young released him in midsummer, and by August Galvin was back in Pittsburgh working as the foreman of a pipe-laying gang.

Cleveland Spiders manager Patsy Tebeau, whose brother George got into a nasty tussle with Dahlen at first base.

As ugly as the Dahlen-Tebeau incident was, it unfortunately typified the kinds of clashes that occurred all too often during this decade. As historian Bill James wrote in his *Historical Baseball Abstract*, "The tactics of the 1880s were aggressive; the tactics of the 1890s were violent. The game of the '80s was crude; the game of the '90s was criminal. The baseball of the eighties had ugly elements; the game of the nineties was just ugly."[5]

Ever since Dahlen contributed three hits and three runs in that May 10 win over Boston, he had been hitting well below his normal pace. The same was true for Anson, although he would eventually find his batting eye and bat .335 for the year. However, for Bill and for many others, 1895 would see a downturn in all offensive categories. Whenever baseball tampers with either the offensive or defensive portion of the game, both sides begin immediately to adapt to the new format. By 1895, most pitchers had adjusted to the longer distance between the mound and home plate and to the new pitcher's slab. That adjustment helped produce a drop in the league's total batting average from .309 in 1894 to .296 in '95. A significant number of players saw their averages decline, though few so precipitously as Dahlen, whose average plunged from .359 to .254. He compensated somewhat for his offensive slide with his continued defensive brilliance. Dahlen did lead the league in errors, but then he got to more balls than any other shortstop, leading in assists for the first of what would be four times. Bill's work at shortstop was also a major contributor to Chicago's leading the league in double plays.

In contrast to Dahlen's offensive decline, two Colts players did exceptionally well at the plate. Bill Lange batted a robust .389, good for fifth place among the league's elite batters, and rookie third baseman Bill Everitt batted .358 for a 10th-place finish.[6] Lange, amiable, talented, graceful, and good-looking, was by far the Chicago fans' favorite player. In a contest to determine the team's most popular member, Lange received more than 26,000 votes, easily winning the prize of a bicycle. A piece in the June 22, 1895, issue of *Sporting Life*, analyzing the social habits of various Colts players, said that "you could find Bill in front of the Chicago Opera House or some other theater any evening." Bill Hutchison, on the other hand, would be inside watching the show, while Adonis Terry, Bert Abbey, Walt Wilmot, and Scott Stratton were "reserved, quiet gentlemen who did not mingle in the gaieties of the town."[7] Everitt, Jimmy Ryan, and Mal Kittridge were never seen without their wives, and Griffith was rumored to be in love. While Dahlen was still a fan favorite, the article said, he did not chase around quite as much as Lange. Anson chose not to say much about the night life of his players, though he repeatedly censured Dahlen and Everitt for their habit of smoking cigarettes. Cigarettes will ruin Dahlen and Everitt in the same way they had led to the death of Kid Camp, said old Cap, a man who usually smoked three cigars a day.[8]

Rookie second baseman Ace Stewart was considered too new to be classified socially, but he was, nevertheless, turning into a very interesting player. Anson had purchased him from the Sioux City Cornhuskers of Ban Johnson's Western League and made him the Colts second baseman. He replaced the highly unpopular and unproductive Jiggs Parrott. Anson had surprised everyone when he began the season with Parrott still on the roster. "I realize that Jiggs is not popular with the Chicago crowds, so we will play him in games abroad only," he said in defense of his decision. [9] Anson soon changed his mind, releasing Parrott after just three appearances.

By July, the *Sporting News* was calling Stewart, along with Lange, the team's two top players. But while Lange was on the way to his greatest season, Stewart faded badly and soon fell out of favor. He and Anson had clashed in late June, resulting in the youngster asking for his release. The manager was always finding fault with his play, Stewart said. The tension may have contributed to his generally poor play, which began soon after. (Everitt also slumped in July as the team struggled all month.) Stewart finished the season with a .241 average and would never again play in the major leagues.

That Anson no longer had the control over his players he had in the past was now obvious to all. Dahlen in particular would do anything he could to rile the "old man." A story in *Leslie's Illustrated Weekly* best exemplified his often juvenile attitude toward Anson.

> Anson never was a good fielder of low thrown balls, and his infielders were wise to his failings as a first baseman. Dahlen was an accurate thrower, and in morning practice he used to shoot them over so they would bound at Anson's feet. One morning Anson dismissed practice, but kept Dahlen out on the diamond throwing over to first base. He didn't know that Bill was kidding him, and of course, Bill never cracked a smile. That's his way when he's having fun. His humor is of the dry variety.
>
> You'll stay here until you learn to throw that ball up to me," said Anson. The other players watched the fun from the clubhouse. A batter would send the ball down to Dahlen and he would shoot it over to Anson. Every throw was hitting the base, and by the time Anson had stopped a few with his shins and chased after balls that got by him he was furious. Finally he let out a bellow of rage that he was going to give Dahlen the beating of his life. Away they went, Dahlen going easily while the ponderous Anson lumbered after him. The other players were thrown into ecstasies of laughter by the chase. Dahlen would pop around a corner, dive over a bleacher wall, and Anson went tumbling after him. All the time the old man was getting more furious. Bill had

Anson gauged so well that he kept only a few feet in front of him and kidded him into thinking he was going to catch up almost any minute. Dahlen kept up the chase for almost an hour, while Anson, with his temper and strength worn to a ragged edge finally gave up vowing dire vengeance on Bill.[10]

But it was not Dahlen alone among his players that Anson could no longer control. Several of them even staged a mini-mutiny during a July 31 game at Pittsburgh. When a twisted ankle forced him out of action in the sixth inning, Anson chose Walter Thornton, a rookie pitcher, to replace him at first base. Dahlen, along with pitcher Griffith, catcher Kittridge, and third baseman Everitt, objected to the move. They gathered together in an attempt to block Thornton's path, while calling for catcher Tim Donahue to come out and play first base. With Thornton and Donahue both standing at the bag waiting to take over, Anson handed his glove to Thornton. "I'm running this club," he said, ordering Donahue back to the bench and the other players back to their positions. The players obeyed, reluctantly, with Griffith continuing to sulk. He served the Pirates three fat pitches, but did not achieve his intended result as each of the surprised batters hit easy fly balls. By the next inning, Griffith's anger had subsided, and he completed the game pitching at full speed.

At the same time Anson was having his problems with Stewart, he also had a run-in with Ryan. Benched by Anson for missing practice, Ryan fell into a slump when he returned, causing the fans to boo him. This was a first for Ryan, a popular player whom the Chicago fans had always supported. When he started hitting again, the boos predictably turned to cheers.

Late August found the Colts in eighth place, neck and neck with Andrew Freedman's Giants. As most of Anson's bets were with Freedman, he was in danger of losing a large amount of money should his club finish behind the New Yorkers. Fortunately, for Anson, a strong final month, coupled with a weak one by the Giants, allowed the Colts to finish fourth, four places ahead of New York. Anson's predic-

Chicago first baseman and manager Cap Anson spent seven years trying to deal with Dahlen's antics on and off the field.

tions, backed with cash, that the Colts would finish in the first division, and that they would have a better record than Brooklyn and Boston, proved lucrative. Rumors had it that the "old man's" total winnings from the various owners were more than his salary.

Another season had passed with no pennant for Chicago, yet, it had been the most successful season of the recent past. For the first time since 1891 the Colts had a winning record, and their fourth-place finish was their highest since they had placed second that year. Success on the field was matched with success at the gate. Attendance rose from 239,000 in 1894 to a new Chicago high of 382,000, the second highest in the league.

Baltimore won its second consecutive pennant, but was again soundly beaten in the Temple Cup series. The Orioles had lost four straight to the Giants in 1894, while this year they managed to win one game from Cleveland. Meanwhile, the Colts' postseason consisted of a two-week barnstorming session through Illinois and Indiana. Anson was off hunting in the Dakotas, so Walt Wilmot led them in his absence. After returning, Anson would make his stage debut in *The Runaway Colt*, a show that most critics panned unmercifully.

Back home in Chicago, all was quiet on the trade front during the offseason. Dahlen's sluggish offensive year aside, he and Bill Lange, the Colts' other young star, were the team's most tradable players. However, Anson and Hart knew that the Chicago fans would not stand for them trading either one: the extremely popular Lange, or even the less popular Dahlen. The two also decided to return to Galveston for spring training. They felt certain that the team's strong start in 1895 had been the result of their preparations in Galveston, as opposed to the wretched start of the year before when they trained at home in Chicago.[11]

Dahlen reported to Galveston from Hot Springs, where he and several teammates had gone to get into playing condition. Bill had done some hunting during the winter, but little else and was obviously overweight when he reported. His girth, when added to his casual style of play, which could easily be mistaken for disinterest and so often was, made him an easy target for the writers. "Fat and lazy Willie Dahlen will attend to matters at short," said the *Sporting News* in one preseason analysis of the Colts. In another, while noting that his salary this year would be $1,800, the paper called him "the hard-hitting, clever, but lazy shortstop."

While individual teams remain the same from year to year, the personnel that makes up those teams is constantly in flux. Players come and players go. Missing from the Colts this season were two men who had been longtime fixtures in Chicago: outfielder Walt Wilmot and pitcher Bill Hutchison. Wilmot had accepted an offer from the Minneapolis Millers of the Western League to be their player/manager, and Hutchison had gone with him. Hutchison had never fully adjusted to the 1893 rule change that increased the pitching distance. He had gone from leading the league in wins for the three seasons before the increase to having losing records in each of the three seasons following it. The winner of only 13 games in 1895 with 21 losses, he blamed his poor showing on his cigarette habit, which he claimed caused him to be excessively nervous. Hutchison vowed that he would never smoke another cigarette, a promise he kept as evidenced by the 20 pounds he gained over the winter. Still, he turned out to be the best pitcher in the Western League, winning 38 games and helping lead Minneapolis to the league title.

Anson expected Algie McBride to replace Wilmot in left field, basing his expectations on the rookie's sensational 1895 season in the Texas-Southern League. McBride was batting .444 for the Austin Beavers before they disbanded in early August, but he would prove not yet ready for the big leagues. McBride played in just nine games before the versatile George Decker took over as the Colts left fielder.

Also gone, for good this time, was second baseman Jiggs Parrott, who had tried to make the team out of spring training but failed. Anson released him, though still echoing his belief that Parrott had major league capabilities. The only reason he was getting rid of him, said Anson, was because the Chicago fans simply did not like Parrott, and he felt some concessions should be made to the fans. Harry Truby, a second-year player, won the second base job, but was injured several weeks into the season. His eventual replacement was onetime Colts star and fan favorite Fred Pfeffer, recently released by the Giants. While he was glad to be back in Chicago, Pfeffer was nevertheless suing the Giants over his release, claiming that it violated a clause in his contract.

Rookie Josh Reilly had filled in briefly at second after Truby was hurt. Unfortunately, Reilly contracted typhoid fever during the season and had to return home to California to recuperate. In line with the practice of the time, Reilly stopped drawing his salary once he left the team. Although he had been with them for only a very brief time, President Hart and all the Colts players contributed money for the young man's benefit. While Reilly would never return to the major leagues, he did recover from his often fatal illness and lived until age 70.

Despite the addition of youngsters like Truby and Reilly, just before opening day the *Sporting News* took issue with the youth and speed inferred by the team's nickname of Colts. The paper suggested that because most of the Chicago players were no longer "coltish," a more appropriate nickname might be "Cart Horses." Not content with that caustic observation, it also criticized the Chicagoans for having the league's ugliest uniforms.

Anson selected left-hander Danny Friend, with only five games of major league experience, to pitch the season opener at Louisville. Friend won 4–2, defeating Chick Fraser, who was making his first big league appearance. Dahlen got off to an excellent start, hitting safely in his first six games. He had nine hits in 24 at-bats including three home runs and two triples. He would finish the season with a career-high of 19 three-baggers, tied for third with Joe Kelley and just two behind the co-leaders, George Van Haltren and Tom McCreery. Three of his triples came against St. Louis on May 3, when a Sunday crowd of more than 17,000 squeezed into the West Side Grounds. With the overflow of fans ringing the outfield, the umpire ruled that any balls hit in among the standees would be a ground-rule triple. Dahlen's three helped the Colts to a 16–7 win.

That game was one of two in 1896 in which Dahlen had four hits (he also had a single). The other was on July 7, when he had four singles in the middle game of a wild three-game series with the Orioles. Chicago scored 13 runs in each game, losing the opener 14–13, winning the second one 13–11, and dropping the finale 15–13. In all, Dahlen had eight hits in 15 at-bats in the three games.

The Baltimore series was in the midst of an incredibly long 46-game homestand, one that began in mid-June with the Colts in ninth place, one game above .500. By the time it ended, they were 16 games above .500 and had climbed to fourth place. Hopes were high in Chicago, but the club was unable to sustain that pace in their final 32 games, all on the road. The Colts ended the season fifth, 18 games behind the Orioles, who won their third consecutive pennant. After two previous failures, Baltimore crowned its 1896 season by sweeping Cleveland to win its first Temple Cup. Anson had bet on the Spiders to defeat the Orioles, a decision that cost him several thousand dollars. He would be more successful that November, winning a similar amount by backing Republican William McKinley over Democrat William Jennings Bryan in the presidential race.

Modern-day fans often think of 19th-century ballplayers as strictly a bunch of hell-raisers. Many of them were, but not all, and not all the time. During homestands, several Colts players and their families boarded at Chicago's Worth Hotel, and one of the ways they passed their evenings was by playing a game called Living Pictures. They would begin the game by placing several tables together, and by making skillful use of the draperies would construct a stage. The players would then mount the stage posed as characters from a famous literary scene. While generally lighthearted and harmless, on one August night this form of entertainment almost cost the Colts the services of Clark Griffith, their best pitcher.

The evening began with a living picture of "Beauty and The Beast," with handsome Bill Lange playing the Beast. Then came "Cupid and Psyche," with Mal Kittridge as Cupid and Barry McCormick as Psyche, followed by "The Noble Fireman," generally acknowledged as the hit of the evening. Bill Everitt played the fireman, Button Briggs was the maiden in need of rescue, George Decker was the ladder, and Tim Donahue played the faithful fire dog.

Next up was "Romeo and Juliet," with an attractive young woman who boarded at the hotel recruited to play Juliet. Dahlen did not usually take part in these skits, favoring the company of the team's other hell-raisers instead. He was, however, taking part this night, and a dispute erupted between Griffith and him over who would play Romeo. Dahlen claimed that Griffith was too bowlegged for the part. Griffith countered that a "fat, pudgy Dutchman" would look ridiculous as Romeo. Griffith eventually won the role, but while he was posing on a ladder during the renowned balcony scene, the ladder gave way and crashed through the stage. Leaning over too far from her "balcony," Juliet also fell through the stage. It took a while, but eventually everyone was safely rescued.

Lusty hitting, led by Dahlen and with major contributions from Anson, Everitt, Lange and Ryan, had again been the Colts' strong point this season. Dahlen had yet another marvelous offensive season, one comparable to his great 1894 campaign.[12] His totals and averages were a bit below 1894, but given that overall batting in the league was down from then, in some ways it was even better. He finished second to Ed Delahanty in both slugging percentage and extra-base hits, categories in which he had finished seventh and ninth respectively in '94. In addition to tying for third place in triples,[13] Dahlen was fourth in the league in doubles, fifth in home runs, and in the top 10 in both total bases and stolen bases. Finishing so high in the latter two categories was evidence of his ability to combine power and speed. His team-leading .352 batting average earned him a gold watch and chain from the club, along with assurances from Hart that the Colts would accept no off-season trade offers for him.[14]

Hart's assurances aside, just how sincere he was in his desire to keep Dahlen is open to question. The two had quarreled in the season's final weeks when Hart refused Dahlen's request for an advance on his 1897 salary. Dahlen countered by requesting his release, hinting that some other club would be willing and happy to offer him an advance. Hart did not appreciate the implied threat, and fired right back at Dahlen. "Don't make yourself believe that we won't give you your release, for we probably will," he said. "We will keep you on the roll until spring, unless we get a chance to trade you, but don't think that Chicago can't get along without you."[15]

Dahlen followed his tiff with Hart with an even nastier battle with Anson during the club's post-season tour. Bill had been a thorn in the old man's side ever since he had joined the Colts as a fresh-faced (and fresh-mouthed) 20-year-old in 1891. The iron discipline that Anson had been able to impose on his players had been deteriorating for years. By now it had just about ceased to exist with most of the veterans, including Dahlen. Anson and his star shortstop had clashed frequently, most recently when Dahlen skipped a practice session at Cleveland a few days before the season ended.

From Cleveland, the club was scheduled to go to St. Louis, where it would finish the season. Anson went down to the train station early and bought tickets for all his players, then boarded the train with the tickets in his pocket. When the rest of the team arrived, the conductors would not allow them through the gates because they had no tickets. While getting word of the situation to Anson would have been easy enough, they thought it would be a fine joke on the old man to let him go to St. Louis by himself. A few miles out of Cleveland, Anson became aware of the situation. He left the train, took a streetcar back to the depot, and after a colorful 15-minute tirade, took his team, en masse, to another St. Louis-bound train.

Pitcher Clark Griffith was Dahlen's teammate in Chicago and his competitor for the lead in "Romeo and Juliet."

Tensions grew even worse a week later, when Anson ordered team practices in Chicago in preparation for a post-season tour. Except for rookie pitcher Button Briggs, all the Colts stayed away. Along with several of his teammates, Dahlen chose instead to spend his day at the racetrack. Then, one night during the tour, on a train chugging its way through the wilds of Indiana, the animosity between Anson and Dahlen boiled over. Dahlen had gone to bed early that night and had skipped the normal procedure of getting his berth ticket from Anson. When the conductor asked him for the ticket, Dahlen told him he did not have one and suggested he get it from his manager. By this time, Anson was completely fed up with his shortstop. "If he wants his ticket, let him come and get it," he told the conductor.

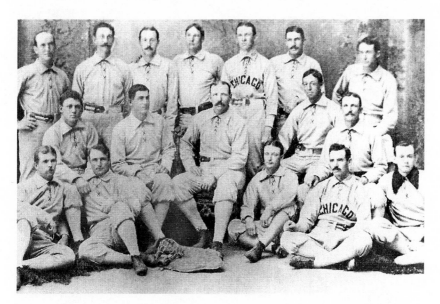

The 1895 Chicago Colts finished fourth, but set a club attendance record.

When the conductor went back to Dahlen with Anson's response, Bill replied angrily that there was no way he was going to get out of bed and go ask Anson for the ticket.

Stuck in the middle of this juvenile dispute, the conductor told Anson the rules required him to put Dahlen off the train if he could not produce a ticket. "Well, put him off," Anson replied, and a few minutes later, when the train stopped at a railway crossing, the conductor escorted Dahlen off the train. According to one newspaper report of Dahlen's unceremonious departure, "He dropped down alongside the raging waters of Cedar Lake, and spent the night in contemplation of a deserted picnic ground."[16]

Still, the question remains of why exactly Dahlen had to be put off the train. The team had already purchased tickets for the trip, tickets that were separate from those entitling them to the sleeper car. Dahlen could have simply left the sleeper car and sat in coach for the trip. Speaking of the incident several days later, Anson attempted to reestablish his managerial control. "The young man simply got gay," he said of Dahlen, "and I simply put him off at Buffalo [*sic*]. Whenever a player thinks he is much better than the common lot it is time to change his views. I had to let him know that he was not running the outfit. There is nothing more to say about it."[17] Hart called it a case of childishness. "Both were probably bluffing and both will probably be sorry when they reflect on their action."[18]

Disregarding Anson's bluster, the players all sided with Dahlen, although some believed he had deliberately arranged the whole affair because he no longer wanted to continue the tour. Many around Chicago also believed that Dahlen had forced the issue as part of his plan to escape the Colts. Anson and Dahlen went a few weeks without speaking to one another until Hart brought them together in his office, where they shook hands and reconciled.

Nevertheless, this latest episode revived memories of Dahlen's desertion in Cleveland two years earlier and spurred some reporters covering the club to campaign openly for the Colts to trade him. The fans, caring only that he was among the best players in the game, felt differently. They mostly wanted their star shortstop to stay, as did W.A. Phelon Jr., *Sporting Life's* Chicago correspondent. Phelon disagreed sharply with those reporters who were urging the club to trade Dahlen because of his disruptiveness. While granting that he could be a difficult player to manage, Phelon believed that Dahlen's hitting, fielding, and running skills far outweighed any attitudinal problems he might have.

"Dahlen may be a kicker and a disorderly element," Phelon wrote, "but any man who can play the ball that Dahlen does is of more value to a team than half a dozen good young men who would observe all the club rules and regulations and bat about 100 points weaker and accept about half as many chances. If Anson had a team full of Dahlens," he continued, "his hair would turn gray in a week, but they would leave Baltimore so far behind that they could not be seen with a spyglass."[19]

Yet, it was general knowledge that Bill himself would have welcomed a trade, preferably to an Eastern team, and if the rumors were correct, specifically to the Phillies. He attended the National League meetings, held in Chicago in mid-November, hoping that it would happen, but it did not. Pittsburgh offered to trade their shortstop, Fred Ely, for Dahlen, but the Colts turned it down cold.

After hinting he would buy a saloon and laze around all winter, as he had a year ago, Dahlen chose to join a local indoor baseball team, one that included several of his fellow Colts. Another teammate was the great Boston shortstop Herman Long, who moved to second base, as Dahlen, by his efforts, claimed the shortstop position. Despite batting left-handed, Dahlen hit very well, and his quickness on the slippery indoor floor made him clearly the fans' favorite performer.

Dahlen also spent much of his winter at Mussey's billiards parlor, in the company of other Colts players wintering in Chicago. Often seen at Mussey's, the city's unofficial gathering place for baseball people, were Griffith, who was also studying law this winter, Ryan, Pfeffer, and even Anson when he was not off hunting somewhere.

FIVE

The Captain Becomes Expendable

Perhaps because so many of their players were now going to Hot Springs to prepare for the season anyway, the Colts chose that city to prepare for the 1897 season. Everyone on the roster reported in accordance with Anson's orders except Bill Lange, who would not arrive until sometime after March 17. On St. Patrick's Day, Lange, wintering in California, would stop off in Carson City, Nevada, to see Jim Corbett defend his heavyweight title against the English challenger, Bob Fitzsimmons.

Corbett had lots of friends in the sports and entertainment worlds, many of whom were at ringside for the fight, including lawmen Bat Masterson and Wyatt Earp. If they were there rooting for and betting on the champ, they went home disappointed. Fitzsimmons, though six years older and 16 pounds lighter, took the title from "Gentleman Jim" with a 14th-round knockout. Corbett was a frequent attendee at ballgames and had numerous acquaintances among the players, many made through his brother Joe, a pitcher with Baltimore. No doubt his loss to Fitzsimmons cost many of his National League friends a sum of money.

A pre-spring training visit to Hot Springs had become an annual ritual for Dahlen, so he was there even before Anson and the other Colts arrived. His indoor baseball pals, Clark Griffith and Herman Long, made the journey with him. Six months had passed since the train incident of the previous fall, but the press had not forgotten it. The *Chicago Inter-Ocean* reminded its readers, perhaps with tongue in cheek, that although Dahlen was now 27 years old, he was "still a youth." They hoped he would learn to take baseball and his responsibilities more seriously as he grew older. It is highly unlikely that Dahlen took the newspaper's admonition to heart; nevertheless, he played the exhibition schedule with a newfound enthusiasm. John Calvin, the Colts correspondent for the *Sporting News*, wrote that Dahlen had "dropped the slouchy don't care" way of fielding the ball, a mannerism for which the press had so often criticized him. He was now going after balls hit in his vicinity aggressively and following up with strong throws to first, said Calvin.

After having his typically excellent spring training, Dahlen continued right into the season, batting safely in Chicago's first seven games.[1] The club, however, started the '97 season slowly, losing the first three games and six of the first eight, all on the road. After winning its home opener against St. Louis, on a day in which the club honored Anson, its longtime star and manager, it dropped the next four. Barely three weeks into the season, the Colts had lost 16 of their first 20 games and were in last place, already eight and one-half games behind Baltimore. Dahlen, batting well above .300 in the early going, was the lone bright spot in Chicago's bleak baseball landscape. He was playing the best ball of his career, wrote *Sporting Life's* W.A. Phelon Jr. "So far Dahlen is the team," he said. "If the rest of the men played with the fire and force of Dahlen, the club would lead the league by a huge margin."[2]

That a reporter who covered Dahlen was praising his physical abilities was not unusual; that he was not countering that praise with some kind of censure for Bill's attitude, either directly or by insinuation, was. Phelon did, however, lament his own failure in getting Bill's personal thoughts on the game he played so well.

"I have frequently tried to get Dahlen to tip off some indication of his ideas on baseball, but it wouldn't go," he wrote. "Of all the quiet, uncommunicative Germans I ever met, Dahlen takes the biscuit. He can say less than any other man of my acquaintance."[3]

Following their miserable start, the Colts would show no great improvement over the rest of the season. A combination of mediocre pitching and injuries to several key players would result in a ninth-place finish. Clark Griffith continued to be the staff ace, winning 21 and leading the league in complete games. However, Danny Friend and rookie Jimmy Callahan each won only 12, and second-year man Button Briggs, 12–8 as a rookie in '96, won just four while losing 17. Only the last-place Browns allowed more runs than the 895 given up by Chicago pitchers.

Injuries also played a part in the team's poor showing, with Jimmy Ryan being the only regular who came close to playing a full schedule. Bill Everitt, who played every inning of every game the year before, missed 32 games this season. George Decker missed 22, including some after his wife's death in early August; Bill Lange missed 18, and Callahan, who doubled as a second baseman, missed 15. Still, the biggest blow was the loss of Dahlen. Bill was batting .314 and fielding as staunchly as ever when he suffered a severe leg wound in a May 30 game against Baltimore. And while the Orioles had a well-deserved reputation as the league's dirtiest team, Dahlen's injury was no fault of theirs, but rather a result of his own aggressiveness.

The Sunday contest against the champion Orioles had drawn another full house to West Side Park. Trailing 1–0 in the bottom of the third, the Colts had a runner at first — pitcher Griffith, who had walked — with two outs and Dahlen at the plate. On the mound for Baltimore was Bill Hoffer, who had made a spectacular entrance into the National League. Now in his third season, Hoffer had compiled the league's best winning percentage in each of the first two. Dahlen connected with one of his offerings, sending the ball into the crowd that was standing in the outfield. Under the ground rules in effect, it was an automatic triple that brought Griffith home with the tying run.

Then, as Hoffer was pitching to Lange, Dahlen broke for home and slid in safely. The Orioles complained heatedly that Lange had interfered with rookie catcher Frank Bowerman, but umpire Tim Hurst disagreed. Following Dahlen's steal of home, Chicago added another run and went on to an easy 9–3 win. The next day's *Chicago Tribune* reported that in sliding home, Bill had "cut his leg open for four inches, almost to the bone."[4]

Dahlen's injury would keep him out of action for two months. Among the games he missed was Chicago's record-breaking win over Louisville on June 29. The Colts swamped the Colonels 36–7 that day, the most runs ever scored by one team in a major league game. Lange, pitcher Callahan, and rookie second baseman Jim Connor each had four hits. Barry McCormick, playing shortstop in Dahlen's place, as he would for most of the time that Bill was out of the lineup, had six.[5] Overall, McCormick did a credible job as Dahlen's replacement. He fielded well, and while he also hit well upon first taking over, he soon faded at the bat. In any case, he was no match for the man he replaced.

Chicago's win over Baltimore on the day of Dahlen's injury moved it into 10th place, but just 12 games behind the first-place Orioles. Despite playing at a .500 clip in his absence, the Colts were still 10th when he returned; however, they had slipped to 20 games behind, and Boston, not Baltimore, was now leading the pack.

During the period he was sidelined, Dahlen spent much of his recovery time at his favorite place, the local Chicago racetracks. An abscess had formed near the cut, and it began to appear as if he would miss the entire season. Fortunately, the wound healed sooner than expected, and on July

25, a gloomy, overcast Sunday, he returned to the lineup for a home game against Louisville. McCormick had injured his leg in practice and was unable to play. When the crowd of 8,000 realized the jaunty walk of his replacement could belong to no other than Bill Dahlen, they began cheering and continued to cheer for a full 10 minutes. In a self-celebration of his return to action, Dahlen played an inspired game in the field and manufactured the only run of the contest. Jimmy Callahan blanked the Colonels, and George Decker contributed a magnificent catch in left field, but it was Dahlen, for this day anyway, who was the darling of the fans.

In a game called after seven innings because of rain, he handled 10 chances flawlessly while taking part in three double plays that stifled Louisville rallies. Batting in his familiar number two position, he had two hits, including a single to lead off the fourth. Pitcher Walter Thornton attempted to bunt him over, but when first baseman Perry Werden's throw to pitcher Bert Cunningham got away, Thornton was safe. Seeing the ball get by Cunningham, Dahlen took off for third and reached there safely. Cunningham retrieved the ball, but Dahlen noticed that he and Werden were arguing. Taking full advantage of the mental mistake, Bill kept running. He scored easily and was credited with an official steal of home.[6] The light rain that had started falling at the beginning of this inning gradually began to increase in intensity. By the seventh inning it had become a downpour, causing umpire Hank O'Day to call the game.

On September 11, Chicago was in seventh place, within striking distance of fifth, when Dahlen culminated this star-crossed season with yet another injury. He sprained an ankle while sliding into second base at Baltimore and played in only one game the rest of the year. Meanwhile, the Colts lost nine of 15 and slipped two places to finish ninth. Their final record of 59–73 left them 34 games behind the champion Boston Beaneaters, who edged out the Orioles to finish first.

Chicago's lowly finish cost Dahlen an additional $100, the result of an off-season bet he had

Inattentiveness by Louisville first baseman Perry Werden led to a Dahlen steal of home.

made. Dahlen and his indoor baseball teammate, Beaneaters shortstop Herman Long, had wagered the money on which of their teams would finish ahead of the other, a wager that in retrospect seemed laughable given the teams' respective positions in the standings. In all, it was a terrible year for the Colts and a frustrating one for Dahlen. A season that started so well for him, with an early summer batting average that ranked among the leaders, ended with his batting .290 and playing just 75 games. The ankle injury had ruined his season, but the fans recognized his effort and showed their appreciation by presenting him a ring.

Because very few players or fans outside Baltimore cared much for the dirty play of the Orioles, Boston's edging of Baltimore for the pennant had been generally popular throughout baseball. The Orioles gained some revenge by winning the Temple Cup in five games. Attendance was again below expectations, and this would be the final Temple Cup series.

The result of having won three consecutive pennants, from 1894 to 1896, and the fame gathered from their notorious style of play, had made the Orioles the most famous team in the nation. Before this season had even ended, they had signed on for a postseason tour of the Midwest and West. Baltimore's opponents would be an "All-American" team, managed by Brooklyn's Billy Barnie and comprising stars from other National League teams. Dahlen, having recovered from his ankle sprain, went along as the All-Americans' shortstop.

Both squads left from Frostburg, Maryland, on October 13, 1897, and played their way across the country. For the series, the Orioles wore their regular gray uniforms with the black and orange stockings, while the All-Americans wore navy blue uniforms with red, white, and blue stockings. Along the way they visited Pike's Peak in Colorado, and some Mormon sites in Salt Lake City. The final destination was California, where the clubs spent several weeks. Boosters in San Francisco and Los Angeles held lavish receptions for them, and the teams responded by playing excellent baseball.

This was no slapdash, put-together-at-the-last-minute type of tour. A great deal of planning went into this effort, resulting in good attendance wherever the teams went. For the players, unlike many other post-season tours, there was no "going through the motions" on this one. Their playing with a purpose was not purely by accident, though. To make sure the players went all out, each had to deposit $100, which they would lose if it were determined that they were either not in condition or not giving their best effort. Dahlen in particular came in for repeated praise for his outstanding play in the field. The games, most of which were closely contested, resulted in 19 wins for the All-Americans and 18 for the Orioles.

As Dahlen toured the West with the Baltimore club, the possibility arose that before the teams returned home, he would be one of them. Supposedly, Orioles manager Ned Hanlon had proposed a trade that would bring Dahlen and some money to Baltimore in exchange for first baseman Jack Doyle. According to the report, Anson saw Doyle, who was unhappy in Baltimore and often at odds with his Orioles teammates, as his successor at first base. A rumor that the Colts would be trading Dahlen was nothing new; a similar report the previous June had him going to the Brooklyn Bridegrooms. Brooklyn club president Charles Byrne had quickly denied that one. Byrne had claimed, to no one's belief, that he was "perfectly satisfied" with his shortstop, George Smith, a .210-hitter finishing his 14th and next-to-last major-league season.

Dahlen was assuredly in favor of the Baltimore deal, having often voiced his preference for being traded to an Eastern team. On the Colts' last visit to Baltimore, he had gone as far as to say he would be glad to play in that city. That the Orioles were among the best teams in the league, probably the best, did not go unnoticed by Dahlen's critics. They had always charged that he sulked with the Colts, who were so often also-rans, and would be a much better player with a contender.

The *Pittsburgh News* echoed that charge in reacting to suggestions by the Chicago press that the Colts trade Dahlen to Baltimore for Willie Keeler. After first claiming that Orioles manager Ned Hanlon would never tolerate Dahlen's indifference and nonchalance, the paper allowed that those negative qualities might evaporate if he were with the Orioles. Dahlen's obsession with horse racing was also something that made some managers leery of having him, but, as it turned out, Hanlon would not be one of them.

Speculation had it that if Baltimore were to get Dahlen, Hanlon would move Hugh Jennings, his current shortstop, to first base and install Dahlen at short. Jennings had been an outstanding defensive shortstop, but an injury to his arm had caused it to grow steadily weaker, and he now found it difficult to make strong throws to first base. Still, Dahlen had been compared unfavorably to Jennings at the start of the recently concluded postseason tour, and perhaps that comparison had been an inspiration to him. There was little doubt that he was now, if in fact he had not always been, a superior fielder to Jennings.

Anson may have wanted Dahlen gone for his own peace of mind, but he did not feel the trade for Doyle, as constructed, was a fair one. If any team should be receiving money as part of the deal, he claimed, it should be Chicago, not Baltimore. "No way will we make this trade," said Anson, and they didn't. Dahlen came back from the tour still a Colt, and returned to playing indoor baseball while telling everyone around him about the wonderful California climate. He also had high praise for 20-year-old Frank Chance, whom he had seen play on the tour and who would be his teammate this coming season.

Anson had been unhappy with the rocky infield and general poor condition of the field at Hot Springs in 1897 and had vowed not to return. Instead, he chose Waycross, Georgia, as the site for the Colts' 1898 training camp. He could not have suspected that by the time spring training came around, he would no longer be the team's manager. The relationship between Anson and President Hart had become so disagreeable that owner Albert Spalding concluded that one of them would have to go. Spalding asked Anson to resign, but Anson refused. Left with no choice, on February 1, 1898, Spalding fired the man who had been his manager since 1879 and chose Tommy Burns to replace him. Burns, manager of the Eastern League's Springfield Ponies, had played for Chicago from 1880 through 1891, and was the third baseman rookie Bill Dahlen had replaced in 1892. With the loss of their longtime leader, the all-knowing "Uncle Anse," some newspapers began referring to the team as the "Orphans" rather than the "Colts."[7]

In early March, Burns took a group of his players (although not Dahlen) to West Baden, Indiana, to get a jump on spring training. Later in the month, the whole club gathered in Waycross, but not for long. Waycross, just north of the Florida state line, was a temperance town with few amenities. On top of that, it had very poor facilities for the players. Not happy there, the team picked up and moved to the larger city of Savannah. However, before leaving, Dahlen pulled a stunt that almost got him run out of town, or worse.

A famous tightrope walker was performing in Waycross and would undertake to do his act above the town's leading thoroughfare. After a few failed attempts, which disappointed the onlookers, his assistant noticed that Dahlen had been mischievously loosening the settings that kept the wire taut. He alerted the townspeople who began chasing Dahlen until he reached the safety of the hotel.[8]

When they reached Savannah, the players were pleased to find it was a very different place from Waycross. Not only were the playing facilities much better, but it was a place where gamblers sold betting pools on horses in the hotel lobby. That, of course, satisfied the horseplayers on the team, foremost among whom was Dahlen. Burns did not approve of these activities, and during the regular season he would break up the players' daily poker game and even attempt to stop their horse race gambling.

Dahlen had turned 28 in January, and he was starting to bald a bit.

Yet in the minds of many, Dahlen still registered as someone who was less than fully mature. In a December 1897 feature on him, *Sporting Life* praised his play, but concluded with these cautioning words. "He is of an erratic disposition and, while sober and careful in his habits, is a hard man to control."[9] Of course, how "sober and careful in his habits" he was is debatable.

Possibly thinking that the best way to control Dahlen would be to give him added responsibility, Burns named him the team captain for the 1898 season. *Sporting Life's* Phelon thought it was a good idea, a way to get Dahlen "out of his lethargy and make him lively as a cricket." However, the gentleman who wrote the "News and Comments" article for that same publication, a man who never missed an opportunity to take a verbal whack at Dahlen, did not agree. He felt that Bill Lange, Jim Connor, Jimmy Ryan, and other candidates Burns was supposedly considering would have been better choices. Dahlen's unstable behavior on the field would eventually prove him correct.

An early indication that Dahlen was not overwhelmed with the honor of being named captain was his refusal of the job until the team kicked in more money. The cash difference between what Hart and the seemingly always financially strapped Dahlen thought the role was worth was $300. After coming to terms on the amount of the stipend, Bill assumed the captaincy and his six-year-old daughter, Corrine, became the team's official mascot. In another family connection, while Cap Anson was no longer the manager, the team continued to employ his father, Henry, who retained his position as a ticket-taker at the West Side Grounds.

During the spring, when Dahlen first undertook his new role, *Sporting Life* grudgingly conceded that he had become "mellow and more accessible to interviews." The praise was short-lived. Once the season began, they were calling him "as obstreperous as ever."

Chicago opened the '98 season at St. Louis, wearing attractive new road uniforms—gray with a maroon stripe on the side of the trousers and maroon stockings.[10] Dahlen showed his ornery side right from the first game, one in which Griffith outpitched the Browns' Jack B. Taylor 2–1. It was Dahlen's stomach-butt of Russ Hall, the St. Louis third baseman playing in his first big league game, that allowed him to score Chicago's first run.

The next day's game got started, but shortly after it did, a fire broke out in the grandstands at Sportsman's Park. Players from both teams noticed the blaze before most of the fans did, and many rushed to help. Several on both teams were singled out for their courage and coolness in directing people to safety and preventing a panic-stricken stampede.

Among the Chicago players drawing praise were Dahlen, Lange, Ryan, catcher Tim Donahue, and rookie outfielder Frank Isbell.

This good deed aside, the 1898 Orphans were on the whole a very combative and quarrelsome team, traits that the Browns rookie manager, Tim Hurst, believed hurt them in the standings. Employing the specific insight of a once and future umpire, Hurst speculated that the constant complaining of the Chicagoans cost the team about five games in the standings. He particularly singled out new outfielder Sam Mertes, veteran first baseman Bill Everitt, and, above all, Dahlen as the main culprits. At one point in the season, Hart had grown so frustrated at having his players thrown out of games he told them that anyone ejected in the future would be fined $25.

The warning (never enforced) apparently did not affect Dahlen. The short-tempered Chicago shortstop went right on complaining, and umpires went right on tossing him out. In all, they dismissed him early a league-high 10 times during the season, a shameful amount for any player, but especially disgraceful for a team captain. The ejections came both in and out of his role as captain, by rookie umpires and by veteran umpires, early in the season and late in the season, early in games and late in games, on balls and strikes and on calls on the bases. Following is a representative sample.

May 22 vs. Washington: By first-year umpire Tom Connolly in the fourth inning for protesting Connolly's decision that Jimmy Ryan had batted out of order. In the seventh, Connolly ousted Bill Lange for continuing to question Dahlen's ejection.

July 29 vs. Washington: By Connolly in the seventh inning for verbally abusing him after being called out on an attempted steal of second base.

August 12 at New York: By veteran umpire Bob Emslie in the fifth inning for arguing a called third strike. Rookie Frank Isbell replaced Dahlen at shortstop and made a throwing error that led to the Giants scoring a 4–3 win.

August 13 at New York: By umpire John Hunt one day later, in the top of the first inning, for protesting an out call at third base on Bill Everitt. Clark Griffith, Chicago's scheduled starting pitcher, cursed Hunt for ejecting Dahlen, and Hunt threw him out too. With Griffith, his best pitcher, gone before making a single pitch, Burns started rookie Walt Woods in his place. The Giants won 9–2.

October 4 vs. Louisville (second game): By umpire Hank O'Day in the fifth inning, after arguing O'Day's call that a pitch had hit his bat and not his person, as Dahlen claimed.

The *Chicago Tribune* called Dahlen's verbal assault on Connolly in the July 29 game "inexcusable," while all the Chicago newspapers berated him often for his lack of self-control. They reminded their readers that losing a player of Dahlen's ability for all or part of any game adversely affected the team's chances of winning that game. The *Sporting News*'s Calvin was especially vehement on this point. Following the August 13 ejection and loss to the Giants, he called Dahlen "the personification of pig-headedness," and blamed him directly for the losses that followed each of his ejections. He also blamed Hart for not enforcing his threat of a $25 fine for each dismissal, a gesture that he believed would have made the "little Pretzel" think twice before getting himself thrown out.[11] As the captain, Dahlen should be advancing the interests of the team, Calvin reasoned. Instead, he was bringing them down.

As deplorable as the 10 ejections were, there probably should have been a few more. The *Brooklyn Daily Eagle* described a June 2 game in which Dahlen sprawled full length on the ground to show his discontent with a decision by umpire John Heydler.[12] "In fact," said the *Eagle*, "throughout the game Dahlen was permitted to kick unmolested."[13] Four days later, in the series finale, he smashed three triples as Chicago crushed the Bridegrooms 15–3, spoiling Mike Griffin's managerial debut.[14]

These accusations of a lack of self-control suggest that the gentlemen of the press thought Dahlen was too intense. Yet, at the same time, they were also charging him, as they had throughout his career, with a lack of intensity, or, more specifically, of not caring. Early in the season, Calvin had given him one of those "left-handed compliments" he so often received from the press. "Captain Dahlen is playing championship ball," he wrote, before lowering the boom, "the kind he can play whenever his heart is in his work."[15]

By midseason, however, it was pure criticism from Calvin. "Captain Dahlen evidently does not appreciate his position," he said. "He is the captain of the team, their chosen leader, and in appreciation of the honor, not mentioning the extra pay it brings him, he should do everything in his power to help the club to a better position."[16] After all, he added, it was not like last year when Dahlen missed those 75 games with a bad spike wound. Most of the games he was missing this season were because of his alleged "stomach problems," an excuse Calvin evidently did not believe. Truth is Dahlen would play in 142 of Chicago's 152 games in 1898, but it was the scattered 10 that he missed because of those "stomach problems" that the press zeroed in on.

Underlying all the criticism was the widely held belief that Bill would rather be spending his time, and money, wherever the horses happened to be running that day. It was a belief well-grounded in fact. One Saturday in late June, he and three of his teammates skipped a home game against Brooklyn. The four chose to spend the afternoon at Washington Park watching the running of the American Derby. All had reasonable excuses, they thought: Dahlen was out with a bad finger, Griffith with a bad back, and Jimmy Callahan was not scheduled to pitch that day. The fourth man was Bill Lange, who told Burns he was the best man at a wedding that afternoon. The four ballplayers had a delightful time watching a horse named Pink Coat win the Derby. While it was Lange that Hart was furious with when he learned the truth, the *Sporting News* reserved its sharpest comments for Dahlen. "Captain Dahlen's interest in the club is not what it should be," the paper proclaimed, "if he can let a matter of a Derby win him away from watching the interests of his club, even though he is on the injured list."[17]

Another of Dahlen's financially inspired public relations blunders occurred in mid-September, which only reinforced his image as a free-spending gambler. Always short of money, he had requested yet another salary advance, this one for $50. When the club refused, reminding him that he was already in arrears, Dahlen stormed angrily out of the office. He played against St. Louis on Saturday, September 10, but told Hart he would not play in the next day's double-header, nor would he accompany his teammates on their final swing through the East. Apparently having reconsidered, he appeared on the field in uniform before Sunday's game, but then returned to the clubhouse and changed into his street clothes. Finding Hart in the stands, he repeated his request, and his threat, but was again refused. By this time, Hart was irate that any of his players would take such a stance, much less the team captain. He wrote out an order decreeing that his star shortstop be benched for the remainder of the season — without pay. Dahlen tried to plead sickness, but Hart told him he must play in that second game — or else. Dahlen did play a couple of innings, thus ending his "strike," but he remained bitter over the whole incident. For Hart, Dahlen's strike threat may have been the ultimate transgression, the one that signaled his end in Chicago.

Rumors of a trade to Baltimore, repudiated in the preseason, resurfaced in late summer. The August 27 issue of *Sporting Life* reported that Hanlon was now offering Hugh Jennings and Joe Kelley in exchange for Dahlen and Bill Lange. Dahlen had made no secret of his desire to be traded in the past, and he repeated that desire after Hart's benching edict. Moreover, he was now convinced that this time it would happen, and that he would be playing elsewhere in 1899. But even if he stayed in Chicago, it now seemed a certainty that the club would strip him of his captaincy.

Speculation about who would captain next year's team began shortly after the season ended. Bill Everitt and Jimmy Ryan were both interested and both were prominently mentioned. (It would be Everitt.)

Despite their contentiousness and their many injuries, Chicago's 1898 season would have to be considered hugely successful overall. After compiling the league's best record in June (19–8), the Orphans remained in the race and occasionally even challenged for the lead. Injuries to key players, especially those to Lange and Mertes, prevented them from keeping up the pace. In fact, costly injuries were so much a part of this Chicago team, that the newspapers took to calling them the "Convalescents" rather than the Orphans. Still, they managed to finish fourth behind only pennant-winning Boston, Baltimore, and Cincinnati. At 85–65, Burns's Orphans were 20 games above .500, a huge improvement over Anson's 59–73, ninth-place Colts of the previous year.

The Orphans also prospered financially. Along with St. Louis, they were the only team whose attendance increased from the year before. But while St. Louis's total of 151.7 thousand was an increase of just over 15,000, Chicago jumped from 327.2 thousand in '97 to 424.4 thousand in '98. For the rest of the league, however, it was another story, and not a good one. America's war with Spain, which broke out shortly after the season started, and a pennant race that in the end involved only three teams, had a devastating effect at the gate. Although the schedule increased from 132 games to 154, total National League attendance declined from nearly 2.9 million in 1897 to just over 2.3 million in 1898, the league's lowest total since 1893.[18]

For Dahlen, the 1898 season was very much a microcosm of his career. He was an outstanding player on the field — probably a much better one than people at the time realized. Still, baseball is a team game, and his ostensibly disinterested attitude, thoughtless escapades, poor judgment, and generally sophomoric behavior made him a less than desirable teammate. "Dahlen, with all his skills, is not a valuable man to a team owing to his peculiar temperament," wrote *Sporting Life* late in the season.[19]

But, oh, those skills. The combination of Dahlen at short, Jim Connor at second, and Bill Everitt at first sparked the Orphans to a major league record 149 double plays, a record that endured for 20 years until the St. Louis Cardinals broke it in 1917. No Cubs team topped that mark until 1922, despite the presence during part of that span of the celebrated Joe Tinker-to-Johnny Evers-to-Frank Chance trio. Batting cleanup, Dahlen repeated his .290 batting average of 1897, while finishing in the top 10 in doubles, extra-base hits, and times hit by pitch. (The 23 times opposing pitchers plunked him is still the Chicago team record.) Not spectacular, to be sure, but combined with his great season in the field, it was sufficient for *Total Baseball* to rate him as the league's outstanding position player for 1898. As in previous seasons, Dahlen's outstanding performance was very likely underappreciated at the time.

Along with his recognized brilliant, if occasionally capricious, play at shortstop, Dahlen had been a mainstay of the offense for all of his eight years in Chicago. He had led the club in runs scored five times, total bases and triples four times, and home runs, doubles, extra-base hits, and slugging average three times. Also in batting average once, hits twice, and times hit by pitch four times. Surely Hart and Burns knew how good a player Dahlen was, but they also knew how very much he wanted to be elsewhere. Clearly, the time had come when it would be in the best interests of all concerned for them to trade him.

Yet when Dahlen announced that he fully expected that he and Lange would soon be traded, Hart objected. Dahlen had no authority to make such a statement, he said, while never denying its accuracy. The decision to trade Dahlen or keep him was Burns's to make, said Hart, although he did expect his manager to consult him. "So far as concerns my personal opinion," he added, "I believe Dahlen and Lange might be exchanged for other players who would be of more service to the Chicago club. I know that the public was dissatisfied with these men this season, and it is on that account that I think it might be well for them to go."[20]

Even Phelon of *Sporting Life*, one of Dahlen's biggest boosters, thought it was time for both Lange and him to move on. "That the two Bills are great ball players goes without denial," he admitted. "That they are not wrapped up in the game as is such a man as Pat Tebeau (the hard-nosed Cleveland player-manager) is also undeniable," Phelon continued. "Possibly they have played too long in Chicago and a change of air would do them good. One thing is certain — the fans regard their exile with less agony than would have been the case two years ago."[21]

Besides the rumors that had the two Bills going to Baltimore for Kelly and Jennings, there was also talk of trading them to Philadelphia for Ed Delahanty and Kid Gleason. These two proposed trades, along with other recent personnel moves got Phelon laughingly to wonder if there was a pattern being established by Hart, a pattern that would "shelve the German element and get a bunch of Irishmen on the team." Along with the likely departure of Dahlen and Lange, he pointed to the impending departures of Fred Pfeffer and George Decker, the hiring of Jim Connor, and the increased use of Tim Donahue behind the plate.

SIX

A Trade to Brooklyn
Brings a Championship

In the second half of the decade of the '90s, the Baltimore Orioles were baseball's most successful team. Future Hall-of-Fame manager Ned Hanlon led a legendary group that included other future Hall-of-Famers, such as Willie Keeler, Hugh Jennings, John McGraw, Wilbert Robinson, and Joe Kelley. The Orioles won consecutive pennants in 1894, 1895, and 1896, and the next two seasons finished second. Yet the Baltimore franchise had been unable to match its great success on the field with comparable success at the turnstiles. Attendance had dropped from a high of 328,000 in 1894 to only 123,000 in 1898, putting the club in severe financial difficulty. Ownership found the solution to their money problems in Brooklyn, a city with a rich baseball history of its own. Well, not really a city. Brooklyn had surrendered that claim earlier in the year. On January 1, 1898, it had accepted an offer that it had refused in 1833 and became incorporated as a borough of Greater New York.

In this era of syndicate ownership in baseball, owning shares in more than one team was legal, and usually desirable. The Orioles took advantage of that arrangement by combining with the Brooklyn Bridegrooms to establish a relationship that each organization saw as mutually beneficial. Under the new setup, Baltimore's principal owner, Harry Von der Horst, and Ned Hanlon, the club's president and manager, would be part owners of the Bridegrooms. Conversely, Brooklyn's principal owner, Ferdinand Abell, and Charles Ebbets, recently elected the team's president, would have a similar interest in the Orioles. Von der Horst and Abell would each own 40 percent of the stock in both the Brooklyn and Baltimore teams, while Hanlon and Ebbets would own 10 percent of each club.

The partners then agreed to move the Orioles' best players to the

Bridegrooms, under the assumption that Brooklynites would turn out in far greater numbers than had Baltimoreans. Or, for that matter, in far greater numbers than they had done in Brooklyn the year before. Attendance at Washington Park in 1898 actually had been lower than it was at Baltimore's Union Park. Unfortunately for the National League, Brooklyn and Baltimore were not alone in their woes. Attendance had been terrible throughout the league, and Brooklyn and Baltimore were just two of the 10 teams suffering declines.

Despite Hanlon's great success in Baltimore and his personal ties to the city, he felt certain he would be managing the Brooklyn club in 1899. So even as negotiations for the Baltimore-Brooklyn merger were underway, negotiations that would allow him to retain the presidency of the Orioles, his major interest was in trying to improve the Bridegrooms. On January 23, 1899, the *Brooklyn Daily Eagle* reported that Hanlon had traveled to New York to meet with Chicago manager Tom Burns. The result of that meeting, wrote the *Eagle*, was Brooklyn's acquisition of Chicago shortstop Bill Dahlen in exchange for second baseman Gene DeMontreville.[1]

Burns, of course, had been trying to trade Dahlen to Hanlon's club for more than a year. At a recent league meeting, he had resurrected a proposal from the previous August: a four-player deal that would have sent Dahlen and outfielder Bill Lange to Baltimore in exchange for Hugh Jennings and Joe Kelley. Hanlon again turned it down, but he still wanted Dahlen, and when Burns suggested an even-up trade for DeMontreville, he jumped at the offer. Burns was happy too, glad that he was rid of Dahlen and pleased to get DeMontreville, an apparently rising star. DeMont, as he was alternately known, had batted .343 and .341 for Washington in 1896 and 1897 and .328 for Baltimore this past season.

Meanwhile, Dahlen, following his lofty .356 average in 1896, had dropped to .290 in each of the past two seasons. He had, however, always played well against the Orioles, especially in Baltimore. Along with many of his players, Hanlon considered him the league's best shortstop. Yet, when the Orioles getting him in a trade for Jennings, their own shortstop, had been rumored, most had opposed it. In their minds Dahlen was an "indifferent" player, while Jennings was always hustling. They acknowledged, however, that if Dahlen had possessed Jennings's temperament, he would be in a class by himself as a shortstop.[2]

But Hanlon did not have Dahlen in mind to be the shortstop in Baltimore. His plan was to bring him to Brooklyn to play third base. By stating his refusal to leave Baltimore for Brooklyn, John McGraw had created a potential vacancy there. It was that vacancy that Hanlon wanted Dahlen, rather than DeMontreville, to fill. In making the trade, Hanlon was indicating that he was certain the Baltimore-Brooklyn deal would go through. But even if it failed and he remained in Baltimore, Hanlon had an alternative plan. Dahlen could play second base for the Orioles, or play shortstop, with Jennings moving to second.

Because the trade involved Dahlen, who along with Lange were the Orphan's best players, the *Chicago Tribune* called it the most important Burns had made since replacing Cap Anson as manager. While Chicago had failed to challenge for a National League pennant since Dahlen's first year there, he nevertheless had established himself as one of the outstanding players in the game. When asked his opinion of the deal, National League umpire Jack Sheridan said that he was surprised to learn that DeMontreville had outhit Dahlen the past two seasons. Still, said Sheridan, "Dahlen is a grand ballplayer, and it will take a mighty good man to fill his place."[3]

Naturally, Burns claimed that Chicago was getting the better of the deal. He cited DeMontreville's four-year age advantage and stressed that he was "a hard, earnest worker at all times."[4] A few days later, Burns went a step further in explaining his reason for making the trade. "I don't want to be quoted as saying that I believe DeMontreville is a better player than Dahlen, but I believe that he will be and that he is now a better player for Chicago than Dahlen. The exchange was made in the interests of discipline and will strengthen the team in other ways as well."[5]

The correspondents covering the Orphans for *Sporting Life* and the *Sporting News* sounded similar themes. William Phelon of *Sporting Life* thought it was a positive step toward breaking up what he called "the good-natured laziness of the Dahlen-Lange combination." Phelon, who always seemed to include a reference to a player's ethnicity in his reports, predicted that "the Frenchman" (DeMontreville) would be far more interested in the club's fortunes than "the German" (Dahlen) had been. John Calvin in the *Sporting News* began by saying there was no one better than Dahlen when it came to "knowledge of the game and the ability to play it," but "that the little man had lost all ambition to do his best."[6]

All these comments, of course, were regarding Dahlen's supposed apathy as a player, a charge that was well known to the New York press. New York newspapermen generally agreed that Dahlen's abilities were superior to those of DeMontreville, but they were already questioning his attitude. The *New York Times*, for one, suggested that the reason "President Hart is anxious to get rid of him" is because "he proved very indifferent to the success or defeat of the Chicago team last year."[7]

Hart, while praising Dahlen's physical skills, elaborated on this alleged indifference when he made his own announcement of the trade. One feature that the baseball public is likely to lose sight of, he noted, is in comparing what Dahlen is capable of doing in the way of ball playing with what he really did do. "In dropping Dahlen from the roll," Hart said, "I do not wish to be considered in any way as reflecting upon Dahlen's playing ability, for a more expert fielder never wore a baseball uniform. If he had greater ambition, I do not doubt but that he would be the acknowledged star of the baseball world. He is a strong player in every department of the game." Hart went on to talk about the need for players to change teams sometimes, predicting that Dahlen's playing in 1899 "will show marked improvement as compared with that of the last few seasons."[8]

"Foxy" Ned Hanlon, one of the three Hall of Fame managers Dahlen played under, had tried for more than a year to acquire him from Chicago.

Western League president Ban Johnson may also have been referring to Dahlen's reputation for indifference in his assessment of the trade. "The deal will greatly strengthen Chicago," said the man who would soon change his league's name to the American League and mount the most serious challenge the National League had ever faced. "DeMontreville is a brilliant player, and Dahlen has not been as valuable a man for the team as those who judge him merely by his work on the field are likely to believe."[9] And in a final swipe at Dahlen, the *Tribune* alluded to DeMontreville's supposed weakness of "not liking the spikes," that is, the failure sometimes to tag base runners because of a fear of being cut. If he did have this weakness, "he will not miss any more men than Dahlen," they said.[10]

Like his teammates, the press, and the fans, Dahlen recognized that it was time for him to leave, but he put the blame on Hart for all the discord between them. "I am sorry to leave Chicago, but it seems to have come to a point where I must go. President Hart and I had some trouble over money matters, and he got sore and determined to get me out of the team. He also set a spy on me, and one or two of the new players who reported to him all I said about him, and reported some things I never did say. He has, so far as I know, found no fault with my playing."

As it turned out, changing Dahlen for DeMontreville would not improve the Orphans. More specifically, Burns would be unable to get along with the "hard drinking" DeMontreville, who became a bigger detriment to the Orphans than Dahlen had ever been. Nor would he be able to get along with several others. The friction between manager and players got so bad that by midsummer, Calvin was writing that Burns had lost control of his team. Jim Everitt, Dahlen's replacement as captain, resigned the post in June, and the dissension-riddled Orphans had trouble finding a replacement. Shortly afterwards, they traded DeMontreville to Baltimore, and at the end of the season replaced Burns with Tom Loftus.

Hanlon was frank in his assessment of the trade, acknowledging Dahlen's difficulty in getting along with some of his Chicago teammates. He was also well aware of what the *Baltimore Sun* called Bill's "reputation of being sulky at times and hard to manage."[11] Still, Hanlon expressed his confidence that the former Chicago team captain would do "gilt edge work" in company more congenial to him.[12]

The deal combining the Brooklyn and Baltimore teams was officially completed on February 4, 1899. Among its provisions was a $10,000 payment to the estate of the late Charles Byrne, the man Ebbets had succeeded as the Brooklyn team's president. The syndicate assigned the players as expected. Most of the best went to the Bridegrooms, including Dahlen, ostensibly to play third base.[13] McGraw, and eventually Wilbert Robinson, remained in Baltimore, with Hanlon naming McGraw as his managerial replacement with the Orioles. Adding players like Bill Dahlen, Willie Keeler, Hugh Jennings, Dan McGann, and Joe Kelley, along with 20-game winners Jimmy "Doc" McJames, Jim Hughes, and Al Maul, raised expectations to a very high level in Brooklyn. Bridegroom fans had seen their 10th-place team of 1898, a team that finished 46 games behind the champion Beaneaters, transformed into one that figured to be among the league's best for 1899. The *Eagle* suggested they might be even more than that. It was conceivable, they believed, that the 1899 Brooklyns might be the greatest National League team ever — better even than the Chicago clubs of the 1880s or the Baltimore and Boston clubs of the past few years.[14]

Most members of the Brooklyn squad traveled together by steamship to their spring training camp at Augusta, Georgia. Dahlen and a few others arrived at the camp headquarters in the Arlington Hotel several days later. With their "confederates" from Baltimore also in Augusta, the two teams played most of their early exhibition games against each other. Even the uniforms of the two teams were almost identical. Each featured a big letter "B" on the left breast — blue for Brooklyn and orange for Baltimore. (While in Augusta, Bill learned of a devastating March 28 fire in Nellis-

ton that burned the homes and busi-
nesses of several Nelliston residents,
including some of his relatives.)[15]

Baltimore showed well in these
exhibition games with Brooklyn. On
April 6, Hanlon got his first look at Joe
McGinnity, a 28-year-old rookie who
had pitched for Peoria in the Western
Association in 1898. Ebbets originally
had signed him to a Brooklyn contract
based on the recommendation of a local
fan, but McGinnity had landed in Baltimore as part of the merger. Dahlen,
batting fifth after having led off in all
the previous games, was the only Brooklyn batter who had any success against
the hard-throwing newcomer. He
touched McGinnity for three hits, but
the Superbas lost 5–1.

Pitcher Joe McGinnity was signed by
Ebbets to pitch for Brooklyn, but the
1899 merger with the Orioles landed
him in Baltimore.

(The Brooklyn club had at various
times in the past been called the
Dodgers, the Trolley Dodgers, and most
recently the Bridegrooms. When Hanlon became the manager, sportswriters began calling them the Superbas after a popular vaudeville act of
the time known as Hanlon's Superbas.)

Overall, the reconstituted Orioles had put together a competitive
team. Beyond retaining McGraw and Robinson, they had held onto
outfielders Ducky Holmes and Steve Brodie, and pitchers Frank Kitson
and Jerry Nops. Coming over from Brooklyn were first baseman Candy
LaChance, shortstop George Magoon, outfielder Jimmy Sheckard, and
pitcher Harry Howell. Led by the pitching of McGinnity, who won a
league-leading 28 games, McGraw's surprising Orioles would finish the
season 24 games above .500 and in fourth place. Yet despite their spirited
showing, attendance dropped below even the 1898 mark. A year later, when
the National League contracted from 12 teams to eight, the Baltimore franchise was among the four eliminated.

Another franchise destroyed by syndicate baseball was the Cleveland
Spiders. Cleveland and the St. Louis Browns had been involved in a merger
similar to the one between Brooklyn and Baltimore. As a result, much of
the former Cleveland team, including such stars as Bobby Wallace, Jesse
Burkett, and Cy Young went to St. Louis. The effects were devastating for

the Spiders. They won only 20 games in 1899 and, like the Orioles, were cut loose in the National League's contraction of 1900.

Third baseman Dahlen was still batting fifth when the club opened the regular season at Washington Park against Boston. Washington Park, Brooklyn's home grounds, was so named because General George Washington had fought the Revolutionary War battle of Long Island nearby. Located in the Red Hook section of the borough, this new structure was the third Brooklyn park to bear that name. The Brooklyn club of the American Association had used Washington Park (I) from 1884 to 1889, and the Bridegrooms had used Washington Park (II) for the 1890 season, their first in the National League. The next year they moved to Eastern Park, in the East New York section of Brooklyn, where they played through 1897. When Charles Ebbets took over the club following the January 1898 death of Charles Byrne, he moved the team to the new Washington Park in time for the '98 season. Washington Park (III) was across the street from number II, bounded by First and Third Streets on the North and South, and Third and Fourth Avenues on the West and East.[16]

In the opener, Kid Nichols defeated Brooklyn's "Brickyard" Bill Kennedy 1–0 in 11 innings. But the game, which Hanlon called, "as fine a game as I ever saw," had greater significance for the Superbas. They had shown the defending world champions, the fans, and most significantly themselves that they were every bit as good as the champs, and maybe better. Boston manager Frank Selee immediately recognized the talent on Hanlon's club. "Brooklyn certainly has got a great team and the race this year will be a warm one among the leaders," he commented after the game.[17]

Dahlen was hitless in his Brooklyn debut, but distinguished himself on the field. He did make an error, but he had nine assists and two putouts. All afternoon, Bill and his Boston counterpart, Jimmy Collins, dazzled the fans with an outstanding exhibition of third base play. Dahlen put all his defensive skills on display in the fourth inning. First he went to his right for Billy Hamilton's sharply hit grounder and threw the speedy Hamilton out at first. Then he grabbed Fred Tenney's foul fly after a long run. Finally, he came in on Herman Long's slow bounder and threw him out at first. Fans remembering the less-than-stellar efforts of Billy Shindle, who played third for the 1898 Bridegrooms, were ecstatic in their acclaim for Dahlen. So was Hanlon. While appraising his infield the next day, one reporter asked him if Dahlen was an acceptable replacement at third for McGraw. "In every respect he is quite as good as McGraw and rounds out an infield which is one of the best in baseball annals," answered Hanlon.[18]

A large and noisy crowd had turned out for the opener, more than 20,000 in a park whose official capacity was 18,000. While they went home disappointed at the outcome, they were aware that a new era had dawned in Brooklyn. After taking two of the next three from Boston, the Superbas moved to Philadelphia, where they lost 4–3. Much of the blame for the loss could be attributed to the three errors made by journeyman Pete Cassidy, filling in at shortstop for the injured Jennings. A sore arm would keep Jennings out of the lineup until July. After he returned, and following a brief "assignment" in Baltimore, Hanlon traded his first baseman, Dan McGann, to Washington for catcher Deacon McGuire, and installed Jennings at first base.

Hugh Jennings as the manager of the 1907 pennant-winning Detroit Tigers. The 1899 "almost trade," sending him to Louisville and bringing Honus Wagner to Brooklyn, would have significantly changed baseball history.

The day after Cassidy's dismal performance, an upset Hanlon moved Dahlen back to his familiar shortstop position. With rare exceptions, he remained there for the rest of his time in Brooklyn. John B. Foster, *Sporting Life's* Brooklyn correspondent, later wrote that Dahlen was so good a fielder, with so good an arm, that if he had stayed at third he would have been one of the best ever at the position. Bill celebrated his return to shortstop with a base-clearing triple against the Phillies, the big blow in Brooklyn's 6–4 win. Cassidy played third that afternoon, but was soon part of a deal with Washington that brought Doc Casey, a mostly untried third baseman, and Duke Farrell, a veteran catcher, to Brooklyn. Casey immediately took over at third, while Farrell became the team's first-string catcher.

Brooklyn had come close to making another deal, one that would have changed the course of baseball history in a most significant way. Had it gone through, Louisville's Honus Wagner would have ended up in Brooklyn instead of Pittsburgh. A story in the July 22 issue of the *Sporting News* declared that the Superbas were working on a trade with the Colonels that would send Hugh Jennings and $2,500 in cash to Louisville and bring Wagner to Brooklyn. Wagner was the Colonels third baseman, the position he would have continued to play with the Superbas had the deal been made, with Dahlen remaining at short. The report added that Louisville owner Barney Dreyfuss wanted Jennings as his shortstop and favored the deal, but that manager Fred Clarke did not. Jennings then killed any possibility of the trade going through by informing Harry Pulliam, Dreyfuss's right-hand man, that he had a sore arm and would be unable to play shortstop for the Colonels.

Two weeks into the season, Hanlon moved Dahlen into the cleanup spot. The move paid immediate dividends. Bill's two hits drove in Brooklyn's only two runs in Bill Kennedy's 2–1 victory at Washington on May 3. Three days later, against Boston's Nichols, he hit his first home run in a Brooklyn uniform. The blow helped the Superbas build a 10–3 lead, but the Beaneaters rallied to tie the score. Farrell's two-run home run in the 10th eventually won it for Brooklyn, 12–10.

Dahlen's average stood at exactly .300 on May 12, when he suddenly came down with a high fever. Dr. McLean, the Superbas' team physician, ordered him to bed, keeping him out of action for 10 days. Joe Yeager, a sometime pitcher and all-around utility man, took Dahlen's place while he rested. After a week's absence, Dahlen returned to the lineup on May 19. Picking right up where he had left off, he doubled, tripled, and drove in four runs in leading the Superbas to a 7–5 win at Cincinnati.

Brooklyn was in the midst of a remarkable 32–4 run when Jack Dunn's 5–2 win at Louisville on May 22 put them in first place to stay. Ten days later, before 2,100 screaming fans at Washington Park, Dahlen's batting and fielding sparked an exciting 8–7 win over the Colonels, increasing the lead to three games. Besides his three hits and two runs scored, Dahlen made several outstanding plays at shortstop, including a game-saver in the seventh inning. With Brooklyn leading 8–6, George Decker and Claude Ritchey opened the Louisville seventh with singles. After moving up on a sacrifice bunt by pitcher Walt Woods, Mal Kittridge followed with a line drive to the shortstop side of second base that appeared headed into center field. Dahlen leaped and speared the ball one-handed. He then stepped on second, easily doubling up Ritchey who was halfway to third. Only the fact that there was already one out kept this from being a triple play, as Decker had almost arrived at home plate. The play, which prevented the Colonels from tying the score, brought the Brooklyn fans to their feet to applaud and cheer their new shortstop. An inning later Dahlen was himself the victim of a great fielding play. Louisville snuffed out his bid for a fourth hit of the afternoon on a sensational grab and throw by third baseman Wagner.

The Superbas provided the home fans even more thrills the next day, overcoming a 10-run deficit to edge the Colonels 11–10. It was their sixth straight win and 18th in the last 21. A win in Cincinnati on June 9 stretched the winning streak to 12. Still, the big buzz in Brooklyn that day was not about the Superbas. The talk among the borough's sports enthusiasts was mostly about the heavyweight championship bout being fought at Coney Island. Englishman Bob Fitzsimmons, the champion, was defending his title against Jim Jeffries, the Ohio-born challenger. Jeffries won with an 11th-round knockout, a result that was extremely popular in Brooklyn and in the rest of the country. The *Eagle* celebrated Jeffries' victory by labeling him the "first real American champion since the days of John C. Heenan."[19] Evidently the *Eagle* did not consider John L. Sullivan, born in Boston, or Jim Corbett, born in San Francisco, both to Irish immigrant parents, as "real Americans."

After several idle days due to rain, the Superbas lost the first game of a double-header at Baltimore, ending the win streak at 12. Brooklyn won the second game, and then the next seven, before enduring its worst string of losses of the season. The team dropped three of four in Chicago, four straight at Pittsburgh, and three straight at Philadelphia. The games in Chicago were the first for Dahlen in that city since the trade. One local reporter noted that he appeared a bit thinner and in better condition than when he had played there. And if he had lost some popularity in his last few years in Chicago, it was not apparent from the reception he received from the fans. Before the first game, a group of his admirers presented him with an imposing four-carat diamond stud, $500 in cash, and multiple bouquets of flowers. His ex-teammates also paid tribute to their former captain by contributing a pair of diamond cuff links. Dahlen had to hire two wagons to carry all the flowers he received back to the hotel. The fans cheered his every move, causing veteran Chicagoans to rank the day's events as the greatest outpouring of applause and gifts ever presented to one player.

The good will shown him did not prevent Dahlen from getting himself ejected in one game at Chicago, and then twice more during the losing streak. Hank O'Day tossed him on June 28 at Pittsburgh for arguing a strike call, and Billy Smith did the honors in the first game of the July 4 double-header at Philadelphia for disputing a call at second base. He also briefly lost his shortstop position, as Hanlon, in a short-lived experiment, shifted him to third and moved Jennings to shortstop. The changes lasted a week before Hanlon returned them to their regular places.

Dahlen's profanity and invective were not reserved just for umpires. He was also a vicious bench jockey. In a September 4 game at the Polo Grounds, Giants pitcher Cy Seymour had a comfortable 4–1 lead when the

Brooklyn bench went to work on him. Seymour had a reputation for being easily rattled, and the expletives thrown at him this afternoon were particularly vile. The perpetrators were many, but Dahlen's remarks were such that umpire Bob Emslie had to warn him to stop. Brooklyn then mounted a rally and won the game, 5–4, and one can only wonder if the bases-loaded pitch that Seymour hit Bill with was accidental.

Over the years, Dahlen and Emslie would have many run-ins. Yet a few days after Emslie censured him for his remarks to Seymour, Bill would come to the rescue of his longtime adversary. After a 2–1 loss to Boston at Washington Park, the Brooklyn fans were irate at what they considered several egregious decisions by Emslie. During the near riot that resulted, Dahlen and second baseman Tom Daly stepped in to help. They shielded Emslie from the crowd, even throwing one particularly crazed fan to the ground as he was about to attack the besieged umpire. All was forgiven the next day, as the Brooklyn fans gave Emslie a resounding cheer when he appeared on the field.

Though the Superbas never relinquished the lead after gaining it on May 22, Philadelphia and Boston stayed close most of the way. Boston actually got to within a game of the lead during the first week in August. Brooklyn finally clinched on October 7, defeating the Giants 13–2 while Boston was losing at Philadelphia. The Superbas would eventually finish eight games ahead of the Beaneaters, with a final record of 101–47 that included a winning mark against each of the other 11 clubs.

Jim Hughes (28–6), Jack Dunn (23–13), Bill Kennedy (22–9), and Doc McJames (18–15) accounted for 92 of the team's 101 victories.[20] On offense, Keeler, with 216 hits, a .379-average, and a league-high 140 runs scored, and team captain Kelley, with a .325 average and 93 runs batted in, were the major contributors.

Dahlen's first year's output in Brooklyn — a .283 batting average, .398 on-base percentage, and .395 slugging average — was very similar to that of his last year in Chicago. On defense, he was steadily solid and often spectacular. Daly, his keystone partner, led all second basemen in errors, but the two men saved countless hits with their sensational play. Time and again, and in every city where the Superbas played, newspaper reports praised Dahlen's brilliance in the field. In a change from their usual complaints, some even praised him occasionally for his attitude. the *Sporting News* commended him late in the season for having played a month, and played well, with a badly fractured toe. Obviously lame, he finally took a few days off in mid-September, but by that time Brooklyn had a good grip on first place.

Although the champion Superbas drew 269,641 to Washington Park,

120 percent more than the previous year, the people of Brooklyn never quite took this team to their hearts.[21] The influx of the Baltimore players had made Hanlon's Superbas a truly great club, but it was not without its consequences. The fans had never fully accepted the business manipulations that produced the merger, nor, surprisingly, were they happy that their team was so good that it hardly ever lost.[22]

In late October, borough president Edward Grout led a local committee that arranged a testimonial dinner in the champions' honor at the Brooklyn Academy of Music. A portion of the money from the more than 10,000 tickets sold, along with other contributions, was presented as gifts to the winning players. Following a series of vaudeville acts, various speakers toasted the pennant winners, including former heavyweight champions Sullivan and Corbett. "Gentleman Jim" had reason to celebrate that went beyond mere fandom. He had bet $3,000 on Brooklyn to win the pennant at odds of 2–1. When they did, he pocketed $6,000.

One speaker at the dinner had praised Dahlen as "the greatest shortstop in the business." However, during the same week, rumors were making the rounds that "the greatest shortstop in the business" would not be playing in Brooklyn next season. The stories originated in Philadelphia, where the Superbas were playing a post-season series against the Phillies. They had Dahlen signing a contract to play in Chicago, but it was not with his old club, the Orphans, nor was it with the new American League team that had relocated from St. Paul. According to these reports, he had signed to play with the Chicago entry in a new American Association that budding magnates in various cities were trying to put together for the 1900 season.

What made the story even more fascinating was that the potential owner in Chicago was none other than Cap Anson, Dahlen's former manager and chief antagonist. Dahlen refused either to confirm or deny the report. "Go and ask Anson," he said. "Perhaps the captain will give you the story."[23] Anson admitted he had not yet signed Dahlen, but insisted he was anxious to have him despite their past rocky relationship. Furthermore, said Anson, he was sure that Bill wanted to play in Chicago.

The proposed American Association never reached fruition; nevertheless, the structure of the game did change radically in 1900. After eight years as a 12-team circuit, the National League paid a cash settlement to its four weakest members— Baltimore, Cleveland, Louisville, and Washington— and liquidated them. The league also reverted from the 154-game schedule back to one of 140 games.

Brooklyn was the reigning champion and had drawn the league's fourth-highest attendance. Nevertheless, rumors had persisted all winter that it was to be one of the teams the National League would be eliminating. But not only did Brooklyn survive, the death of the Baltimore team allowed the Superbas to strengthen themselves even more. They added pitchers Joe McGinnity, Jerry Nops, and Frank Kitson, and infielder Gene DeMontreville from the disbanded Orioles, while reacquiring outfielder Jimmy Sheckard and pitcher Harry Howell from their former syndicate partners.

The addition of McGinnity and Kitson nicely filled the void left by Hughes and McJames. McGinnity's 28 wins (28–16) had tied for the league lead in 1899 and Kitson had added 22 wins (22–16). Hughes McGinnity's co-leader in victories, had chosen to remain in California, while McJames would stay in South Carolina and resume his medical career. Both would return in 1901. Hughes won 35 games over the next two seasons, after which he again returned West. McJames appeared in 13 games in 1901 before dying that September. Only 28, he succumbed to malaria, a disease he had contracted during the '99 campaign. The pitching staff would suffer another blow when Jack Dunn (23–13 in 1899) sustained a sore arm and won only three games before Hanlon sold him to Philadelphia in June.

Dahlen, his pal Willie Keeler, and several other teammates who were wintering in the city had spent part of the off-season umpiring indoor baseball games in the armories of Brooklyn and Manhattan. Although Dahlen had played in such games in his Chicago years, this was his first taste of being on the other side of umpire-player confrontations. He generally drew praise for his umpiring work, and even backed a suggested rule change that he thought would make the game of indoor baseball "perfect." Because runners could steal bases so easily, the proposed rule would compel them to keep a foot on the bag until the ball left the pitcher's hand. In spite of the time spent umpiring, he had gained a little weight, but was less concerned about that than about his wind. To help both, he began taking nine-mile walks into the downtown area from Brooklyn's Sheepshead Bay section, where he was living at the time.

On March 18, 1900, Dahlen left for spring training at Augusta. He traveled on a Pennsylvania Railroad train, accompanied by five teammates living in metropolitan New York. Keeler saw them off, but "Wee Willie" was staying home in Brooklyn for a few days more to care for his seriously ill mother. The train stopped in Baltimore to pick up members of the club living in the Chesapeake Bay area, including Hanlon and Kelley. Hanlon had been pleased with the team's quarters at Augusta's Arlington Hotel the year before, but the Arlington had burned down just before Christmas. Wanting to remain in Augusta, Hanlon booked the Superbas into another local hotel, the Planters.

After a productive and injury-free training period, the team reached the District of Columbia on April 10 for a game against Georgetown University. By then, the consensus was that this group of Superbas was even stronger than the champions of the year before. As well they should have been. For while former Orioles John McGraw at $9,500 and Wilbert Robinson at $6,000, both now with St. Louis, would soon become the highest-paid players in the league, Brooklyn had the overall highest total payroll.

Right from the start of the season, Dahlen and second baseman Tom Daly were playing as marvelously as they had in '99. At third, Gene DeMontreville was fitting in well as the replacement for the diminutive Doc Casey. DeMontreville seemed to work well under Hanlon's discipline, and they were praising his strong throwing arm as the equivalent of Dahlen's back when he had played that position. First baseman Hugh Jennings was still holding out, but the club was confident it could sign him. Meanwhile, Hanlon switched team captain Joe Kelley from left field to first, with Sheckard replacing Kelley in left. When Jennings finally signed, Kelley went back to left field, and with Fielder Jones in center and Willie Keeler in right, Brooklyn again had an excellent outfield. Duke Farrell and Deacon McGuire, both acquired from Washington during the 1899 season, would again split the catching duties.

Along with the shape of the league changing, so had the shape of the game's focal point. Rule makers had converted home plate, which had long been a diamond-shaped 12-inch square, into the five-sided, 17-inch-wide design still in use today. The change, while not widening the plate any, was done to give umpires a better look at both sides of it. In the opinion of most observers, this would benefit pitchers rather than hitters. Pitcher Bill Kennedy of the Superbas agreed with that supposition. "I've been looking the matter over carefully," the loud-voiced but illiterate Kennedy said, "and I tell you there won't be as many bases on balls once the boys get their arms in all right."[24] Kennedy proved to be prophetic, as walks would drop from an average of 415 per team in 1899 to 379 per team in 1900.

SEVEN

One of the Great Teams of All Time

A large crowd packed the Polo Grounds stands for the 1900 season opener between the Giants and the visiting Brooklyn Superbas. Many more fans, unable or unwilling to find seats, stood behind the outfield ropes or looked on from the surrounding bluffs. The New Yorkers took the field wearing their white home uniforms with white caps. They wore blue stockings, and the "New York" spelled out in block letters across their shirt fronts was also blue. The Superbas were in their gray road uniforms and caps. They too wore blue stockings and had their city name printed in blue block letters on their shirt fronts.

The Giants stood at the opposite end of the talent spectrum from the champion Superbas. They had finished 10th in the 12-team league of 1899 and would finish eighth in the eight-team league this year. Still, it was a well-played game between the intracity rivals. Brooklyn's Bill Kennedy bested New York's Bill Carrick 3–2 with Dahlen's eighth-inning two-run single driving in the winning runs. Despite the Superbas having to come from behind to win, Abe Yager in the *Brooklyn Daily Eagle* felt the outcome was never in doubt. "It was the clashing of up-to-date scientific baseball and the obsolete methods of ten years ago and science won out," said Yager in a gibe at the Giants organization.[1]

Dahlen's game-winning hit highlighted what had been a wonderful two days for him. The night before, a group of friends from his off-season residence at the Pierrepont Hotel had presented him with a silver loving cup. Then, with the Superbas trailing, 2–0, in the opener, he led off the seventh with a hit, stole second, and scored on Kennedy's single. An inning later, he drove in the game-winning runs. Dahlen's opening-day work on the field was also eye-catching. He handled 11 chances (nine

74

putouts and two assists) without an error. And to cap it all off, he made each of the three putouts in the ninth inning, ending the game with a nifty shoe-top grab of Kid Gleason's low liner. His nine putouts at shortstop is an opening-day record that still exists.

Dahlen was also involved in the game's only controversial play, which occurred in the Giants half of the third inning. Win Mercer, who had singled, was at first, when Charlie Frisbee laid down a bunt. Kennedy fielded it, but his throw went over the head of first baseman Hugh Jennings and down the right field line. As Keeler chased after the ball, Frisbee rounded first base and headed for second. However, Mercer, assuming that Frisbee had been thrown out, had stopped at second. Not until Frisbee was just a few feet from him did he realize what had happened. He started for third, but on his way there he collided with Dahlen. Umpire Bob Emslie ruled that because Mercer would have been an easy out in any case, Dahlen had committed no interference. The call, correct though it was, did not prevent the Giants fans from hurling their usual abuse at one of their least-favorite Brooklyn players.

The next day the Giants shelled Brooklyn pitchers Frank Kitson and Jack Dunn to win 12–8. In addition to losing the game, the Superbas also lost Tom Daly, their second baseman. New York's George Van Haltren spiked Daly, forcing him to miss the next two months. Hanlon temporarily adjusted his infield by moving Gene DeMontreville from third to second, with Joe Yeager taking over at third. DeMontreville was the player that Hanlon, then the manager at Baltimore, had traded to Chicago the year before to get Dahlen. The Orioles had gotten him back in an August 2 trade for shortstop George Magoon. Now, with Baltimore's demise, he and Dahlen were playing side by side, as they would until Daly returned. The move pleased DeMontreville, who believed playing with Dahlen would make him a better second baseman. "You can't help but play ball when you get by the side of Dahlen," he said. "He knows everything that is going on and after he has made a move or two you know just where to catch him."[2]

Beginning with his outstanding showing on opening day, and carrying through to the end of the post-season series with Pittsburgh, the 1900 season was one of Dahlen's finest as a shortstop. As early as April 28, the *Brooklyn Daily Eagle* heralded a play in which he turned a line drive by Boston's Fred Tenney into a double play for being "as pretty a play as is likely to be seen this season."[3] Later in the year, also against the Beaneaters, the *Eagle* called him "a whole team in himself" after a game in which he had seven putouts and eight assists. Hardly a day passed without the local newspaper making a reference or two to one or more of his spectacular stops, catches, or throws.

Along with his great physical prowess, Dahlen was also playing smart baseball. It was his baseball wisdom that allowed him to devise a particular play that became known around the league as the Sacrifice Killer. The Superbas would use it when the opposition had runners on first and second, no one out, and an obvious sacrifice situation in effect. First baseman Jennings and third baseman Lave Cross would play in close, in the standard positions for defending against an anticipated sacrifice bunt. Then, just before the pitcher released the ball, Dahlen would dart toward the bag at second. His move would usually drive the runner back in that direction, setting up an easy force-out at third when the ball was bunted. The Brooklyn club used the Sacrifice Killer several times, even though their opponents had been warned to prepare for it. Yet because the play called for great coordination between Dahlen, the pitcher, and the rest of the infield, no other club seemed ready to try it. Another reason may have been that if it did not work, it increased the chances of a ball being hit through the infield. To prevent that, a very fast infield was necessary, and none of the others matched Brooklyn's in that category.

Jennings had not signed his contract until the morning of opening day, and then surprised the crowd by taking his place at first base. By July, *Sporting Life* was calling him "the best fielding first baseman ever," though this was just his second season at the position.[4] Because of the Daly injury, the versatile Kelley had been filling in at third base, but with the mid-May purchase of Cross from the St. Louis Cardinals to play the position, the Brooklyn infield was set. The addition of a player of Cross's quality made a great team even greater. Historian Bill James wrote that the 1900 Superbas had six players with Hall of Fame credentials. Four — Willie Keeler, Hugh Jennings, Joe Kelley, and Joe McGinnity — are already in Cooperstown, while two others of comparable quality — Bill Dahlen and Lave Cross— are still waiting admission.[5]

The first of Dahlen's three ballpark evictions this season came on May 4 at Washington Park, during a 6–5 loss to New York. Brooklyn had already scored three runs in the fifth inning when Dahlen batted with two out and Jennings at third base. Pitchers Carrick of the Giants and Dunn of the Superbas had been disputing umpire Tom Connolly's ball and strike calls all afternoon. So had many batters from both teams, including Dahlen. When Connolly called a strike on a pitch that he thought was outside, Bill let him know about it in his usual caustic manner. As the next day's *Brooklyn Daily Eagle* noted, when Dahlen complains to an umpire, he does it "with a sarcasm that is more biting than a howl of discontent from several others." [6]

Dahlen continued with his surly comments throughout the at-bat, until Carrick retired him on a fly ball to Van Haltren. Then, as he almost always did, he continued with his complaints. It seemed inevitable that one of Bill's nasty remarks would trigger an expulsion. Ultimately it did, and Connolly threw him out of the game. Dahlen, who never left quietly, was still shouting abuse at the umpire even as he headed to the clubhouse. While no one can dispute that Dahlen was naturally hotheaded, there may have been a contributing factor. He may just have had too much sugar in his body. The *Eagle* of May 8, 1901, reported that his pregame lunch consisted strictly of desserts.

Hanlon's team was 9–7 on May 12, two and a half games behind Philadelphia and tied for second place with Cincinnati, when they began their first swing through the West. The initial stop was St. Louis

Third baseman Lave Cross, who played alongside Dahlen on the great 1900 Superbas team, is another Deadball Era star that the Hall of Fame has neglected.

where four days earlier the newly organized Street Railway Employees of America, Local 131, had demanded recognition of their union from the St. Louis Transit Company. Along with recognition, they were also asking for higher wages and a 10-hour work day. The transit company refused, and the city was now in the grip of a bitter and violent transit strike, one that would cost several lives and last all summer.

An inability to get to Robison Field by streetcar did not prevent a capacity crowd from showing up for that afternoon's game against Brooklyn. What drew most of them to the park, however, was not the appearance of the champion Superbas. What they had come to see was John McGraw, the feisty third baseman who was now the game's highest-paid player play his first game in a St. Louis uniform. McGraw, who had ended his holdout on the same day the strike began, would have an unfortunate debut for the team now known as the Cardinals. His ninth-inning error led to three runs, allowing Brooklyn to overcome a 4–2 deficit and win 5–4. Three days later, in the finale of the St. Louis series, Dahlen had another of his sensational days at shortstop. He chalked up 10 assists, four putouts, and participated in two snappy double plays. At Cincinnati, the next stop of the Western swing, he continued displaying what the *Eagle* called his "phenomenal" fielding.

On the morning of May 30, the Superbas were still in second place, now a game and a half behind Philadelphia. They fell three and a half behind after losing both games of the Decoration Day double-header to the Cardinals while the Phillies were winning two from Chicago. A win by Philadelphia the next day, while Brooklyn was idle, stretched the Phillies' lead to four games, but it would be downhill for them after that. An injury to Nap Lajoie, suffered in a fight with teammate Elmer Flick, caused Philadelphia's great second baseman to miss several weeks. During that time the Phillies played at a below-.500 pace. By the end of June, they trailed the Superbas by three games and were never again a factor in the race.

Earlier in June, the New York City Buildings Department had ordered Washington Park's 25-cents bleacher seats taken down, reducing the park's bargain seats from 6,000 to 3,000. The reduction came as a terrible blow to a club already experiencing disappointing attendance, and rumors began circulating that the club would be moving to Washington. Even league president Nicholas Young seemed amenable to the transfer, although he continued to deny it publicly. It would not happen, this year or ever, but suggestions of moving the Brooklyn club to the nation's capital would resurface again a few years later.

With the downfall of the Phillies, Brooklyn's greatest challenge came from Pittsburgh, a team that had finished in the middle of the pack for most of its 13-year existence. Yet just as Brooklyn had benefited from the death of the Baltimore Orioles, Pittsburgh had benefited when the same fate befell the Louisville Colonels. Barney Dreyfuss, a distillery executive with a major interest in both clubs, had simply transferred the best of the Colonels to Pittsburgh. Moving north were such stars and future stars as Honus Wagner, Fred Clarke, Tommy Leach, Claude Ritchey, Rube Waddell, and Deacon Phillippe.

After trailing Brooklyn by seven games on the morning of September 1, the Pirates closed the gap to two and a half games by September 12. At that point they had played five games more than the Superbas and lost them all. The closeness of the race induced the Superbas to put up a scoreboard in right field so that patrons at Washington Park could monitor the scores of Pittsburgh's games.

By September 25, after five straight losses, three to the last-place Giants and two to the Phillies, Brooklyn's lead was down to one game. All three losses to New York were by one run and all featured daily run-ins with umpire Pop Snyder. The trouble began after Dahlen objected to a third strike call in the ninth inning of the first game at the Polo Grounds. When his fussing continued into the home ninth, Snyder tossed him out. An inning later, the Giants pushed across a run to win 3–2. That incident was merely a prelude to what happened at the next day's game in Brooklyn. Trailing 4–3 in the last of the ninth, the Superbas had two runners on base. The batter, pitcher Joe McGinnity, hit a ground ball to George Davis that the Giants shortstop turned into a game-ending double play. It was a very close play at first base, and the out call led to a violent reaction among the Brooklyn players.

Kelly threw his glove at Snyder, while McGinnity began shoving him. Meanwhile, the angry crowd started surging onto the field. Snyder, who had discharged the Giants' Pink Hawley an inning earlier for arguing an out call on the bases, had to have the police escort him from the field. Both teams continued their complaints about Snyder's decisions into the next day. And while there was no repeat of the rowdyism of the day before, Dahlen and Sheckard sure seemed to be trying their best to initiate some. Both men led their teammates in showering Snyder with sarcasm before Captain Kelley finally ordered them to stop. Adding to the "peaceful" atmosphere was a large contingent of police, who held the crowd in check.

Snyder, a big-league catcher between 1873 and 1891, made no secret of his dislike for Dahlen's style of protest. "There's a man that is more troublesome than the player that lets out a holler and stops. Dahlen keeps nagging at a man even when he is in his position at short."[7] John Montgomery Ward had been the same way, said Snyder. He would come off the field smiling, but saying something nasty to the umpire as he passed him. Dahlen, he said, had been that way since his early days in Chicago.

Tim Hurst also had reason to oust Dahlen from a game this season. However, a September 1 encounter between the two at Washington Park was even more interesting, in spite of it not resulting in an ejection. It took place with Dahlen at bat in the fifth inning of a game against Philadelphia. While protesting a strike called against him, he stood on home plate to assure that Phillies pitcher Bill Bernhard would not quick-pitch him. "Get off the plate or I'll call you out," roared Hurst. When Dahlen refused to move, Hurst ordered Bernhard to pitch. Bernhard did, but it was a slow toss that Dahlen reached out one hand for and caught easily. "Yer out," said Hurst. Jennings and Kelley came rushing out to inform Hurst that he had no right to call Dahlen out for what he had done. The argument went on for a few minutes, but when it was over, Dahlen was out.

Unlike this almost comical skirmish with Hurst, Dahlen had a notorious clash this year with another umpire, Ed Swartwood. Although Swartwood was a former big league outfielder and the 1883 American Association batting champion, he was a very bad umpire. In an entire article devoted to the poor quality of umpiring in the league this season, *Sporting Life's* John B. Foster called Swartwood the worst offender in the bunch.

Foster cited *Philadelphia Inquirer* writer Frank Hough, who said Swartwood "was incompetent, always had been incompetent, and promised no better for this year than he had in years." [8]

Swartwood had been living up to his reputation during a July 16 game at the Polo Grounds, when a particularly egregious call in the eighth inning triggered the incident with Dahlen. After first ruling that the Superbas had completed an inning-ending double play on a ground ball hit by New York's Mike Grady, Swartwood reversed himself. He decided that Grady was safe, a ruling that allowed Jack Doyle to score and give New York the lead. The call was one of several bad ones, with all of them having favored the Giants. This one, however, was the proverbial last straw. The entire Brooklyn club exploded in rage, led by Dahlen. When Bill's truculence became more than Swartwood could tolerate, the umpire aimed a punch at him. Dahlen avoided that blow, and was spared any future ones when McGinnity grabbed Swartwood in a bear hug to prevent him from trying again.

The next day's *New York Times* placed most of the blame for the ruckus on the Superbas. They described the incident as a disgraceful row between the Brooklyn players and the umpire. "Dahlen became so abusive," they said, "that Swartwood would have given him a thrashing but for the intervention of the players."[9] Probably so; as tough as Dahlen was, Swartwood was several inches taller and weighed more than 200 pounds. Nevertheless, while Dahlen could be extremely abusive, it is unlikely that he said anything Swartwood had not heard before. Striking a player is an unforgivable act for an umpire, and by 1901 Swartwood was gone from the National League's staff.

Following their late September five-game losing streak, the Superbas rallied to win nine of their final 12 decisions. Simultaneously, the Pirates were losing seven of 13, including four of five to seventh-place Cincinnati. Brooklyn finally clinched on October 6, with an 8–6 win at Philadelphia's Baker Bowl. Their final margin of victory would be four and a half games, although their .603 winning percentage was the National League's lowest yet for a pennant winner. We should remember, however, that 1900 was a unique season. The contraction of the four weak franchises, with their best players dispersed to the remaining clubs, gave the National League eight strong teams in 1900. The eighth-place New York Giants, for instance, finished only 23 games behind Brooklyn, and the Giants .435 winning percentage is one of the best ever for a last-place team.

That Brooklyn could win against such tough company, following its domination in 1899, surely places them among the all-time great teams of baseball. Yet because so many "historians" never look at the 19th century, this Superba mini-dynasty has been largely forgotten. They are clearly among the most neglected of baseball's great teams.

A group of well-connected Brooklyn rooters arranged for a private party at the borough's Continental Hotel to celebrate the pennant clinching. Every member of the team was present at the dinner. Many made speeches, including Kelley, Jennings, and Keeler, though Dahlen and Sheckard begged off speaking to the group. In his address, Hanlon declared that despite the late clinching he had never doubted his team would win. He remained confident, he said, even after the five straight losses to New York and Philadelphia. "When it gets down to cases of that kind where nerve is needed, the best team will always win out. And I never had any doubt which was the best."[10]

Although the pennant race was over, the season-long rivalry between Brooklyn and Pittsburgh was not. The *Pittsburgh Chronicle-Telegraph* had invited the champions to play a best-of-five post-season series against the runner-up Pirates. They would play all the games in Pittsburgh, with the winner to receive a silver cup valued at $500. Additionally, all the players would share in the gate receipts, which would be split evenly no matter the winner. The Pirates were certain that they were a superior team to the pennant winners. They had good reason to believe this. Pittsburgh had been the only club to win the season series from the Superbas, taking 11 of 18 from them. Now they were anxious for another chance to prove their superiority.

Hanlon, meanwhile, was anxious to confirm that his club was the better one, and he quickly accepted the challenge. The Superbas manager had an additional incentive for wanting to play this series. Dreyfuss had been making snide and disparaging remarks all season about the Brooklyn club in general and Hanlon in particular. *Sporting Life* printed some of his remarks in its June 30 issue.

"Yes it is a fast club," Dreyfuss said about the Superbas, "but I never saw a crowd of men quit sooner than that same team. Why the day that Phillippe pitched against them on their own grounds they let down in a way that actually made me mad. I hated to see such a display of weak-heartedness for the sake of the people who had paid their money to see men give a display of the national game."[11]

Dreyfuss was likely referring to Phillippe's June 7, 7–4 victory at Washington Park. The home team had indeed looked lifeless for eight innings before rallying for three ninth-inning runs. Dreyfuss further questioned the Brooklyn team's courage by proclaiming that "whenever you get the lead on them, they are not in the running."[12]

Even Hanlon, known as "Foxy Ned" for his baseball cleverness, was not immune from Dreyfuss's criticism. "Oh yes, it is a great team," he said. "Hanlon will tell you that without giving him a chance." Dreyfuss went on to question the credit given to the Brooklyn manager for his supposed cunning use of pinch runners: "A Brooklyn paper came out and gave Hanlon credit for his alleged craftiness in having a fast man run for (Duke) Farrell in the game. It said the plan was original with the manager of the champions. That's funny. We made the move early in the season and had (Tommy) Leach go onto the bases several times for (Pop) Schriver."[13]

The Pirates owner also had a ready answer when a reporter praised Hanlon for Dahlen's spirited play under his management. Dahlen has been "showing energy" daily, said the reporter, while pointing out that this was not always the case in Bill's Chicago days. "I can not see where he has been improved so much," replied Dreyfuss, claiming that Hanlon had tried twice this season to trade Dahlen. "He has offered him to us at least once that I know of. People tell me that there is no love lost between the men, and has not been for some time past. You always hear of the efforts Hanlon makes to buy a player. He will give that to the papers, but I take notice that you do not hear of him giving out any stories of the Dahlen kind. He is too slick for that."[14]

If Dreyfuss was correct that Hanlon had wanted to trade Dahlen, such a deal never took place, and Bill completed a very solid season in Brooklyn. He batted .259, and his 69 runs batted in were tied for second highest in the club. On August 30, against Philadelphia, he tied a National League record by hitting two triples in an inning (the eighth). In the field, Dahlen led all shortstops with 517 assists and handled more chances than any other player in the league, excepting first basemen. *Total Baseball* has adjudged him, retroactively, as the National League's fourth-best player in the category of fielding runs for 1900.[15] His fielding average was second among shortstops to the Giants' George Davis, but Dahlen handled close to 200 chances more than Davis. In a post-season column, Foster praised both shortstops, but again countered his praise of Dahlen's physical abilities with insinuations about his attitude.

"I don't believe that any baseball enthusiast has ever seen Dahlen play in any season when he exerted himself harder to win than he did the past summer," wrote Foster. "There was nothing on the field that he would not go after, and as a general rule he was very successful in what he attempted. When Dahlen feels the humor for good work, he can go as far as the best shortstop whoever walked on the diamond," Foster continued, alluding both to Bill's abilities and to his moodiness. "There are days when William holds a grudge against himself. He is inclined to be peevish and sulky. He had a great many of those days when he was with the Chicago nine."[16]

In truth, he did have a great many of those days when he was with the Chicago nine, particularly that night in 1896 when a conductor put him off a train for exhibiting just such peevish and sulky behavior.[17] Yet a similar situation had arisen this season, and this time Dahlen, along with his teammates, had acted anything but "peevishly." After the club booked them on a train from Chicago to New York that had no dining car, the players, including Dahlen, made do. They took turns jumping off at the many stations along the way, picking up food, and occasionally Bromo-seltzer, wherever they could. Dahlen even joined a quintet with Farrell, DeMontreville, Kelley, and Daly that entertained the others with a series of ragtime ditties and sentimental ballads.

The Chronicle-Telegraph Cup series began at Pittsburgh's Exposition Park on October 15. Despite the Pirates' confidence, Brooklyn surely seemed the stronger team with a lineup of .300 hitters like Keeler, Jones, Kelley, Sheckard, and Daly, and a 28-game winner in McGinnity. Beyond leading the league with a .293 batting average, they had also been number one in stolen bases, slugging average, and on-base percentage. Moreover, the Superbas were a veteran club that knew how to play the game. Dahlen, Kelley, Jones, Jennings, Pitcher Bill Donovan, and McGuire were all future major league managers, while Dunn would become one of the most successful minor league managers ever.

The younger Pirates, meanwhile, had Wagner, who had emerged this season as the league's best player, as their only .300 hitter. He had won the first of his eight batting championships with a .381 average while also leading the league in doubles, triples, total bases, and slugging average. However, Pittsburgh's greatest strength was in its pitching, which was deep and varied. Right-hander Phillippe and lefthander Jesse Tannehill had each won 20 games to lead a sensational staff that also had on it right-handers Jack Chesbro and Sam Leever, and left-hander Waddell.

Hanlon, evidently believing his Superbas did not need him there to win this series, had gone home to Baltimore. Captain Kelley, the acting manager, made the obvious choice to pitch the opening game. Kelley selected Joe McGinnity, 28–8 on the season with a league-leading 343 innings pitched. Not so obvious was Pirates manager Fred Clarke's selection. Clarke chose Rube Waddell, bypassing his two 20-game winners and two others who had won 15 each. Waddell had won only eight games this year (8–13), but his 2.37 earned run average was the league's lowest. The unpredictable left-hander had missed a good part of the campaign after Clarke grew weary of his erratic and buffoonish behavior and suspended him.

An early season incident between Waddell and Dahlen had added to the bad blood between the two clubs. During the May 23 game at Pittsburgh, the Brooklyn players had so rattled Waddell that he had to leave a game the Pirates eventually won, 8–5. Dreyfuss wired a complaint to National League president (Nick) Young, complaining about the tactics and language used against his pitcher. He singled out Dahlen as the worst offender, alleging that he had stood along the first base line shouting vile epithets at Waddell. Dahlen denied the charges, as did his teammates. All contended that at no time was Dahlen coaching at first base. The only coaching he had done, they all agreed, was at third base, and that was for only one inning. And when he was coaching at third base, they insisted, he had used only the normal "razzing" techniques that were common to all "coachers." Dreyfuss had also taken after Hurst, the umpire that afternoon, for allowing what the Pittsburgh president called "rowdy baseball." He asked that the league not permit Hurst ever again to umpire in Pittsburgh.

The Brooklyn players, while admitting that they had been trying to rattle Waddell, argued that it was a common practice done to all pitchers, especially the good ones. You try to find their weaknesses and you work on them, they said. An article in the *Brooklyn Daily Eagle* blamed the whole fuss on Waddell, saying he "cried" and looked to blame others when he failed on the mound. The writer of the story also suggested that because more betting on baseball went on in Pittsburgh than in any other National League city, the fans took losses harder there.[18]

Young had not only turned down Dreyfuss's request about Hurst umpiring games in Pittsburgh, he assigned him to work the Chronicle Cup championship series. Dahlen had also turned Dreyfuss down, refusing his demand for apologies to Waddell and to him. However, Dreyfuss was not finished. Before the final game of that May series, Pittsburgh police officers had surrounded the Brooklyn bench with instructions to arrest any player who did anything much beyond going on and off the field. This attempted intimidation was just the beginning. Before the first pitch was thrown, Dreyfuss appeared in front of the bench and ordered the players to gather round and hear him out. To a man, the players refused. So did Captain Kelley when Dreyfuss called for him to come out. Hanlon, who managed from the bench in street clothes, was furious at all that had gone on and finally ordered Dreyfuss to leave. "You have no more right to interfere with the running of this team than I have to go over to the Pittsburgh bench and force them to do my bidding, or one merchant has to try to run another's store."[19]

This residue of bitterness between the two clubs still existed when the Chronicle Cup series got underway. Game one took place on a lovely autumn day, although recent rains had left the field wet and muddy. An estimated 5,000 fans attended, most of whom were confident of a home team victory. A group sitting along the left field railing had put up a sign that said: "The Cup Will Stay in Pittsburgh, Sure Champions of the World." The Superbas shook that sense of bravado some by taking the opener, 5–2. They used well-placed bunts to capitalize on the slippery conditions, scoring three runs in the third inning and single runs in the fourth and sixth.

McGinnity was magnificent. He limited the Pirates to five hits and two harmless ninth-inning runs, runs that a collision with Waddell an

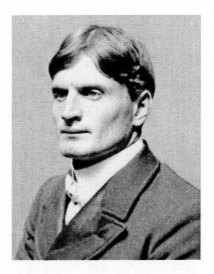

The Pirates accused Dahlen of using vile epithets to rattle their pitcher, the erratic Rube Waddell.

inning earlier may have precipitated. Caught off third base when Waddell fielded a bunt by Keeler, McGinnity, attempting to avoid the tag, had slipped in the mud with his head crashing into Waddell's knee. Several minutes passed before he could stand up and leave the field, leading several Superba players to advise Kelley to bring in a new pitcher. Kelly decided to send McGinnity out for the ninth inning, but ordered Kitson to warm up, in case he needed him. Despite the two runs, Kelley allowed McGinnity to finish the game.

Dahlen contributed two hits to the win, including a leadoff triple in the sixth inning that led to his scoring Brooklyn's final run. He also made the Superbas' only error of the game, although the call was questionable. In going after Jimmy Williams's second-inning ground ball, he slipped in the mud and then threw wild to first. The next batter was Chief Zimmer, and Dahlen atoned for the "error" by turning the Pirates catcher's ground ball into an inning-ending double play.

For the rest of the series, both the temperature and the attendance fell precipitously. Fewer than 2,000 Pittsburghers came out for game two, possibly due to the much cooler weather. Brooklyn won again, 4–2. With Kennedy, their second leading winner, out with an injury, Kelley used Kitson, who pitched a four-hitter. Sam Leever pitched well for the Pirates, but his defense collapsed around him, committing six errors. One was his own, one was by catcher Jack O'Connor, and four were throwing errors

by third baseman Jimmy Williams. Two of Williams's miscues, along with
the one by O'Connor, aided in Brooklyn's scoring the three runs in the
sixth that broke a 1–1 tie.

Game three was all Pittsburgh. Facing elimination, the Pirates
thrashed the Superbas 10–0. They battered Harry Howell for 13 hits and
all 10 runs, while Deacon Phillippe held the visitors scoreless. Pittsburgh's
decisive win was not without controversy. Many fans believed Brooklyn
had allowed the Pirates to win this game in order to extend the series.
Many in the betting crowd concurred in that belief. The skeptics cited as
"proof" the fact that McGinnity had warmed up before the game, but that
when the time came to take the mound, it was the seldom-used Howell
who did so.

The Superbas denied participating in any such conspiracy, and won
the next day to end the series. This time McGinnity not only warmed up,
he pitched, besting Leever 6–1. People in Pittsburgh, confident that their
Pirates were the better team had bet heavily on them to win. Gamblers
took advantage of their certitude to relieve the locals of a great deal of
money. So did a few of the Brooklyn players, chiefly Dahlen, Keeler, and
Kelley.

Brooklyn's team batting average for the four games was .231, slightly
lower than Pittsburgh's .233. Keeler, at .353, and the catching duo of Duke
Farrell and Deacon McGuire, each at .375, were the only regulars to hit
above .300. Dahlen had only one single over the final three games to finish

Dahlen as a member of the Brooklyn
Superbas, one of baseball's unrecognized great teams.

the series at .176. He did, however, play
his position flawlessly, handling 19
chances without an error, and the one
hit he had drove in the first two runs of
the final game. Brooklyn's strong pitching and Pittsburgh's erratic fielding —
it made 11 errors in the four
games — were the deciding factors in
the Superbas' victory.

Before the series, the Brooklyn
players had decided that if they won
they would draw straws to see who got
to keep the actual cup. But after
McGinnity's two commanding com-
plete-game outings, they reversed
themselves and awarded it to the "Iron
Man" unanimously. McGinnity, one of
the league's best-liked men, thanked

everyone, but hinted that because of his business interests in the Oklahoma Territory, this might be his final season as a player. His iron and forge works in McAllister had lost money in his absence, he said, and his pitching salary was insufficient to cover the deficit.

Clarke, who had not played in any of the games because of a leg injury, called the series both a disappointment and a financial failure. Because of the poor attendance — fewer than 11,000 for the four games — the players' shares came to just more than $100 per man. The meager payoff made the players nearly unanimous in saying that mid- to late October was just too late for a post-season series.

Fred Clarke's Pittsburgh teams were great rivals of the Superbas and later the Giants, but a leg injury kept the Pirates player/manager out of the 1900 Chronicle Cup Series.

Despite again winning the championship, this Brooklyn team had failed to generate much excitement among the hometown fans. Newspapers blamed the locals' indifference on the club's importation of the players from Baltimore. The Orioles and their style of play had never been popular with the Brooklyn crowd, and some people were still unhappy with the former Orioles' players, even though they were now wearing Brooklyn uniforms. Others blamed it on the fact that the Superbas were so clearly the league's best team. Because everyone expected them to win, it removed much of the interest from the games. Whatever the reason, the fans had not turned out in numbers commensurate with a winning team. Nor, it seemed, did this group of players inspire the loyalty that fans had shown to previous Brooklyn teams. The club drew just 170,000 to Washington Park, an amount that exceeded only one other National League team — the seventh-place Cincinnati Reds.

Sporting Life's Foster summed up the problem this way: "You can't buy your way to the championship of the National League by corralling the best players in sight and expect that by holding a monopoly of playing talent you are going to induce very many to become fevered over your team's performance."[20]

Yet the race had been close, and the Superbas had been forced to overcome a rash of injuries. Because of that, Hanlon deserved credit for having juggled his lineup sufficiently to keep the team in first place. Still, the indifference to this team, so obvious in the attendance figures, occasionally went beyond the fans. Several Superba players complained that Hanlon had been the only team official to congratulate them after the October 6 pennant-clinching.

A week after winning the Chronicle Cup, supporters of the team held another dinner, this one to salute their latest victory. The site was Brooklyn's tony Carleton Club, where the symbols of triumph, the 1900 pennant flag and the Chronicle Cup trophy, were set in places of honor. Speaking on behalf of the team, President Ebbets made a speech to the local politicians and fans attending. Each player received a pair of sleeve buttons (cuff links) upon which was mounted a miniature bat and ball. A small diamond was embedded at the center of the ball, which was surrounded by the inscription, "Brooklyn B. B. C."[21] Inscribed on the bat were the words "Champions 1900." Several of the Superbas, including Hanlon and Kelley, had already returned to their winter homes and would get their trophies by mail. Dahlen, who lived in the city, chose not to attend.

Two days after the reception, Dahlen and 19 other National Leaguers boarded a steamer in Manhattan bound for Cuba. Most were from the Superbas and the Giants, but players from other National League teams were also part of the assemblage. Those players would fill out the rosters of the two squads, one of which would represent Brooklyn and one New York. The teams would play a series of games against each other in Havana, the capital, and in the lovely city of Matanzas, known as both the Athens and Venice of Cuba. While long popular on the island, interest in baseball had been booming there since the United States helped liberate Cuba in the recent war with Spain. The Cuban National League had several strong teams, and the big leaguers would be playing games against them too.

Besides Dahlen, the Brooklyn position players making the trip to Cuba were Jennings, who would serve as the team captain, Keeler, Sheckard, and Daly. Other nonpitchers were Shad Barry of Boston and Pop Schriver of Pittsburgh. Jimmy Callahan of Chicago was one of three pitchers. The other two were from the Superbas: Harry Howell, whose shelling in game three against Pittsburgh would be his last official game for Brooklyn; and young Bill Donovan, with three wins in three big league seasons but on the verge of stardom. The New York squad had George Davis, who had replaced Buck Ewing as manager of the Giants in midseason, Jack Doyle, Charlie Hickman, Pop Foster, Mike Grady, Cy Seymour, Kid Gleason, and pitcher Win Mercer, all of the Giants, along with Jesse Tannehill and Tom O'Brien of Pittsburgh.

Among those on the dock as the steamship *Havana* set sail were catcher Tim Donahue of Chicago and pitcher Pink Hawley of the Giants. Both had contracted to be part of the delegation, but both had backed out, with Howell and Schriver taking their places. Donahue was forgoing the trip because of a badly swollen hand, and Hawley because of a fear of yellow fever. "Why the island is full of the fever," said Hawley, "and it attacks big men quicker than anybody else. Even the mosquitoes carry it around."[22]

Fear of yellow fever was a legitimate concern. The disease had wreaked havoc in Cuba for centuries, but a cure was near. The United States Army Yellow Fever Commission was part of the American occupation force that had remained in Cuba following the war with Spain. Led by Colonel Walter Reed, this group of medical researchers was in the process of proving (as Pink Hawley had surmised) that it was the *Aedes aegypti* mosquito that was responsible for the yellow fever virus. Their discovery would put to rest a theory, long believed by many, that direct contact with infected people or "contaminated" objects caused the disease.

Just as the ship was about to get underway, Grady and his wife, who had both been in Philadelphia, came rushing out of a hack. A gangway was let down and they were able to board. Then, as the ship was ready to leave, Sheckard and Callahan began protesting their assignment to cabin 13. Tommy Simpson, the secretary of the Brooklyn club, finally assuaged their "fears" and the big steamer left its moorings and headed into the Atlantic.

While the trip down from New York to Cuba met with some rough seas, Dahlen, for one, handled it in good humor. "I've found that this boat riding is all right; the only trouble is that the ocean is paved very poorly," he joked. "If they hadn't put so many creases in it, you could get from one side to the other without being shaken up."[23] Nevertheless, he took part in the general horseplay and ballad singing the players engaged in to pass the time.

Nor did the "rough seas" end after the ship docked in Cuba. Simpson felt that Abel Linares, who was running the Cuban end of the tour, had not lived up to previously agreed-upon financial arrangements. He threatened to turn around and head home, at which point the mayor of Havana stepped in. Fearing bad publicity for Cuba back in the United States if the players should return under these circumstances, the mayor assured Simpson that his demand for $2,000 in American money would be satisfied. But it was not until he actually received the money that Simpson agreed to go on with the tour.

Not surprisingly, the two American clubs won all the games they played against the Cuban National League teams. Simpson felt that the Cubans "knew the rudiments of the game," but nothing about "the inside workings of baseball." He praised their fielding and running ability, but felt they had "lots to learn" about hitting, pitching, and teamwork.

Half the American contingent left early, but Dahlen was among those who stayed for the whole tour. He and the others who had stayed sailed home aboard the Ward Line steamer *Seguranca*. Crowds of Cubans gathered on the docks to cheer them as they left, and as the ship steamed past Morro Castle, the fort at the entrance to Havana Harbor, the American soldiers now stationed there waved their swords and caps in salute. On December 1, the *Seguranca* arrived in New York, and Dahlen summed up the feelings of the players about their Cuban adventure.

"We didn't make any money, but had a pleasant time. Our last game, played last Sunday, was fairly well attended," he added, "but we thought it would be better to return to New York than to make any more attempts to get the Cubans' hard-earned dollars for value received."[24]

However, an assessment of the trip was not all that Dahlen had on his mind upon returning home. He was perturbed at being the lone Superba not to have received a pair of sleeve buttons from that group of Brooklyn rooters who had gathered at the Carleton Club following the Chronicle Cup series.

"I was upset when I got back to Brooklyn to learn that I was the only member of the Brooklyn team who was barred out of the sleeve-button presentation engineered by a few admirers of the champions," he said. Aware of how big a role he had played in the Superbas success, he then wondered at the possible reasons for the omission. He did so in the sarcastic manner to which reporters following the team had become accustomed. "I have yet to learn whether I didn't play good enough ball last season to warrant the present, whether the supply of buttons gave out, or whether I unconsciously offended one of the admirers in some way or other. I suppose I will have to bear the blow, play better ball next season, and be extra polite to any of the admirers I may meet."[25]

Foster took up Dahlen's cause, explaining that if the sleeve buttons were strictly personal mementoes, the givers were free to give them to whomever they liked. If, however, they were a reward for good playing by members of the team, he said, then "Dahlen was as much entitled to be remembered as any player, for he contributed as largely to the success of Brooklyn as any man on the nine."[26] Foster could have well had in mind a game like the one in Cincinnati on July 5. Jerry Nops was the star of the game, pitching a 2–0, one-hit shutout. But it was Dahlen who almost single-handedly accounted for the two runs the Superbas scored against Reds pitcher Doc Newton. He scored both, the first in the seventh on Lave Cross's single after he had tripled, and then in the ninth on Daly's fly ball after he had doubled and stolen third.

Then, as he usually did after complimenting Dahlen's skills on the field, Foster contrasted them with his temperament. "Dahlen is of the opinion that he was slighted because somebody did not like his conduct on the field," Foster continued. "If he wants to know it, there were plenty of persons who did not like it, and have not liked it for a long while. By and by, Dahlen, Kelley, and a great many other players will recognize the fact that a revulsion of sentiment has taken place as to what constitutes snappy baseball, and they will give greater pleasure to twice the number of patrons by counting out of their game that which is offensive to even some who are supposed to have rhinoceros hides when it comes to a matter of public behavior."[27]

As it turned out, Dahlen was not alone in being bypassed for the sleeve-button award. Neither Tom Daly nor Bill Kennedy had received them either. The reason, it seemed, was a feeling by the committee that while they were not the only players who had not attended the Carleton Club dinner, they were the only ones who had done so despite still being in town. To make it even worse, all had given their promise to attend. Their awards were withheld, said the *Eagle's* Yager, who covered Brooklyn baseball for *Sporting Life*, because of "their unmannerly conduct and gross lack of courtesy" to the rooters organization.[28]

Committee member George Mason, speaking for the rooters, clarified the reason for the omissions: "The committee went to considerable trouble and expense to get up the testimonial, and if Dahlen wanted the buttons, he should have attended. He told me on the day of the affair that he would be there, but he did not show up."[29]

Dahlen made a personal appeal to Ebbets, which began with his claim that he had a previous engagement, and ended with his accusing the committee of "fourflushing." He wanted the buttons, he said, only because the Brooklyn rooters were considerate enough to have made them for the members of the team.

The accusation of "fourflushing" did not sit well with Ebbets. "If Dahlen was so anxious to get his buttons, he would have attended the testimonial," he said, "particularly as he had personally promised a member of the committee that he would be present. He did not even send a message of regret. Furthermore, he insulted the members of the committee, all of whom are personal friends of mine, by saying they were "fourflushing."[30]

Despite the disappointing attendance and the unpleasantness surrounding the sleeve-button incident, Ebbets and Hanlon had to be pleased. The Brooklyn fans too, and why not? They might have lost their status as an independent city, but for the last two seasons the best team in baseball represented their borough. Unfortunately, there would be leaner times ahead for the Brooklyn fans, beginning with the arrival of the American League the following year. The 1900 pennant had been Hanlon's fifth in seven years, but it would be his last. Pittsburgh would replace Brooklyn as National League champions in 1901, making them the first Western team to win a pennant since the 1887 Detroit Wolverines. The Pirates would dominate the league in the first three seasons of the new century, while for Brooklyn the glory days would be gone for a long time. Ebbets's club would not finish first again until 1916, while Brooklynites would be unable to celebrate another world championship until 1955.

EIGHT

The American
League Comes Calling

The National League had survived the 10-year challenge of the American Association (1882–1891) and the short-lived ones of the 1884 Union Association and the 1890 Players League. They had been "the only game in town" since 1892, but that distinction ended with the start of the 1901 season. Ban Johnson's declaration of major league status for his newly reorganized American League ended the National League's monopoly forever. The first beneficiaries of the competition between the two leagues were the players. The addition of eight new teams bidding for their services meant that the Nationals were no longer able to dictate salaries in the same way they had previously.

Johnson's league had been the topic of much discussion at the October 1900 dinner celebrating the Superbas' Chronicle Cup victory. The Brooklyn supporters present were deeply concerned about a previous day's report that some prominent Superba players would leave the club to sign with the upstart league. According to the rumor, three would become managers: Joe Kelley in Washington, Hugh Jennings in Philadelphia, and Lave Cross in St. Louis, if that city got a team. Dahlen, along with Willie Keeler, Fielder Jones, Deacon McGuire, Frank Kitson, Joe McGinnity, and Bill Kennedy were the others supposedly ready to jump to the new league. All denied the rumors; nevertheless, McGinnity, Cross, and Jones would be American Leaguers in 1901.

Since that October night the Americans had firmly established that they were here to stay by signing a host of National Leaguers. Among those players making the jump to the new league were such luminaries as Nap Lajoie, Cy Young, Jimmy Collins, Clark Griffith, Harry Davis, Buck Freeman, and John McGraw. The Americans tried hard also to sign Honus

Wagner, the National League's best player, but Wagner stayed loyal to the Pirates. Overall, Pittsburgh was the team least affected by the American League raids. The Pirates lost only one regular to the new league, third baseman Jimmy Williams, who "jumped" to Baltimore. It was no coincidence that Barney Dreyfuss, the league's most enlightened executive, owned the National League team retaining the largest number of its players.

McGinnity had been the National League's leading winner in 1900, and his defection was a serious blow for Brooklyn. He and fellow pitcher Harry Howell left to rejoin John McGraw, who was managing the American League's new Baltimore club. Both had worked under McGraw in 1899 when he managed the Baltimore club that was then in the National League. Hanlon was left hoping that the loss would be offset, at least partially, by the return of Jim Hughes, a 23-game winner for Sacramento of the California League in 1900. Centerfielder Jones, a .300 hitter in four of his five seasons in Brooklyn, signed with Charles Comiskey's Chicago White Stockings. St. Louis did not get a franchise in the new league, so instead of going there, third baseman Cross joined Connie Mack's Philadelphia Athletics as a player.

Hanlon predicted that Frank Gatins, whom he had purchased from the Hartford Indians of the Eastern League, would make the fans forget Cross. Gatins was already 29 years old, and he had only 17 games of big league experience; still, his manager at Hartford, former Brooklyn manager Billy Barnie, had recommended him strongly. Out with a sore arm when the season opened, Gatins eventually returned and played in 50 games. His .228 batting average and .255 on base average were certainly not enough to make the fans forget Cross, or even enough to earn him another year in the majors. In July, Hanlon purchased Dahlen's old Chicago teammate Charlie Irwin from Cincinnati to play third base.

The Pirates were the team least affected by the American League's early player raids, thanks to the enlightened ownership of Barney Dreyfuss.

Two other contributors to the 1900 pennant-winners— Hugh Jennings and Gene DeMontreville — were also gone, but they would be working for other National League teams this year. Jennings had informed the club that he would join them on June 1, after he ended his law studies at Cornell University. Unwilling to wait, Hanlon sold him to Philadelphia in February and moved Joe Kelley in from the outfield to take over at first base. The same month, Hanlon sold DeMontreville to Boston. In a four-game series in May, DeMontreville would come back to haunt his old team, helping the Doves won three of the four.

Willie Keeler expressed regrets about the loss of his outfield mate Jones, but looked forward to playing with his replacement. He assumed (correctly as it turned out) that it would be veteran Tom McCreery. Keeler made those statements on April 2 as he, Bill Kennedy, and Duke Farrell prepared to board a train that would take them to Charlotte, North Carolina, for the start of spring training.

"Dahl,"[1] as they often called Dahlen, was supposed to be part of this group, but was nowhere in sight. Then, just minutes before the train was to leave, Bill came sauntering down the hall as if there were hours to spare. He had been out of town, he explained, and had arrived home just the day before. His teammates were delighted to see their shortstop, whom the *Baltimore Herald* reported had received a favorable raise to remain in Brooklyn. As they were greeting him, team secretary Tommy Simpson handed Keeler, the designated leader of the group, the tickets for all four, and they were on their way.

Baseball officials had not made a consequential change to the offensive-defensive balance since 1893, when they helped the offense by moving the pitching mound back to 60 feet, six inches. Now they would do something for the defense. For years, the game's best hitters had been wearing out pitchers by fouling off good pitches without consequence. Beginning in 1901, the National League, but not the American, approved a rule making the first two foul balls hit by a batter count as strike one and strike two.[2] The main argument in favor of the new rule was that it would speed up games. It would prevent hitters from staying at the plate for interminable lengths of time fouling off pitches, while waiting for the "perfect" one to hit. (One-time Oriole teammates McGraw, Kelley, and Jennings were among those who were particularly adept at this maneuver.) Of course pitchers loved the new rule and batters hated it, while the fans, and even the sportswriters, split almost evenly in their preferences.

The Superbas started the season slowly, splitting their first six games. Dahlen continued to be a marvel in the field, handling 43 chances without an error. "His stops and throws were perfection," said the *Brooklyn Daily Eagle*, adding that "he was the greatest judge in the league of the pace of men running to first."[3] He was able, they said, to loaf against slow runners and hustle with the fast ones. Throughout the season, newspaper game stories would remark on Dahlen's exceptional abilities at shortstop.

This from the *New York Times* of May 5 was typical. "Dahlen's work was as usual a feature of the play."

And there was this from the *Eagle*, which stressed the oft-repeated distinction between Dahlen's fielding proficiency and his fielding manner. "The more one watched Dahlen's work at short field, the more he wonders at the ground the star covers. Far from a graceful poser in the field, and apparently wholly indifferent to all that is going on, Bill suddenly awakens when a ball is hit anywhere in his direction and becomes alive with animation and fire. Nothing seems too difficult for Dahlen to undertake, and he is wide awake at every point of play."[4] Again the contrast between his being "apparently wholly indifferent to all that is going on," to becoming "alive with animation and fire."

The key word to remember in the phrase, "apparently wholly indifferent to all that is going on," is "apparently." In reality, Dahlen was anything but indifferent on the field. One of Hanlon's pet phrases was "to always keep the other fellows guessing and work in the unexpected at the most critical time."[5] Dahlen gave a great example of "working in the unexpected at the most critical time" in a May 2 game against Philadelphia. Brooklyn, behind rookie Gene McCann, led the Phillies 5–4 with two out in the top of the ninth, but the Phillies had runners at first and second with slugger Ed Delahanty coming up. It was a match-up that did not necessarily favor the home team. McCann was making just his third big league appearance, while Delahanty had long been one of the league's most-feared batsmen.

Delahanty took his place in the batter's box, as the crowd in Washington Park nervously awaited the confrontation. The players on the field also seemed focused on "Big Ed"— all, that is, but Dahlen. Bill had slipped quietly behind Roy Thomas, the runner at second, and had signaled catcher Deacon McGuire to have McCann throw the ball to him. McCann, looking in at the fearsome Delahanty, caught the sign, whirled and threw. Dahlen was waiting to put the ball on Thomas for the third out. As the crowd cheered, and McCann congratulated Dahlen, Delahanty slammed the bat down and gave Thomas a most unappreciative look.

Plays like this notwithstanding, the *Eagle* would still often comment on the contrast between Dahlen's abilities and his style. They did it again after a particularly brilliant effort in a game at Cincinnati on June 19. "Dahlen is not an ideal shortstop in practice," they noted. Or does he "believe in working when there is no necessity for it, saving all his energy for the proper time. As soon as the ball is heard, however, his ears go up and he is alert active like a thoroughbred waiting for the barrier to raise."[6]

By mid-June, Hanlon's men were a game below .500 (21–22) and in sixth place. Pittsburgh had just taken the lead, a lead it would hold over the final 16 weeks of the season. Several Brooklyn players were suffering nagging injuries, including Dahlen. A cold had settled in his back, preventing him, the *Eagle* said, from stooping over for grounders or "kicking" at the umpire. The illness caused him to miss a four-game series at St. Louis (June 13–16), in which Brooklyn lost three of four to the Cardinals. Gatins subbed at short, but just did not have the range to get to balls that Dahlen could.

Bill returned on the 18th, going nine-for-19 as the Superbas won four straight to move into third place. The fourth win, on June 21, was a 21–3 thrashing of the Reds at Washington Park. Keeler had five hits and Dahlen four — plus four runs batted in. In all, the Superbas racked up 26 hits against Harley "Doc" Parker, who went all the way for Cincinnati. This was Parker's first outing of the season, and his performance was so poor — the 21 runs and 26 hits are both still National League records— the Reds released him the next day. He never again pitched in the major leagues.[7] Cincinnati was also the victim on September 23, when Brooklyn crushed the Reds 25–6. The 25 runs tied the club record for most runs scored in a game, set on May 20, 1896, and not equaled since.

Cincinnati had been particularly inept against Brooklyn the past two seasons, losing 29 of 39 games played to the Superbas. The 1901 Reds had hard-hitting veteran Jake Beckley and some excellent young players in Harry Steinfeldt, Sam Crawford, and pitcher Noodles Hahn, but overall they were a bad team. Dahlen had his own theory as to just why they were so bad. He blamed it on their home park, League Park, which had an all-dirt infield. Not only was an all-dirt infield hard on the eyes, said Bill, but it reflected the heat in the summer, thereby tiring the Reds players. Maybe Dahlen was on to something. In 1902, when the Reds moved into their new park, the Palace of the Fans, they finished fourth.

Along with the addition of Irwin to play third base, Hanlon purchased outfielder Patrick "Cozy" Dolan from the Cubs in June and pitcher Doc Newton from the Reds in July. The three midseason additions helped the club to an excellent final two months. They won 35 of their final 53 games, but it was not nearly enough to overtake the Pirates. Bill Donovan led the league with 25 wins; Kitson had 19, and Hughes 17. But Kennedy and the fatally ill Doc McJames, who had won 40 games between them two years earlier, won only eight this year.

After having batted in the low .200s for most of the first half, Dahlen had an excellent August and September that brought his season's average up to .266. Though he had not hit for a high average, he usually made his hits count. (His 82 runs batted in was the league's ninth-highest total.)

As early as July, the *Eagle* had noted that Dahlen was making his hits at the most opportune times. While Dahlen had yet to "strike his batting gait," they wrote, he had, nevertheless, done some "extremely timely hitting."

In an attempt to raise his batting average, the right-handed hitting Dahlen had even experimented briefly with becoming a switch-hitter. Frustrated at his trouble connecting with high fastballs thrown by right-handed pitchers, he resorted to occasionally batting left-handed against them. The first time was against Philadelphia's Red Donahue in the second game of an August 20 double-header. A double off Donahue convinced him to try it again, which he did a few days later against the Giants' Dummy Taylor, but he soon gave up the experiment.

Donovan and Hughes had pitched Brooklyn to a sweep of that double-header in Philadelphia, moving Brooklyn into third place, four and a half games behind Pittsburgh. A week later, Hughes and Kitson won a double-header against Boston. Combined with Philadelphia's double loss to New York, it moved the Superbas past the Phillies and into second place. The next day, Newton beat Kid Nichols while the Pirates were losing to St. Louis. With a record of 61–46, Brooklyn trailed the 61–39 Pirates by just 36 percentage points. It would be the closest they would get to repeating as champions. A final record of 79–57 left them two games behind second-place Philadelphia and nine and a half behind the pennant-winning Pirates. They could take some satisfaction, however, in being the only team to win the season series from Pittsburgh, taking 11 of 19.

By the time the Superbas closed the 1901 season with a double-header against the Giants, Hanlon was already thinking of 1902. Among the things he was considering was finding a place for newcomer John Gochnauer. Wanting to get an advanced look at Gochnauer, he played him at shortstop in both games, moving Dahlen to second, a position he had not played since appearing in 10 games there for Chicago in 1893. After the season, Bill went home to Fort Plain for a brief visit before joining other big leaguers on a cross-country exhibition tour that took them all the way to California.

Bill had been mostly well behaved this past season. Bert Cunningham had administered his lone ejection on July 12 in Chicago. Cunningham, in his one season as a National League umpire, was substituting for Frank Dwyer and not doing it very well. The *Eagle* went as far as to call his decisions "farcical." The play that resulted in Dahlen's ejection came in the fifth inning, and began when Brooklyn catcher Deacon McGuire hit a ball that the Superbas all believed was foul. Cunningham, however, ruled it fair, a ruling that resulted in a double play. When McGuire objected to the call,

Cunningham threw him out, the first time in the soft-spoken veteran catcher's 17-year career that anyone had ejected him.

Any umpire who could throw the courtly Deacon McGuire out of a game, would have no problem in tossing out the feisty Bill Dahlen. Bill's departure, an inning after McGuire's, was triggered by Cunningham's calling the Cubs' Frank Chance safe on an attempted steal of second. Thinking he had tagged Chance in time, Dahlen objected in his usual manner and Cunningham told him to leave. He did, without further incident, unlike teammate Jimmy Sheckard, who spat in Cunningham's face to protest a decision at Cincinnati a month earlier.

Dahlen had also set off the Superbas' biggest row of the season, although he had done so inadvertently. Brooklyn was trailing the Giants 7–6 in a May 13 game at the Polo Grounds, when they loaded the bases with two outs in the ninth. His line-single to left "scored" Sheckard and Keeler, but Tom Daly, the runner from first, was out on a throw from left fielder Kip Selbach to second baseman Sammy Strang. When the Brooklyn players discovered that umpire Hank O'Day had ruled that only Sheckard's run counted, they angrily charged onto the field. Surrounding O'Day, they began "gesticulating and throwing their gloves on the ground to add force to their arguments."[8] O'Day reacted by ejecting Joe Kelley, but when that did nothing to end the protests, O'Day forfeited the game to New York, 9–0.

In late September, Hanlon had promised he would hold a banquet for the club if it could beat out Philadelphia for second place. Hanlon-led teams had finished first five times and second twice over the last seven years, and "Foxy Ned" did not want to break that string. Most of all, he did not want to finish behind a team that had Hugh Jennings on its roster. Hanlon had managed Jennings both in Baltimore and Brooklyn before selling him to Philadelphia before the current season began. The Superbas came close, but Jennings and the Phillies did finish second, by two games.

Several reasons can be offered for why Pittsburgh replaced Brooklyn at the top of the standings, but Pirates executive Harry Pulliam had his own theory. He traced the Superbas' undoing back to May, when they allowed rookie outfielder Lefty Davis to go to Pittsburgh. Whether or not Pulliam was right, the move of Davis from Brooklyn to Pittsburgh would have historic importance. Manager Fred Clarke had been unhappy with shortstop Fred Ely, so upon getting Davis, he installed him as his right fielder and moved Honus Wagner from right field to shortstop. A few days later, Clarke gave Ely his unconditional release. Meanwhile, Wagner eventually became the full-time shortstop, still recognized by historians as the greatest ever at that position.

Davis had originally signed to play with Connie Mack's new American League team in Philadelphia, but jumped to Brooklyn before the season started. He had been a bust in his 25 games with the Superbas, compiling a .209 batting average and a horrendous .822 fielding percentage. After the consequences of his poor play led directly to several Brooklyn losses, Hanlon finally gave up on him, giving him his 10-day notice of release on June 14. Oddly, Davis would have his best performance as a Superba just two days later, going four-for-four in an 11–5 loss at St. Louis. When the 10 days were up, the Pirates signed him, and he batted .313 in 87 games for them.

Davis was an excellent addition to an already powerful lineup. Along with Clarke and Wagner, the Pirates also had outfielder Ginger Beaumont, third baseman Tommy Leach, first baseman Kitty Bransfield, and second baseman Claude Ritchey, all of whom were top-notch performers. Yet their greatest strength continued to be in a pitching staff led by Deacon Phillippe, Jack Chesbro, Jesse Tannehill, Sam Leever, and Ed Doheny.

Davis's blossoming in Pittsburgh, following his miserable start in Brooklyn, was among the biggest surprises of the season. A possible explanation for Davis's poor performance with the Superbas emerged in John B. Foster's September 21, 1901, column in *Sporting Life*. Foster wrote of a conversation he had with a Pittsburgh reporter who blamed Davis's Brooklyn troubles on his teammate, center fielder Tom McCreery. Davis would have done fine, he said, had he been playing alongside anyone but McCreery.

The hazing of rookies by veterans was an accepted practice then, as it still is, although to a far lesser extent. But while present-day hazing, where it does exist, is often good-natured, it was not so a century ago. Positions on a major league club were highly valued and difficult to attain and then retain. This was even more the case in 1901. In attempting to hold down costs in their war with the American League, the Nationals had mandated a roster of just 16 men. Veterans guarded their choice status by whatever means necessary. Some were particularly vicious, and according to that Pittsburgh newspaperman, McCreery appears to have fit that category. "It's the same old story that happened in Pittsburgh," said the reporter. "When Beaumont first joined the Pittsburghs, McCreery did everything he could to make it impossible for the new man. I am told that he did the same thing for Davis on the Brooklyns."[9]

Dahlen spent another two seasons in Brooklyn, but the Superbas never again came close to preventing the Pirates from winning their second and third consecutive pennants. The 1902 Pirates had again been the team least affected by the American League's raids. Being able to keep their roster largely intact, the defending champions won a then-record 103 games in a race whose outcome was never in doubt.[10] The Pirates finished 27 games ahead of the second-place Superbas, which remains the largest pennant-winning margin in major league history.[11] Chesbro (28), Tannehill (20), Phillippe (20), Leever (16), and Doheny (16) were responsible for 100 of those 103 victories.[12] Chesbro was the ace, leading the league in wins, compiling a record 14-game winning streak, and throwing a league-leading eight shutouts.[13]

Perhaps it was the players' loyalty to Barney Dreyfuss, or perhaps it was, as rumored, a deliberate scheme by Ban Johnson to avoid signing Pittsburgh players, or maybe it was a combination of both. Whatever the reasons, while the Pirates remained off limits, the American Leaguers considered players on the other seven clubs to be fair game. Buoyed by their success in 1901, they had continued signing many of the National League's best players for 1902. Particularly hard hit were Philadelphia and St. Louis.

The Phillies lost future Hall-of-Fame outfielders Ed Delahanty and Elmer Flick; Delahanty went to Washington, and Flick to Cleveland. Also leaving the Phillies were their three 20-game winners from 1901: Al Orth signed with Washington, Red Donahue with St. Louis, and Bill Duggleby with the crosstown Philadelphia Athletics.[14]

The Cardinals lost pitcher Jack Powell, along with three regulars from their 1901 squad: Bobby Wallace, their great shortstop; Jesse Burkett, the defending batting champion; and Dan McGann, their first baseman. McGann went to Baltimore, while Burkett, Wallace, and Powell all signed with the new St. Louis team, recently relocated from Milwaukee. Philadelphia, which had finished second in 1901, and St. Louis, which had finished fourth, both landed in the second division in '02. Two other prominent National Leaguers leaving to sign with the Americans were shortstop George Davis, from the Giant to the White Sox; and pitcher Bill Dinneen, from the Boston Beaneaters to the Boston Americans.

Brooklyn had three major defectors: the two .300 hitters that made up the right side of their infield and their first-string catcher. First baseman Joe Kelley went home to Baltimore; 35-year-old second baseman Tom Daly, a member of the team since 1890, its first year in the league, went to Chicago; and 37-year-old catcher Deacon McGuire went to Detroit. Hanlon would shift McCreery from the outfield to first base to replace Kelley, and an energetic, acrobatic rookie named Tim Flood would win the second base job. The Brooklyn club disputed the McGuire move, but on June 25, 1902, a federal court judge ruled that the Superbas had no legal claim to him. Jimmy Sheckard also left, signing with Baltimore, but returned after just four games with the Orioles.

Yet, it could have been worse for the Superbas. The previous August, reports had circulated that the Americans had specifically targeted four unidentified Brooklyn players. Dahlen denied being one of the four. "No, I'm not one of the chosen band," he told the *Eagle*. "I've heard footsteps in the distance, but they haven't reached me yet. I haven't heard of any of the boys going out. As for myself, there's a hard winter coming, and I guess I'll hold out for a fat salary and eat snowballs."[15] In contrast to the way the press often pictured him, the *Eagle's* Yager went to great lengths to describe a Dahlen who was both cooperative and exceedingly gracious.

"Dahlen in visiting attire is not the same Dahlen in uniform on the ball field. With the change to street clothes, Bill's face is transformed from the 'eat em up' cast of countenance, which has made many an umpire quail, to a really sweet exterior, and he is not only an easy graceful conversationalist, but is even inclined to be jolly."[16]

Later in the '01 season, the paper reported that a group of Brooklyn players, led by Keeler, Kelley, and Dahlen, had given an ultimatum to Ebbets and Hanlon. You have first choice on our services, they all said, but

unless you meet our salary demands, we will leave. The three men denied the story. "I am not in any clique," said Dahlen, who was asking for a $400 raise, twice the amount that Hanlon was offering. "To show that, I am ready to sign now, if the club comes up to my figure. The difference between my figure and that offered by the club is $200, and the club can have my services right now, regardless of the demands of the other men, if it will pay that difference."[17]

Keeler, the team's biggest star, naturally was the most sought after, receiving solicitations from six of the eight American League clubs. Chicago was one, with an offer of a two-year contract at $4,300 per year. Another was Detroit, which was willing to pay him $5,000 to play with the Tigers. Hanlon did not expect Keeler to take any of those offers, but he did worry about one that came from John McGraw in Baltimore. McGraw, Keeler's ex-teammate with the National League Orioles and now the manager of the American League Ori-

Six of the eight clubs in the new American League were trying to lure Willie Keeler from Brooklyn.

oles, had already lured two old Orioles, Kelley and Joe McGinnity, back to Baltimore. No doubt McGraw lobbied hard for Keeler too when "Wee Willie" served as an usher at his second marriage in January 1902. But in the end Keeler chose to stay home. In February he re-signed with the Superbas, whereupon Hanlon named him Kelley's successor as team captain.

Hanlon himself had not been immune from the baseball rumor mill. One story that surfaced the previous summer had him taking over the presidency of the Chicago Cubs from James Hart. Nothing came of that rumor, or of another one going round at the same time that was even more ominous for Brooklynites. Word had leaked out that league president Nick Young was making inquiries about National Park in Washington, D.C., the past home of that city's National League entry. The purpose of Young's inquiries, some suspected, was in preparation for the league's moving the Brooklyn franchise to the nation's capital for the 1902 season.[18] Other teams in the league were complaining that gate receipts earned when visiting Brooklyn were just not sufficient.

Of course, Young denied that he had any intention of moving the Superbas, and to the relief of the borough's fans, the team was back in Brooklyn in '02. Dahlen was back too, in spite of having been heavily wooed by the American League. One postseason rumor had him headed to St. Louis to play for the new American League team there, while another said he was ready to sign with Charles Comiskey's Chicago White Stockings. However, one afternoon in early November, Dahlen ran into Ebbets at the Aqueduct racetrack, where the two men agreed on a 1902 contract. Also at Aqueduct that day was Jesse Burkett, who told Dahlen about the $10,000 he had received for jumping across town from the National League Cardinals to the American League's Browns.

Undeterred by Burkett's tale, and those of other "jumpers," Dahlen claimed to be content to remain with the Superbas, although he had hoped for a higher salary than the one he finally agreed to. The main reason he had chosen to stay in Brooklyn, he told one reporter straight-faced, was because of its nearness to the ocean. Such a pleasant location, he claimed, was worth the few hundred dollars he might have gained by signing with one of the American League's western clubs.

Assuming Dahlen was being humorous when he stated his preference for being near the ocean would be easy, yet he really may have meant it. Teammate Charlie Irwin was equally convinced of the advantages of being near the sea. "There isn't anything on the top of earth that is better for a ballplayer than baths in the ocean," said Irwin.[19] Another teammate, pitcher Doc Newton agreed, as did umpire Frank Dwyer. "I always like to get around New York," said Dwyer, "for this means a chance to get at least one day off, for that means a trip to salt water."[20]

Sporting Life's Foster, while always quick to criticize Dahlen when he felt that Bill was not giving his best, applauded the signing. The praise heaped upon him for his work at shortstop aside, 1901 had not been one of Dahlen's better fielding seasons, at least from a statistical standpoint. Nonetheless, Foster chose to look beyond the numbers. "Not a shortstop on the diamond played better ball than Dahlen played last year," he said. "There seemed to be nothing that could get away from him, whether on the ground or in the air, and he used better judgment in playing for batters than ever he did before."[21]

Keeler spent the early spring coaching the Harvard College baseball team before joining the 21 others that reported to manager Hanlon for spring training. Dahlen was not among them. Rather than joining his teammates in Columbia, South Carolina, at the beginning of April, he chose to remain in Hot Springs, where he had been since late February. Although in excellent condition overall, his throwing arm had been causing him pain. Past visits to the spa convinced him that a few weeks in Hot Springs would cure the problem, which it did. During his stay there, several American League clubs continued trying to talk him into "jumping," but despite the offers of a higher salary, Dahlen turned them all down. However, before joining the Superbas in Columbia, he did play in several games for another team, the rival Pittsburgh Pirates, who were holding spring training in Hot Springs. In one intrasquad contest, playing for the Pirates second stringers, he had four hits in a win against the regulars.

Dahlen finally arrived in Columbia on April 12, five days before the season opener. His late arrival may have disturbed Hanlon, but given the American League's attempts to sign him while he was in Hot Springs, the manager was just relieved to have him at all. When the Superbas returned from the South, Bill settled in at Brooklyn's St. George Hotel, which was now his in-season residence. He missed the first preseason game at Washington Park, against Columbia College, but played in the final one against Manhattan College. The times were such that even now, a day before the opener, some sources were still claiming that he had jumped his contract and would be playing in the American League, either with Boston or Washington.

The next day he was at shortstop as Brooklyn opened the season at home against Boston. In recent years, the Superbas' home uniforms had featured a bright red ornate "B" on their left breasts, bright red stockings, and all-white caps. But Washington Park patrons saw a new look on opening day. The stockings and the "B" were now blue, as were the caps, although the caps now had a white "B" on the front. Superba fans seemed to like the new uniforms, but of more interest to them was Bill Donovan's 2–1 win over Boston's Vic Willis. When Doc Newton and Gene McCann followed with wins over the Beaneaters, the Superbas were 3–0, but they then lost nine of the next 11. On May 19, following three straight defeats at St. Louis, Brooklyn descended into the league cellar.

Their previous stop, at Chicago, had been an especially tough one for Dahlen. On successive days in the series' final three games, the 12-year-veteran fell for the hidden-ball trick, was ejected, and then imploded defensively and was again humiliated on the base paths.

After Newton and Frank Kitson had thrown back-to-back shutouts in the first two games of the series, Pop Williams and Jock Menefee combined to do the same to the Superbas in game three. Chicago had only one hit, but beat Donovan 2–0 thanks to "Wild Bill's" wildness and his throwing error. The Orphans had already scored their two runs when Dahlen singled in the seventh inning, stole second, and reached third on Tim Flood's fly ball to center fielder Jimmy Slagle. It was a close play at third, but umpire Bob Emslie ruled that third baseman Charlie Dexter had failed to tag the sliding Dahlen. Second baseman Bobby Lowe, now with Chicago after 12 years in Boston, disputed the call, but Emslie stayed with it.

Meanwhile, Dexter slipped the ball under his arm and resumed his position. As Charlie Irwin stepped in to bat, and Menefee took the sign, Dahlen danced down from third. As he did, he was kidding Dexter about his having missed the tag. Suddenly Dexter jumped between Dahlen and third base. This time he clearly applied the tag for the third out, while no doubt doing some kidding of his own. Bill also heard it from the Chicago fans. He had been mostly popular with them in his many years there. Nevertheless, those who had always referred to him as "Bullhead," or "Bullet Head," or similar endearing names, took great satisfaction in jeering at his base-running "boner."

Dahlen's blunder had hurt the team, yet his ejection the following day was even more detrimental. Emslie chased him for complaining long and loud after Bob Rhoads struck him out in the fourth inning. Hanlon replaced Dahlen with rookie Ed Wheeler, who went on to commit five errors over the next six innings. Two of the errors led directly to Chicago runs in a game Hughes lost to the Orphans 3–2.

Back at short the next day, Dahlen made four errors of his own, greatly contributing to the Orphans' 12-inning 8–7 win. On top of the four errors, Dahlen suffered the indignity of another base path embarrassment. Dexter, the same man who had caught him napping two days earlier, was also the perpetrator of this one. In the top of the 12th, Dahlen was on second when Hughie Hearne ripped a single to right. As Bill raced past third, headed for home with the potential winning run, Dexter stuck out his foot and tripped him. After sliding several feet on his chest and then being tagged out, an enraged Dahlen complained to Emslie. Unfortunately, for the Superbas, Emslie had not seen Dexter execute the trip. Assuming Dahlen had stumbled, he called him out. After threatening Dexter with future retribution, Dahlen then committed the error in the home 12th that led to Chicago's winning run.

Dahlen was frequently accused of "not having his head completely in the game," and there might have been some truth to that charge in this series. An item in the *Eagle* of May 15 stated that Bill's former wife had attended each of the five games, while a Chicago reporter wrote that he had seen them chatting together after one of them. He even speculated that the two were in the process of reconciling, but it was purely speculation. They had married when both were very young, and while their brief union had produced a daughter, Corrine, who lived with her mother, there was no chance of their getting back together.

Another Dahlen ejection and another poor performance by his replacement, Wheeler, led to another tough loss in Hughes's next start, five days later in St. Louis. This time, Dahlen could not make it past the first inning, his ejection coming after just one Cardinal had batted. Leadoff man John Farrell had swung at and missed a pitch. It should have been strike three; however, rookie umpire Charles Power ruled that because the ball hit Farrell on the arm, he was entitled to first base. When Dahlen objected, Power tossed him. Not satisfied, Dahlen continued shouting at Power from the bench until the umpire ordered him off the premises. Wheeler came in and, as the *Eagle* said, "made another severe mess of it at short." He contributed several more errors, including one that led to the winning run for St. Louis. "His fumbles and throws were as weird and as costly as those in last Wednesday's game in Chicago," wrote the *Eagle*.[22] Power later ejected center fielder Sheckard, whose replacement, Rube Ward, another rookie, made several outfield mistakes and went hitless.

Brooklyn had hit Cardinals pitcher Bob Wicker freely in this game, so Hanlon was particularly perturbed after the loss. He was not only angry with Power, but also with Dahlen and Sheckard. Along with questioning Power's ability, he thought the rookie was being far too severe on the players as a way to establish his authority. His complaint with Dahlen and Sheckard was over their not heeding his warnings about Power's capricious decisions and his imperious manner. President Young must have agreed with Hanlon's assessment, because Power umpired just this one year in the National League. The Board of Discipline headed by Cincinnati Reds owner

John T. Brush reacted to Dahlen's latest early termination by slapping him with a one-day suspension.[23]

As for Wheeler, this would also be his only season as a big-leaguer. A hard worker and a hustler, he just did not have the talent to stick — not with a .125 batting average and an .852 fielding average. Wheeler did, however, have one moment of glory. Playing second base against Philadelphia one afternoon, he made what the *Eagle* called five really brilliant plays and had to doff his cap repeatedly for an appreciative home crowd. "Dahlen too, covered himself with glory," the *Eagle* added, "but this is so common an occurrence with the star shortstop that his splendid fielding was accepted as a matter of course."[24]

Yet as common as Dahlen's fielding brilliance was, he did have his "off days." Such was the case on August 9, a game in which Hughes defeated St. Louis 4–1. Hughes was terrific, allowing only one hit, a single by Homer Smoot with two out in the eighth inning. But he had lost any chance at a shutout in the very first inning thanks to Dahlen making errors on the first three Cardinals hitters. Roy Brashear, Smoot, and George Barclay all reached on ground balls to short that Bill fumbled, and Brashear eventually came around to score.

Brooklyn's early season stay at the bottom of the standings had been brief. Nevertheless, local fans were quick to realize that this team was neither the equivalent of the one that had won championships in 1899–1900, nor even one that was on a par with the Superbas of 1901. Clearly, the defections to the American League had hurt, but defections had hurt the other teams too. All except Pittsburgh. By the end of May, the Pirates were 30–6, and already seven and a half games in the lead. The race in the National League would be for second place, and Brooklyn was very much in it. Newton's 8–0 win over Philadelphia on May 29, launched an eight-game winning streak and a run of 18 victories in 22 games. By June 19, Hanlon's squad had reached second place. They would occupy that position on and off for the rest of the season and eventually finish there.

The bottom half of the batting order sparked many of the Brooklyn victories during this run, beginning with Dahlen, who batted fifth. Impressed with the scrappiness of the group, the fans took to calling them the "gas house gang," a name later made famous by the Cardinals of the 1930s. Bill was the hero of one game in which the Superbas would have dropped back to third had they lost, and he earned $5 in the process. On July 2 at Washington Park, Bill Duggleby, back with the Phillies, and Hughes had each pitched seven scoreless innings before Philadelphia broke through with a run in the eighth.

Brooklyn went quietly in the home half, and when Dolan fanned to open the ninth, the chances of winning seemed nearly hopeless. Keeler got the fans stirring with a single off Duggleby's glove. Then when Duggleby hit the next batter, Sheckard, the crowd, so quiet just moments before, was up and roaring for a Brooklyn victory. Up came McCreery, but Duggleby got him on a slow roller to shortstop Rudy Hulswitt. On the out, Keeler moved to third and Sheckard to second. So with two out and the tying and winning runs in scoring position, the outcome rested with Dahlen.

"Bring in the run and I'll give you a five spot," Hanlon shouted as Dahlen grabbed a bat. "Count out the money. It's as good as mine," Bill replied while heading toward the plate. True to his word, Dahlen lashed Duggleby's first pitch to deep left field. The ball landed well beyond the reach of left fielder George Browne, bringing home both runs. After turning second, Bill ran to the clubhouse, although he could have easily made third had it been necessary. "I'll give a five spot every time for these kind. Just consider it a standing offer," said Hanlon as he handed over the money.

Two weeks later, after seeing his club shut out three times in five days by Cincinnati's Noodles Hahn, St. Louis's Stan Yerkes, and Chicago's Jack W. Taylor, Hanlon shuffled his lineup. Dahlen, who had batted cleanup early in the season, returned there and would rotate between the third, fourth, and fifth positions for the rest of the year.

The Superbas' final game of the season, scheduled at Philadelphia, was rained out. Before the players began to scatter for home, Hanlon attempted to sign as many of them as possible. Dahlen, for one, refused. He would like to stay in Brooklyn, said Bill, but he had an offer from Detroit that was just too tempting to turn down. He was to confer with Detroit officials in Manhattan the next day, he said, and unless Brooklyn met his demands, he would sign with the Tigers. Hanlon probably did not fully meet Bill's asking price, but he was able to satisfy him, and the following day Dahlen signed with the Superbas. *Sporting Life's* Foster was pleased that Bill would be back in 1903. "He has played the position of shortstop for Brooklyn in a manner that could scarcely be improved upon," he wrote. "In some respects, he is one of the greatest ground coverers who ever worked on an infield."[25]

Yager, who earlier had commended Dahlen's off-field behavior in the *Eagle*, echoed those thoughts in *The Sporting News*. "Dahlen, despite his outwardly surly manner on the ball field, is not half the bad boy the fans have been led to believe he is. There is not a more easily approachable man on the diamond today and he never ignores anybody, be he the poorest dressed or the most misshapen. No charitable deed is proposed, but Bill immediately becomes a prime mover in the undertaking and all collections for benefits and such are placed in his hands."[26]

Dahlen's 1902 numbers—a .264 batting average, .329 on base percentage, and .353 slugging average —were almost identical to his 1901 totals. And again he made his hits count, finishing fourth in the National League with 74 runs batted in. He was also fourth in doubles (25), seventh in triples (8), and fifth in total extra base hits (35).

Meanwhile, Dahlen's unsigned teammates, Keeler, Donovan, and Irwin, headed to Indianapolis, where they would join other players en route to play a series of exhibition games on the West Coast. Dahlen was supposed to be part of the group, but left instead for Fort Plain to be with his sick mother and would catch up with the group later.

Despite finishing so far from first place, Brooklyn's season had to be considered an artistic success. Most experts had laughingly dismissed Hanlon's preseason predictions of a second-place finish for his Superbas. Yet by holding off a late challenge from Boston, he turned out to have been right. Financially, the picture was not so rosy, but, as all in the Superbas' front office agreed, the losses were not as heavy as they might have been. Home attendance was up slightly in 1902, as just under 200,000 made their way to Washington Park. League attendance overall, however, was down significantly, and so the Superbas were leaving most cities with lower paychecks than the year before. Philadelphia and St. Louis, the teams most affected by defectors to the American League had the most substantial declines.[27]

Because Harry Von der Horst, who owned 40 percent of the team, chose not to involve himself in its day-to-day operations, Hanlon and Ebbets continued to battle for its control. And while Ebbets was the team president and Hanlon the manager, Hanlon's salary was likely three times as high as Ebbets's $4,000 per year. Ebbets would eventually buy out von der Horst and Ferdinand Abel and take complete control of the Brooklyn franchise.[28]

NINE

"It Has Always Been My Ambition to Play in New York City"

Dahlen had been among the handful of players that attended the National League's annual meeting in New York in December 1902. In a break with tradition, the league's moguls held the meeting at the Victoria Hotel rather than the Fifth Avenue Hotel, its usual site. As their major order of business, the eight team presidents elected 33-year-old Pirates executive Harry Pulliam as their new president. Pulliam succeeded Nicholas Young, who had occupied the position for 18 mostly ineffectual years.

In another break with tradition, the league announced its 1903 schedule, something it normally did not do until the spring. The early announcement date was just the latest maneuver in the ongoing public relations war between the two leagues. By making their schedule public now, the Nationals were attempting to one-up the Americans, who in 1902 had issued theirs first.

Yet less than a month after the Nationals enacted this and a few other Machiavellian manipulations, their bitter two-year battle with the American League ended. Some skirmishes would still be fought, but for the most part the interleague war, begun when the Americans declared themselves a major league, was over. The end came on January 10, 1903, at the St. Nicholas Hotel in Cincinnati. Coming together at a joint meeting, representatives of the two leagues signed a peace pact that had as its basis two major stipulations: each league would respect the other's territories, and each would agree (with a few notable exceptions) about which players belonged to which teams.

Another significant outcome of the meeting, one whose ramifications are still with us, was the American League's transfer of its Baltimore franchise to New York. In return for the Nationals accepting a competitor for the Giants in New York, American League president Ban Johnson guaranteed that his league would stay out of Pittsburgh. Agreeing to share the market in the nation's largest city to insure a monopoly in Pittsburgh may strike the modern-day fan as a poor bargain, but it was not necessarily so a century ago. Pittsburgh, a hotbed of baseball interest, was the National League's best team and one of its premier drawing cards.

The agreement to place a second major league team in Manhattan was achieved over the determined opposition and vociferous objection of Tammany Hall operator Andrew Freedman, the owner of the National League's New York Giants. Johnson offset the Tammany opposition to an American League team in New York with some well-developed political skills of his own. He arranged clandestinely for two men to own the club who had enough Tammany Hall connections between them to more than neutralize Freedman's opposition. One was Frank Farrell, a major figure in the New York gambling trust that operated more than 200 betting parlors. The other was "Big Bill" Devery, a one-time bartender who had gotten himself appointed to the police force by Tammany and later became New York City's chief of police.

While the new club, the Highlanders, would be playing in Hilltop Park, less than a mile from the Polo Grounds, it would be the Superbas, not the Giants, who would feel their impact first. After several failed attempts by American League teams to lure Brooklyn's biggest star, Willie Keeler, the Highlanders succeeded in signing him for the 1903 season. Keeler's batting average had gone down for four consecutive years; still, he remained one of the game's great batsmen. (His .333 mark in 1902 had been the league's third best.) Keeler's departure, a serious loss for Brooklyn, was doubly so for Dahlen. Not only was he losing a man who had been his teammate for the last four seasons, he was also losing his closest friend in baseball. By joining the Highlanders, Keeler, who began his career with the Giants, became the first man to play for all three New York City teams.

The second would be Jack Doyle, the feisty and controversial first baseman whom the Superbas had purchased from the American League's Washington Nationals. Doyle, a member of the Giants on three separate occasions, would later play one game for the Yankees in 1905. Hanlon went after Doyle because he had been dissatisfied with the first base play of Tom McCreery. In June, he sold McCreery to Boston, while accusing him of a fear of being involved in collisions. Hanlon was a temperate man and

would not make such damning charges offhandedly. Nor was he the first
to make them. McCreery had a well-developed reputation for fearing collisions, not only defensively but also as a runner on the base paths. Rather
than slide, he would often just accept the fielder's tag, which, of course,
did not make him very popular with his teammates.

Doyle, by contrast, was absolutely fearless. More important, he was
a better hitter than McCreery and better defensively. Hanlon expected
Doyle's alert and nimble-footed play at first base to strengthen his entire
infield, and especially Dahlen. He anticipated Doyle being more alert to
receive the often quick throws Bill would make after getting to balls that
might have eluded other shortstops.

Besides losing Keeler, its best hitter, Brooklyn also lost four pitchers
who had accounted for 66 of their 75 wins in 1902: Frank Kitson (19–13)
and Bill Donovan (17–15) signed with Detroit of the American League;
Doc Newton (15–14) and Jim Hughes (15–10) decided that they preferred
to play in the Pacific Coast League, Hughes for the second and final time.
Ebbets protested the signings of Kitson and Donovan, claiming that he
had valid contracts with both. He argued, unsuccessfully, that Detroit
should return both men to Brooklyn as part of the peace agreement. The
loss of these four pitchers would prove a severe blow to the Superbas, as
all would have excellent seasons in 1903. Kitson and Donovan combined
to win 32 games for the Tigers; Newton won 35 for Los Angeles, and
Hughes won 34 for Seattle.

Dahlen was back in 1903 for what would be his final season in Brooklyn, primarily because of his preference to remain in the New York area.
Though outwardly always short of money, he nevertheless turned down
what may have been higher salary offers to remain there. Dahlen's reluc-
tance to leave New York was well-known, but it did not prevent other
teams from trying. The September 20, 1902, issue of *Sporting Life* reported
that Washington manager Tom Loftus was trying hard to sign him for the
1903 season, as were representatives of the Detroit Tigers.

Another factor in his remaining was the Superbas' failures in their
attempts to get a shortstop to replace him. *Sporting Life* revealed that the
Brooklyn club had tried to sign Tigers shortstop Kid Elberfeld, but had
been unsuccessful. The article went on to say that the club was now
rumored to be after Cleveland's John Gochnauer, a former Superba, and
would not offer Dahlen a contract until they were certain they could not
sign Gochnauer.

Elberfeld was an excellent young player, and the reasons why Hanlon would want him are obvious. But other than his also being young, one
can only wonder why Hanlon would want Gochnauer back. This was the

same John Gochnauer, then a rookie, whom Hanlon had played in Dahlen's place in both games of the in 1901 season-ending double-header. After playing in those two games and one previous for Brooklyn, Gochnauer had moved on to Cleveland, where he had batted a lowly .185 in 1902. He would duplicate that mark in 1903, which, although he was just 27 years old, would be his final big league season.

Meanwhile, Dahlen had enjoyed another fine year in 1902, and if he had slowed any at age 32, it was not apparent. John B. Foster wrote that the "peevish one," as he called him, had played the position of shortstop in a manner that could not be improved on. "There isn't a man in the National League or American that is in his class this season," said Foster in late June. "Always a good ground coverer, he gets over more this summer than ever he did in his life."[1] Foster attributed Dahlen's range to his ability to get a good start on balls hit to either side of him. He suggested that more players would reach more balls if they, like Dahlen, could get moving the moment the ball left the bat.

One of Foster's colleagues at *Sporting Life* made his own attempt at interpreting Dahlen's alleged split personality on the field. This correspondent noted that while Dahlen was "brilliant as a meteor in the heat of conflict," he was "slow and indifferent" in his preparations. "To see Dahlen in practice before a game, you would imagine him to be one of the poorest and most indifferent players in the business," he wrote.[2] John McGraw, his future manager with the Giants, had another slant on Dahlen's seeming indifference. "It made him an iceberg on the field, keeping the others cool in the tightest situations," said McGraw.[3]

Dahlen professed innocence, claiming that he really did not know why he appeared lazy and inattentive in practice. Yet, he often did, and his fumbles of ground balls and poor throws to first gave the impression that he just did not care. The slipshod play made those unfamiliar with him wonder how he had become such a star player. However, as *Sporting Life* pointed out, everything changed once the game began. Then he becomes "as near perfection as a player can get."[4]

Contrary to his lackadaisical attitude in pregame practices, Dahlen was always one of the hardest workers at spring training. This led Hanlon to try several times to get him to carry that pre-season zeal into the regular season. He had never been successful. Once opening day arrived, Dahlen would revert to his old habits, idling his way through practice while devoting all his interest and his energy to the actual games.

Columbia, South Carolina, was again the site of spring training this year, with the players using the University of South Carolina's grounds for their workouts. Before reporting, Dahlen returned to Hot Springs, which he always claimed was the best place for him to get his throwing arm in shape. Also in Hot Springs were Clark Griffith, his old Chicago teammate and newly named manager of the Highlanders, and Giants manager and fellow horseplayer John McGraw. (Hot Springs was not only good for Bill's arm, it allowed him to spend time at the racetrack.)

Dahlen was the last man to report to Columbia, yet in his first day there he played in midseason form, as Brooklyn crushed the university team 12–5. Although he had reported looking a bit overweight, everyone connected with the Superbas registered surprise at the enthusiasm he showed in practice. Even Hanlon had a few kind words for Bill regarding his preparation.

The 1903 Superbas were a much different team from any they had fielded in the past few years. When the season opened, Dahlen was one of only four players on the 20-man squad who had been with the club for more than a year. A Superba since 1899, he was the oldest member of the squad in point of service, and the logical choice to succeed Keeler as captain. Hanlon dutifully made the offer, but, because it contained no financial reward, Dahlen turned it down. Bill felt that the additional work he would have to do as captain entitled him to receive extra money.

Hanlon disagreed, arguing that the Brooklyn club had already paid him well enough. He reminded everyone that by raising Dahlen's 1903 salary to an even $4,000, they had amply rewarded him for his exhibition of loyalty in the face of American League offers in 1902. After Dahlen's refusal of the captaincy, Hanlon offered the position to Doyle, who accepted without further inducement. Bill had no hard feelings about Doyle assuming the captain's role. The two veterans got along well and even roomed together.

Having lost his four best pitchers, Hanlon chose Henry Schmidt, a 29-year-old rookie, to face Christy Mathewson on opening day at the Polo Grounds. Brooklyn won 9–7, but Mathewson revenged the defeat four days later, defeating Schmidt 2–1 at the Washington Park opener. Hanlon would get 41 wins out of Schmidt and another rookie, Oscar Jones, this season, in bringing the Superbas home a respectable fifth. Jones, an undersized righthander from Pennsylvania, won his first six decisions on his way to a 19–14 record. The Texas-born Schmidt went 22–13, but after the season he informed the club of his dislike for "living in the East." His rookie year would be his only one as a major-leaguer. Veteran Ned Garvin won 15 games (15–18), but Roy Evans, another veteran, of whom much was expected, failed to produce. Evans had accumulated only three wins when Hanlon sold him to the St. Louis Browns in July.

Though he made four errors in Brooklyn's first three games, Dahlen's overall play at shortstop remained impressive. "Dahlen is in as good form as he ever was in his life," said Abe Yager in *Sporting Life* on April 25. "He can throw the ball with the same easy grace, and when it comes to a matter of picking up ground hits, Bill does it so easily that he fairly looks lazy while he is working." That "easy grace," so often mistaken for laziness, had plagued Dahlen throughout his career, just as it would plague players with similar styles in the future, most often African-Americans. Hugh Jennings, then the very successful manager of the Detroit Tigers, may have hit on the reason for this apparent laziness in an interview he gave after Bill retired. He called Dahlen the best judge of distance that he had ever seen. "Dahlen could judge a runner by a fraction of a second and never hurried a throw unless it was absolutely necessary," Jennings said.[5]

A few weeks into the season, Yager continued his acclaim for Dahlen's talents with this accolade. "Bill Dahlen is playing the game of his life this season. He is doing sensational work in the field and is batting over .300."[6] And this the following week: "Billy Dahlen's fielding of late has been of the sensational order."[7] But while they loved him in Brooklyn, sportswriters in Chicago seldom missed an opportunity to take a dig at the onetime Colts star. The press there was completely enthralled with the play of Joe Tinker, their second-year shortstop, with one writer going as far as to claim that "Tinker was worth two Dahlens."[8]

The loss of so many players to the American League, particularly the very popular local boy, Keeler, adversely affected the Superbas' early season attendance. So did the racing fever that gripped the borough's sporting populace each spring. Rather than take in a ballgame, many fans headed instead to the Sheepshead Bay Race Track to try their luck with the horses.[9] Those that did come out to Washington Park in April and May were often treated to sloppy and erratic play, leading Hanlon to accuse his charges of lacking "baseball brains."

The pitching of rookie Schmidt was one of the few bright spots of the spring. Following his split with the Giants, he pitched three consecutive shutouts. Two were against Philadelphia and one against Boston. Schmidt was threatening to erase Jack Chesbro's one-year-old National League record of 41 consecutive scoreless innings pitched when he faced Boston again on May 8. But the Beaneaters scored four runs in the second inning on their way to an easy 8–1 win, and Chesbro's record remained intact.[10]

Another rookie that impressed Hanlon early was infielder Dutch Jordan. Hanlon used Jordan to replace second baseman Tim Flood when Flood failed to hit. However, Jordan would find big league pitching too much for him, limiting his stay in the majors to only two seasons. Hanlon had purchased Sammy Strang from the Colts to play third base, but while Strang was a decent hitter, he was a defensive liability. He also had an attitude problem. One August afternoon, while Joe McGinnity of New York was beating Brooklyn in both ends of a double-header, Hanlon got so upset with Strang's listlessness he benched him.

Pittsburgh had escaped the American League raids of 1901 and 1902, but it was not immune to its 1903 incursions. Two of its leading pitchers, 28-game winner Chesbro and 20-game winner Jesse Tannehill, had joined Keeler on the new team in New York. The loss was damaging, but not fatal. Though the race was not the runaway it had been in 1902, Pittsburgh still captured its third consecutive pennant. The Fred Clarke-led Pirates finished six and a half games ahead of a New York Giants squad that John

McGraw had reinvigorated with his leadership. Unable to abide by Ban Johnson's rules, McGraw had abandoned the Orioles and the American League in mid-1902 and signed to manage the Giants. McGraw's desertion was a big part of the collapse and eventual relocation of the Baltimore franchise. Ironically, that franchise was now in New York and would eventually overtake McGraw's team in popularity.

The climax to this first season of peace came when Pittsburgh and the American League champions, Boston, agreed to meet in what we now recognize as the first "modern" World Series. Boston struck a huge blow for the new league's prestige by winning the scheduled best five-of-nine series in eight games.

Dahlen remained in New York after the season ended, eschewing an offer to barnstorm through the south with a team organized by Doyle. He spent as many days as possible indulging his favorite pastime, visiting the racetrack, usually in the company of his good pal, Keeler. The two friends, along with several other

Dahlen with the 1904 Giants, fulfilling his ambition to play in New York City.

Brooklyn and former Brooklyn players who lived in the borough, would often spend their evenings at Charlie Ebbets's spectacular new "Superbas Bowling Parlors."

Ebbets's bowling establishment was so lush that at the conclusion of the National League's winter meeting, the league's executives crossed the Brooklyn Bridge to attend a banquet there. Prominent among the attendees at the December 10 extravaganza were league president Harry Pulliam, and team presidents Barney Dreyfuss (Pittsburgh), James Hart (Chicago), Garry Herrmann (Cincinnati), Frank Robison (St. Louis), and team secretary Fred Knowles of the Giants.

Ebbets, Harry Von der Horst, William G. Byrne, and George H. Watson represented the Brooklyn club. Many members of the press were also there, as were several players. The seemingly inseparable Dahlen and Keeler; their former teammate, Joe Kelley, now with the Reds; and outfielder Patsy Donovan of the Cardinals were among them. One reporter remarked that Dahlen, at the then advanced baseball age of 33, looked to be in excellent shape and likely would need only a couple of days to be ready to play. This was not out of the ordinary for Bill, who worked hard to stay in good condition during the fall and winter.

Two tables had been set up for the banquet, with no specific seating designations made. This allowed players, press, and magnates to intermingle freely, though there was little chance that Pulliam and Dahlen would be sitting together. In mid-September, Pulliam had suspended Dahlen for using some particularly vile epithets during an argument with rookie umpire Augie Moran. His suspension was supposed to last for 10 days, but Bill was back after sitting out just one game.

The meal itself was a veritable feast, with each course honoring a league member and served in the order of that member's 1903 position in the standings. It was a dining experience typical of the era, but one that would make a cardiologist blanch. The menu consisted of:

> Superba cocktail a la Pittsburgh
> Blue points a la New York
> Haute Sauterne
> Chicken gumbo a la Chicago
> Olives   Salted almonds   Chow chow
> Amontillado
> Bluefish sauce a la Hollandaise
> Lyonnaise potatoes
> Peaches a la Conde
> Niersteiner

Prime ribs of beef au jus a la Cincinnati
Browned potatoes   French peas
St. Esteph
Rhode Island turkey a la Brooklyn
Chestnut dressing   Giblet sauce
Mashed potatoes   String beans
Champagne a la Harry Pulliam
Mince pie a la Philadelphia
Roquefort   Crackers   Camembert
Coffee a la Boston
Cordial a la St. Louis

This lavish affair would mark the end of Dahlen's five-year stay with the Superbas. Later in the month, his status would change, both as a member of the Brooklyn baseball club and as a bachelor. On December 13, the Superbas traded him to their bitter intracity rivals, the Giants, in a deal that shocked New York sports fans. Dahlen had been the greatest shortstop ever to wear a Brooklyn uniform, an honor he held until Pee Wee Reese came along 37 years later. When famed sportswriter Hugh Fullerton was picking his all-time franchise teams for a 1936 series in the *Sporting News*, he had Dahlen at shortstop for Brooklyn.[11]

The uncertainty surrounding George Davis, their former shortstop and onetime manager, had galvanized the Giants into making the trade. In 1902, Davis had jumped from the Giants to the American League's Chicago White Sox. When the season ended, he violated the January 1903 peace treaty between the two leagues by signing a two-year contract to play for the Giants.

Unwilling to let Davis leave, White Sox president Charles Comiskey and American League president Ban Johnson took the case to court. Former Giants star John Montgomery Ward, who the year before had argued for Davis's right to break his contract and sign with Chicago, now argued for his right to return to New York. Davis did return, but he would be of virtually no use to the 1903 Giants. Because of a series of court orders, Davis appeared in just four games for McGraw's club. New York would eventually, and reluctantly, accept his return to Chicago for the 1904 season. The gesture by the Giants was similar to those made by various other clubs, all to keep peace between the two leagues.

The strong likelihood that the Giants would be unable to keep Davis in 1904 motivated McGraw to look elsewhere for a shortstop. His first choice was Pittsburgh's Honus Wagner, the league's best shortstop (and best player), although McGraw knew he had no chance of getting him.

Neither owner Barney Dreyfuss nor manager Fred Clarke had any intention of trading Wagner, and if they had, they surely would not be sending him to McGraw's team.

Knowing the acquisition of Wagner was out of the question, McGraw decided to go after Dahlen, the league's second-best shortstop. The Giants, who had risen from eighth place in 1902 to second in 1903, were now conducting battles on two fronts. Not only were they trying to break Pittsburgh's three-year hold on the National League pennant, they were also intent on maintaining their supremacy in New York against the challenge from the American League's Highlanders.

In exchange for Dahlen, the Superbas were getting Jack Cronin, a journeyman right-handed pitcher, and Charlie Babb, a rookie shortstop. Cronin had been with six teams in six years and had a lifetime 31–35 record. Babb had batted .248 in 1903 as a fill-in for Davis. A rumored $5,000 accompanied Babb and Cronin to Brooklyn, a rumor that both McGraw and Hanlon denied. Even if it had, money in the team's treasury was irrelevant to the Brooklyn fans who were irate at losing yet another one of their favorites. Losing him to the hated Giants, and getting what they perceived as so little in return, made the deal even more intolerable for them.

On the surface, the exchange seemed so one-sided that it led the *Brooklyn Daily Eagle* to wonder if Hanlon had "lost his cunning." Dahlen was, after all, a steady hitter, among the game's fastest and smartest base runners, and had just led the league's shortstops in fielding percentage.

"To give up the best shortstop in the league and the most popular player of the Brooklyn team for one average fielder and a second-rate pitcher is apparently not upholding the reputation for cleverness maintained by Hanlon in the past," claimed the *Eagle*.[12] Had McGraw, his former pupil, outwitted the Brooklyn manager, the paper wondered?

However, the writer reversed himself in the next paragraph, hinting that because of the many successful trades Hanlon had made in his career, he perhaps knew something no one else did. He cautioned his readers not to judge the trade too quickly. Still trying to look on the bright side, he suggested that though Dahlen was still in good shape, he was 33 years old and very likely nearing the end of his career. Meanwhile, Hanlon was proclaiming that Babb would eventually be the equal of Dahlen, and although he was a scant three years younger, would be playing long after Dahlen was through.

As it turned out, this trade, which appeared so one-sided in favor of the Giants on the surface, was exactly that. Babb played only two seasons, and Cronin one, before they were gone from the big leagues. Meanwhile, Dahlen would begin a most successful stay with the Giants. McGraw would

The unavailability of Honus Wagner, the league's best shortstop, led John McGraw to go after Dahlen, the second best.

later call the Bill Dahlen for Jack Cronin and Charlie Babb trade with Brooklyn the most successful deal of his 33-year managerial career. "It gave me just what I wanted — a great defensive shortstop," said McGraw. "There were mighty few better than Dahlen."[13]

Yet even after "stealing" Dahlen, Mc-Graw was not completely satisfied. He then asked the Superbas about their one remaining high-priced player, outfielder Jimmy Sheckard. Feeling that the loss of Dahlen was just about all the fans would accept, Brooklyn chose to keep Sheckard.

While McGraw was still only 30, leg injuries had just about ended his playing career. He had been in only 12 games in 1903 and would play in only 12 more over the next three seasons. Having just completed his first full season as manager of the Giants, McGraw saw in Dahlen, three years his senior, someone who could be a team leader on the field while he ran things from the dugout. "Now I have the man I've wanted ever since I've had charge of this team," he said.[14] He talked about how much Babb and Cronin would help Brooklyn, but was unable to hide his glee at getting Dahlen.

"I think he is one of the greatest shortstops that ever played the game and will greatly strengthen our infield. He is the style of player that suits me. His ears go up when the bell rings and thereafter is always in the game until the last man has been retired. Dahlen is an aggressive player and knows how to get what he is entitled to. He is a perfect iceman when playing before a big crowd and we expect to have a few of those at the Polo Grounds next year."[15]

McGraw's praise for Babb and Cronin aside, Hanlon no doubt knew he was not getting fair value for Dahlen. Nevertheless, he had other reasons for making the trade. Mainly, it was his resentment of the way Dahlen flouted the rules he had laid down for the club, which he believed hurt morale. Over the years, Hanlon had largely ignored Dahlen's challenge to his control, but he had already decided that if Dahlen were back in 1904, things would be different. However, when Dahlen refused the club's attempt to cut his salary below the $4,000 he had earned in 1903, a move designed to help the Superbas with their own financial difficulty, they decided to deal him. One day after the trade, Dahlen signed with the Giants for at least the same $4,000 salary he had received the year before.

"I hope Dahlen would have every success in his new place," said Charlie Ebbets. "He stuck by us when others quit us. He gave us a chance to make him an offer when men like Keeler, Donovan, and Kitson jumped to the American League without allowing us time to meet the offers of the opposition. Dahlen is a great player and I am sorry to see him go, but in manager Hanlon's judgment the deal is for the best interests of the club."[16]

Hanlon parroted the party line. "I've parted with Dahlen, and somehow, I feel I have just parted with half my team," he said. "I cannot have any but the kindest recollections of the transactions between Dahlen and myself, but I am not selfish, and when I saw that Bill could benefit himself by the interchange I was only too willing to let him have any advantage that came his way. He is a fast and reliable player, ever and always watchful to benefit his team and his club, and I hope that in his efforts in behalf of his new manager he will be equally as successful and useful as he proved to be when he was on my team."[17]

Sporting Life's Foster took the trade as another opportunity to contrast Dahlen's ability with his attitude. A prediction that he would play the best ball of his life under the spotlight in New York followed a summation of Dahlen's negative effect in Brooklyn. Claiming that he was impetuous, nonchalant, and had an aversion to rules, Foster asserted that Dahlen had been a poor influence on Brooklyn's younger players.

Would the Giants have made the trade for Dahlen had they been able to retain Davis? Probably not. For New York area fans of the 1950s with long memories, arguments over who was the best shortstop in town were nothing new. Half a century before there were differing opinions about whether that distinction belonged to Pee Wee Reese of the Dodgers or Phil Rizzuto of the Yankees, similar debates raged concerning Dahlen and Davis. Between 1899 and 1901, when Dahlen was the Superbas shortstop and Davis was the Giants shortstop, fans of the two teams argued over who was the better shortstop with the same heat and intensity that the Reese-Rizzuto controversy later generated.[18]

Moreover, there is an uncanny parallel between the careers of these two great five-foot-nine shortstops, both of whom were born in 1870, just

40 miles apart in upstate New York. Both were outstanding defensively, and there is an almost eerie closeness to their respective offensive accomplishments.[19] The one major difference between them is that in 1998 Davis finally earned entrance to the Hall of Fame, while Dahlen is still waiting.

Although Davis left town in 1904, the arguments among New York fans about who was the city's best shortstop would continue unabated. Giants fans would now claim it was Dahlen, while those rooting for the "Yankees" (a name the newspapers were beginning to use in place of Highlanders), insisted it was the fiery Kid Elberfeld, whom they had obtained from Detroit in June of 1903.[20]

Less than a week after Dahlen made the symbolic journey across the East River from Brooklyn to Manhattan, the new Williamsburgh Bridge opened. This magnificent structure linked the two boroughs, even as work was underway on a tunnel that would connect them via the city's new subway system. Yet, no more than their incorporation into Greater New York five years earlier had done would these new methods of easier access to Manhattan generate any greater love for the colossus across the river among Brooklynites.

Ignoring that 1898 measure, which had in fact made Brooklyn a part of the city, Dahlen exacerbated the borough's sense of inferiority by announcing that, "It has always been my ambition to play in New York City. Brooklyn is all right, but if you're not with the Giants, you might as well be in Albany."[21] No doubt those in the state capital, a mere 55 miles from Bill's neighbors in Nelliston, and the fans in Chicago, where he had played for eight years, were similarly offended.

Dahlen's second venture into matrimony took place four days before Christmas, when he wed the for-

Not content with stealing Dahlen from Brooklyn, the Giants also wanted the Superbas' best remaining player, Jimmy Sheckard.

mer Jeannette Hoglund of Third Street in Brooklyn. Dr. Robert B. Hull, pastor of the borough's Greenwood Baptist Church, performed the ceremony at his home. Hull was an ardent baseball fan who often attended games at Washington Park. He was also the rare clergyman for that time who considered the game a "legitimate pastime and perfectly proper sport."[22] Keeler, of course, was Bill's best man. The honeymoon trip included a visit to Nelliston, after which they set up housekeeping in Manhattan.

Willie Keeler, Dahlen's Brooklyn teammate, neighbor, and best friend, was also the best man at his wedding.

TEN

The Most Hated Team in Baseball

In the 14 years since winning the pennant in 1889, the Giants had gone downhill, finishing mostly in the lower half of the league standings.[1] Their fortunes began to change in July 1902, even as they were in the midst of their second last-place finish in three years. Andrew Freedman's hiring of John McGraw as manager had energized both the Giants players and the New York fans. In 1903, his first full season at the helm, McGraw had engineered a spectacular turnaround. Boasting the league's only 30-game winners— veteran Joe McGinnity (31–20) and 22-year-old Christy Mathewson (30–13)— he had parlayed their success into a second-place finish.

McGraw believed he needed only a few changes to make up the six and a half games the Giants had finished behind Pittsburgh. Adding Dahlen had been the major one, but he also added three rookies to the roster: left-handed pitcher George "Hooks" Wiltse, third baseman Art Devlin, and outfielder Harry "Moose" McCormick. Wiltse (13–3) and Devlin (.281 in 130 games) would emerge as two of the National League's best rookies in 1904. McCormick would benefit the club in another way. In July, the Giants would trade him to Pittsburgh in a three-way deal that brought them high-living, hard-hitting outfielder Mike Donlin from Cincinnati.

McGraw spent most of January at Hot Springs, during which time he paid several successful visits to the racetrack. Spring training began in March, with Dahlen, the recent groom, joining his new teammates in Savannah, Georgia. McGraw had counted on Dahlen steadying the Giants infield, and he was not disappointed. Bill was also generally well behaved, despite unintentionally setting off one rhubarb. In an April 2 game at Nashville, against the Southern Association Volunteers, minor league umpire Tony Mullane called him out on an attempted steal of third. The

New York Times reported the next day that Mullane, a former big league pitcher, "did not see the play," and that Dahlen was "clearly safe."[2]

Roger Bresnahan, the Giants third baseman that afternoon, was doubling as the team's third base coach. Bresnahan voiced his disagreement in words that led Mullane to throw him out of the game. Enraged, Bresnahan confronted Mullane face-to-face as both the Giants from their bench and a group of fans from the bleachers rushed onto the field. The local police soon joined them and eventually restored order. They then cajoled Mullane and Bresnahan into shaking hands, and the game continued.

Meanwhile, Charlie Babb, Dahlen's replacement, was doing a creditable job over at the Superbas training camp in Columbia. Pleased with Babb's work, at least thus far, Hanlon repeated his belief that he had made a good trade, while refusing to "badmouth" Dahlen. Hanlon took issue with the remarks of those in the

Manager John McGraw's aggressiveness and abrasiveness made the Giants the most hated team in baseball.

Brooklyn organization who had prophesied that Dahlen had faded so badly he would be out of baseball within a year. "Barring accident, I will make a bet that he is playing as good ball five years from now as he is at present," Hanlon said of the man he had traded. "Most people forget that Dahlen began to play ball at a very young age and that he has many a good year before him in professional company."[3]

Hanlon's prediction that Dahlen would be playing well "five years from now" was irrelevant to McGraw; his mind was strictly on the 1904 pennant race. Whenever reporters asked him to assess his club's chances, he would stress two factors in the Giants' favor. One was pitching, where he expected Mathewson and McGinnity to be even better than they were a year ago. The other was the addition of Dahlen. McGraw claimed that with Dahlen at short, his infield was now as good as any in the game. In his opinion, said McGraw, Dahlen had no superior at shortstop, and in praising Bill's ability to perform when it counted, called him "an iceberg in tight places." He predicted that Dahlen and second baseman Billy

Gilbert would remind fans of the great play of shortstop Hugh Jennings and second baseman Heinie Reitz of the old Baltimore Orioles. For McGraw, the quintessential "old Oriole," there was no higher praise.

Dahlen played his first home game as a Giant on April 11. The opponent was the Jersey City Skeeters, the defending Eastern League champions. Fans entering the park that afternoon did so through a new entranceway, one feature of the newly redesigned Polo Grounds. New stands had been added in the 25-cent areas of right and center fields, and all the rooms in the building now had electric lights. As part of the renovation, the club installed business offices for the staff and a dressing room for the Giants players.

The 2,000 fans that showed up to welcome the club home saw Christy Mathewson (with five scoreless innings) and Joe McGinnity easily defeat the Skeeters 7–1. Mathewson was back on the mound three days later for the season opener at Brooklyn. A large crowd at Washington Park braved the bitterly cold weather, but went home disappointed when Mathewson allowed just three hits in defeating the Superbas 7–1. To the delight of the Brooklyn fans, Dahlen went hitless against his former teammate, Oscar Jones, and also failed to hit in the next two games. He did field with his usual brilliance, though, as the Giants swept the three-game series. With Dahlen replacing Babb at short, Devlin replacing Billy Lauder at third, holdovers Dan McGann at first and Gilbert at second, the Giants believed they now had the National League's best infield.

Dahlen recorded his first hit as a Giant the following day at Philadelphia. He had a double as the club won its fourth straight, a hard-fought 7–6 win. After then battling the Phillies to a 15-inning 1–1 tie, the two clubs traveled to New York where the Giants were scheduled to open their home season the next day. Cold weather caused a 24-hour postponement, but a record crowd was in place for the rescheduled opener.

The Giants listed their single-day attendance record at 32,240 for a game against Pittsburgh in June 1903. But when the off-season renovations and newly added seats raised the Polo Grounds' capacity, that record was in immediate danger. It fell on opening day. The gates opened at 1:00 p.m., three hours before the scheduled first pitch. Fans quickly filled the 18,000 seats, and then began lining up in rows behind the outfield ropes. By 3:00 P.M., most of the huge throng was in place. "Probably the largest crowd that ever attended a baseball game in this city," said the *New York Times*.[4] The tremendous gathering embodied a greater percentage of women than usually attended baseball games. This was customary for an opening-day game, an event that many fans viewed as much a celebration and a social occasion as it was a baseball game. New York's own Seventh

Regiment Band entertained the crowd with popular tunes before the game, and Mrs. De Wolf Hopper, wife of the famed stage performer and ardent Giants fan, threw out the first ball.

The pregame festivities turned out to be the highlight of the day for the local fans, who saw the Giants lose their first game of the season. Driving Mathewson from the mound in the fifth inning, the Phillies, behind Chick Fraser, humbled the home team 12–1. Dahlen scored the Giants' only run, drawing a seventh-inning walk and coming around on singles by Devlin and Frank Bowerman. Bill had been a favorite target of Giants fans when he appeared at the Polo Grounds in the uniforms of the Colts and Superbas. However, now that he was one of their own, they forgot all past animosities and cheered him as heartily as they did the rest of the Giants players.

After annihilating the Phillies the next two afternoons 18–3 and 10–1, then taking two of three from Brooklyn and four of five from Boston, the Giants' record stood at 12–3. As they headed to St. Louis for their first swing through the West, they had a two-game lead on the Superbas. Dahlen experienced his first ejection as a Giant on May 12 at Cincinnati. In the second inning, with the Giants trailing 4–0 (in a game they would lose, 13–7), umpire Bob Emslie called him out on strikes. When Dahlen strongly disagreed with the call, Emslie, who had already tossed McGraw in the first inning, ordered him to leave. Dahlen did leave, but only after a long delay in which he simply refused to go. His actions resulted in another suspension from league president Harry Pulliam, this one for the next three games.

When Dahlen returned to the lineup, on May 17 at Pittsburgh, the Giants' lead over the second-place Reds was down to half a game. The champion Pirates, hampered by the illness of ace pitcher Deacon Phillippe, were already seven games behind. Though their goal of a fourth consecutive pennant was beginning to look doubtful, Pittsburgh remained a very formidable team. They took two of three from the struggling New Yorkers, who then went to Chicago and dropped two of three there too. The May 22 game against the Cubs, played on a Sunday, drew the largest crowd at Chicago's West Side Grounds in five years. The opposing pitchers were Mordecai "Three Finger" Brown for the Cubs and Luther "Dummy" Taylor for the Giants. Brown's right hand had been mangled in a farm accident at age seven, and Taylor was a deaf-mute. It would be many years in the future before deformities and disabilities were not considered fair game for nicknames. Chicago, behind Brown's two-hitter, won 3–1, allowing it to move past New York into second place.

As they headed east, the third-place Giants trailed both the Reds and the Cubs. But by the time Cincinnati came to town for a three-game series on June 2, the Giants and Reds were in a virtual tie for first place. The teams split the first two, both of which were decided by one run: Mathewson over Jack Sutthoff 2–1, and Noodles Hahn over Taylor 3–2. In that second game, Dahlen had gone from hero to goat in half an inning. His long home run in the seventh had put New York ahead 2–1, but his error in the Cincinnati eighth led to the Reds scoring the winning run. Red player-manager Joe Kelley was on third base and Cy Seymour was on second with one out, when Cozy Dolan flied out to right fielder George Browne. Kelley scored easily as Browne threw to third to try to double up Seymour. It was an accurate throw, but in his haste to get Seymour, Dahlen attempted to deflect the ball toward third baseman Devlin. Instead, the ball rolled past third allowing Seymour to score.

The deciding game of the series the next day featured opposing pitchers who were both unbeaten. McGinnity had won his first 10 decisions, and the Reds' Jack Harper his first seven. Throw in a lovely Saturday afternoon, and the result was another record-breaking crowd. The 37,223 who attended did more than shatter just the Polo Grounds record. Veteran observers adjudged it to be the largest crowd ever to have seen a baseball game anywhere. After playing to a 2–2 tie, in a game that lasted 11 innings, the Giants, Reds, and Cubs took turns at the top over the next three weeks. With the Cubs in town on June 11, the Giants' attendance record, set one week earlier, was broken again. The crowd of 38,805 that squeezed into the park was duly rewarded. They witnessed a sensational pitching duel in which Bob Wicker of Chicago allowed one hit in 12 innings in besting McGinnity, 1–0.

Upon completion of the Western clubs' first visit to New York, the Giants led the league by half a game. Yet many of their players were struggling at the plate. Several of them blamed their hitting problems on the new stands in center field, which were filled with patrons wearing white shirts and straw hats. That sea of white, they complained, was making it difficult for them to pick up the flight of the ball after it left the pitcher's hand. Surprisingly, considering the potential loss of revenue, management listened. Forgoing the income provided by keeping those seats available, the club erected a fence in center field to provide the hitters with a better background.

The Giants were not alone in their batting woes. Offense was down throughout the National League. Baseball people attributed some blame for the decline to the increasing use by pitchers of spitballs and other "trick" pitches. However, they cited the introduction of the "foul strike" rule in 1901 as the major cause. Statistics bore them out; the league batting average in 1900, the year before the new rule, was .280. It had dropped to .267 in 1901, and would sink to a lowly .250 this season. W.F. Koelsch of *Sporting Life* was one of many voices calling for the abolishment of what he called the "foul strike monstrosity." Included among those voices was McGraw, who thought the 10 or 15 minutes that it cut from a game's length was not worth the price of the reduced offense it produced.[5] Not coincidentally, McGraw and many others believed that it was his ability to continually foul off good pitches that had inspired the law.

Dahlen's ninth-inning single off the great Cubs righthander Mordecai Brown drove in the game's only run in Christy Mathewson's June 13, 1905, no-hitter at Chicago.

St. Louis had been the final club to visit New York in that first Western invasion. The Cardinals dropped two of three, with their lone win coming in the middle game. Jack W. Taylor, in the midst of his prodigious streak of 187 consecutive complete games, beat McGinnity 5–2. Mathewson's win over the Cardinals in the finale launched the Giants on an 18-game winning streak. Matty also won the final game of the streak, defeating the Phillies in the second game of a July 4 double-header at the Polo Grounds. Both teams traveled to Philadelphia the next day, with McGinnity scheduled to face Philadelphia's Bill Duggleby. Because the Giants were in first place and the Phillies were last, and because opponents had battered Duggleby in his last two starts, gamblers listed the odds on the streak continuing at 5–1. But baseball games are played on the field, not in bars and pool rooms. The Phillies pulled out a 10-inning 6–5 victory, bringing the streak to an end. Chick Fraser, in relief of Duggleby, got the win, and Dummy Taylor, in relief of McGinnity, took the loss.

Chicago and Cincinnati, tied for second, a half game behind the Giants when the streak began, remained tied for second when it ended. Only now they were 10 games behind. The Cubs had reduced the margin to seven games by July 21, when the Giants arrived in Chicago for the final four games of a 16-game swing through the West. By winning all four, the Cubs could have pulled within three games and put themselves back in the race, but they won only one. The Giants left Chicago with a nine-game lead and never looked back. Dahlen sparkled throughout the trip, batting above .300, fielding with his usual brilliance, and serving as the team leader in the field, just as McGraw had anticipated. "Bill Dahlen, on the Western trip, probably played better ball than at any time in his long career. His wise head controlled the infield," remarked *Sporting Life*.[6]

Just as Chicago had been the focal point of the world's attention in the summer of 1893, St. Louis was its focal point in the summer of 1904. The city was playing host to two major events of worldwide significance. One was a World's Fair to celebrate the centennial of the Louisiana Purchase by President Thomas Jefferson, and the other was the Summer Olympic Games. Originally scheduled for Chicago, the games had been moved to St. Louis so they could be held in conjunction with the centennial.

Leading the league by 11 games, the Giants rolled into St. Louis in late August and swept a four-game series. The sweep of the Cardinals began yet another long winning streak, one that lasted for 12 games and continued past Labor Day. Win number six, a particularly disruptive first game of the August 31 double-header at Cincinnati, included a near riot. The Giants had been unhappy with umpire Chief Zimmer's decisions right from the opening pitch. Their anger exploded in the fourth inning when Zimmer called the Reds' Fred Odwell safe at second on a steal attempt. Both Dahlen and McGann reacted by loudly objecting to the call. Dahlen, who had made the tag on Odwell, punctuated his anger by tossing the ball away. Zimmer's reaction was to eject both him and McGann. Pulliam again suspended Dahlen for three days, and McGann indefinitely, but he later also limited McGann's suspension to three days.

Boisterous as it was, the Dahlen-McGann incident was just a prelude to the big blowup that occurred two innings later. With Jack Warner catching the opener for the Giants, Frank Bowerman, the team's other backstop, was on the bench. (This was the same Frank Bowerman who as a rookie with Baltimore had been behind the plate when Dahlen injured himself on a steal of home back

First baseman Dan McGann was Dahlen's teammate in Brooklyn, New York, and Boston, and another frequent victim of umpire ejections.

in 1897.) Through five innings, fans sitting behind the Giants bench had been showering Bowerman with a steady stream of abuse. By the sixth, Bowerman had grown tired of the invective and went into the stands, where he punched one of the offending patrons. The man he hit, inflicting cuts on his jaw, was Albert Hartzell, a public school music teacher and the son of a member of the Cincinnati Board of Education.

At 6' 2 inches and 190 pounds, Bowerman was one of the biggest players in the league, and one of the toughest. The year before he had beaten up Pittsburgh's Fred Clarke in a Polo Grounds office. Zimmer apparently felt that attacking a patron was not as serious as disputing his decisions, and was content to have Bowerman return to the bench. The umpire's leniency did not please the city's acting mayor, who happened to be at the game. When he saw a group of Giants players advancing menacingly toward eight policemen who had come onto the field, he ordered the police to arrest Bowerman. Mr. Hartzell decided not to prosecute, and Bowerman was later released.

This was not the first time Zimmer, the longtime big league catcher, had thrown Dahlen out of a game. He had done so as recently as the nightcap of a July 29 doubleheader at Washington Park. Zimmer, who was in his first and only season as an umpire, had warmed up in the first inning by discharging the right side of the Brooklyn infield—first baseman Pop Dillon and second baseman Sammy Strang. Their crime was protesting a ball/strike call against McGann. So when Dahlen erupted over a third strike called on him during his second at-bat, out he went too. McGraw, appearing in one of his two games at shortstop this season, filled in admirably the rest of the way.

These 1904 Giants had aroused the fans of New York like no other Giants team in years, if ever.[7] Still, they were not the only reason baseball excitement was running high in New York. Contributing to the city's baseball mania were the pennant-contending Yankees, in just their second season in Manhattan. Ban Johnson had done all that he could to build a strong American League franchise in New York. He wanted a team there that could battle the well-established Giants for the devotion and the dollars of New York's fans, and he had succeeded. Johnson had begun by arranging for former Chicago White Stockings manager Clark Griffith to manage the team. Furthermore, many American League fans in Boston suspected that it was Johnson who had been behind the trade this June that sent their star outfielder, Patsy Dougherty, to New York.

Needing a replacement for Dave Fultz, whose football-related leg injuries were severely limiting his playing time, the Yankees got Dougherty from Boston in exchange for Bob Unglaub. On the face of it, the trade was

heavily one-sided in favor of New York. Dougherty had batted .342 and
.331 in his first two seasons, while Unglaub, an untested rookie, had played
in just six games this year, with four singles in 19 at-bats. Dougherty joined
a lineup that included such stars as Willie Keeler, Kid Elberfeld, and Jimmy
Williams. The Yankees also had the league's best pitcher, Jack Chesbro, who
was on his way to a post-1900 record 41 wins.

Unlike the National League, where the Giants were making a sham-
bles of the race, the Yanks entered September in a tight race with Boston.
Chicago, Cleveland, and Philadelphia were all close behind. With the
Giants an almost sure winner, and the Yankees a possible one, New Yorkers were relishing the idea of an all-Manhattan World's Series.[8] Yet as early
as the first week of July, there were indications that a Giants-Yankees series,
or, for that matter, any series at all, would not be taking place that fall.
The July 9 issue of *Sporting Life* was the first to report the ominous news.
According to a very close friend of new Giants owner John Brush, his team
would absolutely refuse to meet the Yankees should the Yanks win the
American League pennant. Brush, the friend revealed, was fully prepared
not only to violate the agreement between the two leagues to play a seven-
game championship series, but also to disappoint the baseball fans of New
York City.

Soon after announcing their refusal to play against the Yankees,
McGraw announced that the Giants would be unwilling to participate in
a World's Series against any American League team.[9] "The Giants will not
play a postseason series with the American League champions," he declared
on July 27. "Ban Johnson has not been on the level with me personally, and
the American League management has been crooked more than once,"
said McGraw, whose fanatical hatred for Johnson was common knowledge.[10]

Meanwhile, Johnson blamed the Giants' refusal to play on Brush,
believing that McGraw was not highly placed enough to make such a decision. "No thoughtful patron of baseball can weigh seriously the wild
vaporings of this discredited player who was canned out of the American
League," he said of McGraw.[11] Johnson found allies for this theory among
the Giants players, most of whom agreed that McGraw was not responsible for the decision. They, of course, were eager to participate in a
World's Series, both for the glory of victory and for the money. "Our
manager is being held back by the powers that be," one of them said in
an interview.[12]

Brush confirmed everyone's worst fears when he announced in late September that by winning the National League pennant, his team was already
the world champions. "Nothing in the constitution of the National League

requires its victorious club to submit its championship honors to a contest with the victorious club in a minor league," he haughtily announced.[13]

The following day, Frank Farrell of the Yankees and John I. Taylor of the Boston Americans, responded to Brush's condescending statement. Farrell and Taylor, owners of the American League's remaining contenders, issued a joint challenge to Brush to have his Giants meet whichever of their teams won the pennant. When Boston won, defeating the Yankees on the season's final day, Taylor gave the Giants a final chance to change their minds. He challenged McGraw to meet his team for the championship, with all the receipts going to the players, but McGraw turned him down.

In a way, although on a much higher level, this was the same position Brush and McGraw had taken following the 1903 season. While Boston and Pittsburgh were meeting in the World's Series, National and American League teams from St. Louis, Chicago, and Philadelphia were meeting each other in their own intracity post-season series. These confrontations delighted local fans and put extra money in the players' pockets. Griffith had proposed that the two New York teams do the same, but Brush and McGraw refused.

With their obstructionism, overly aggressive style of play, unrelenting taunting of the opposition, and wide-ranging assault on authority, the Giants had become the most hated team in baseball, with McGraw as its most hated man. Johnson went as far as to publicly denounce Brush and McGraw as more detrimental to baseball than the game's worst enemies.

The Giants and the Yankees did get to meet in the fall of 1904, but it was in a hotel rather than on the ballfield; namely the Quincy House, where both clubs stayed when they were in Boston. On September 13, the Giants were getting ready to take the steamship back to New York just as the Yankees, trailing Boston by one-half game, were arriving in that city for a crucial four-game series.

McGraw may have hated the American Leaguers, but his animosity had not spread to his underlings. Several chose to stay and chat with the Yankees players and return home later, on the midnight sailing. Personnel from the two teams participated in a general intermingling, including Dahlen and Keeler. The two close friends took the opportunity to catch up with each other's latest doings. Also seen chatting were Giants second baseman Gilbert and Jimmy Williams, his counterpart on the Yankees. The two infielders were likely reminiscing about their time together with the 1902 Baltimore Orioles.

"How nice it would be if these boys were to shake hands on the field before the first game of the championship series," said a wistful Abe Nahon, the Yankees secretary.[14] Farrell, exhibiting a lot more class than Brush or McGraw, capped the day by inviting any of the players on either team who cared to attend to be his guests for the show at the Hollis Theater that evening.

A 7–5 defeat of Cincinnati in the first game of a double-header on September 22, was the Giants 100th win of the season, and the pennant clincher. Fittingly, the win went to McGinnity, his 34th of the season. McGinnity and Mathewson had combined to form what was arguably the most productive one-two pitching duo of the 20th century. The "Iron Man" finished this season with a league-leading 35 wins, while Mathewson was second with 33. In the five years between 1903–1907, the two produced 272 victories for McGraw's Giants: 140 for Mathewson, and 132 for McGinnity.

Four days after the clincher, a double-header sweep of the Pirates allowed New York to tie Pittsburgh's 1902 record of 103 wins, a record it broke the next day against the Cubs. Seemingly satisfied that it had set this new mark, the club played listlessly the rest of the way, losing eight of their final 10 games. One loss was a forfeit to St. Louis in the second game of an October 4 double-header at the Polo Grounds. Only about 2,000 fans showed up for the home finale, but they made up in raucousness what they lacked in numbers. Sloppy play had cost the Giants the first game and the fans' rowdyism cost them the second. The cause of the forfeit came in the Cardinals' fourth, and Dahlen was right in the middle of it. Earlier, umpire Jim Johnstone had thrown utility player Doc Marshall out of the game. Marshall, coaching at first base at the time, had protested too vigorously Johnstone's call that Jack Dunn had missed first base on what appeared to be an inside-the-park-home run. Dunn, the onetime Brooklyn pitcher, was finishing his career as Giants position player.

In the fourth, St. Louis had scored a run to take a 2–1 lead, when Cardinals shortstop Danny Shay reached on a Dahlen error. When Johnstone called Shay safe on an attempted steal of second, Dahlen and Gilbert complained so vociferously that Johnstone ejected them both. A long delay followed, and when the Giants gave no evidence that they planned to continue, Johnstone forfeited the game to St. Louis. The forfeiture so enraged that portion of the crowd inclined toward hooliganism, they began to attack Johnstone as he made his way to the dressing room. The beleaguered umpire was about to strike back at one "fan" who had pushed him, but the police intervened. Johnstone chose not to press charges.

Although they were clearly the best team in the league, leading in almost every batting and pitching category, it was their enormous success against the three other Eastern teams that triggered the Giants' runaway.

New York's record against Boston, Brooklyn, and Philadelphia was a com-bined 56–9.[15] Overall, they finished with a mark of 106–47, 13 games ahead of second-place Chicago.[16] Moreover, there is a clear correlation between the Giants' accomplishments on the field and their roughneck style of play with their profits at the box office. Added to the more than 600,000 fans they drew to the Polo Grounds, their notoriety attracted record crowds wherever they played. Fans in other National League cities turned out with the hope of seeing the rowdy New Yorkers get their comeuppance. The Giants estimated their net receipts for the season at $100,000, which was more than the two next most profitable teams combined.

Among the categories in which the Giants led the league was their 283 stolen bases. Dahlen and Sam Mertes, who had been his teammate on the 1898 Chicago Orphans, were the co-leaders on the team. Each had 47, which also tied them for second in the league behind Pittsburgh's Honus Wagner, who had 53. Bill's 47 stolen bases were his most in a season since he stole 51 for Chicago back in 1895.

Beyond his base-stealing laurels, Dahlen batted a solid .268 and was fourth in the league with 26 doubles. Batting mainly in the sixth position, Dahlen led all National Leaguers in the yet unofficial category of runs bat-ted in, with 80, which remains a post-1893 low for a full-schedule season.

McGraw, perhaps in a fit of hyperbole, was calling him the best short-stop in the game, although everyone agreed that distinction belonged to Wagner. McGraw himself had predicted the Pirates star eventually would be remembered as the greatest player ever. But if Wagner was the best, Dahlen was most surely the next best, at least in the National League, which was the only league McGraw considered worth discussing.[17]

ELEVEN

From "Bad Bill"
to "Bill the Wizard"

An unusual story had reached the public in the summer of 1904, alleging that Giants star Bill Dahlen had been receiving letters from an evangelist in Illinois. The letters were in the form of suggestions that the notorious "Bad Bill" change his heathen ways and consider the religious life. Dahlen had dismissed the appeals with the aid of some very unholy type language; nevertheless teammates with whom he had shared the letters, began to notice a change in his demeanor. He reportedly had kept the letters, reading and rereading them, and seemed to be setting himself apart from the other players. Finally, the story reported, Dahlen informed McGraw that he had decided to quit baseball right then and become an evangelist himself. McGraw had begged Dahlen to remain with the Giants for the rest of the season, it said, and Dahlen had eventually relented and agreed to stay.[1] It may have been around this time that Dahlen, a heavy drinker, gave up the habit. He would return to it after his playing days were over.

Those who knew him best never believed Dahlen had ever seriously considered quitting baseball, pointing out that he had worked harder for McGraw in 1904 than at any time in his life. If Dahlen had ever thought about giving up the game, the idea quickly faded. However, his association with evangelism stayed with him. References to Dahlen as "the evangelist," rather than by his name, remained commonplace in newspaper game stories for the rest of his career.

With his religious fervor having apparently subsided, he re-signed for 1905 shortly after the '04 season ended and was in Savannah for the start of spring training. A group of Giants living in the New York area had sailed down aboard the steamer *City of Macon*, but Dahlen and Frank Bowerman chose instead to go by train. After 10 days of practice and intrasquad games in Savannah, the Giants switched their headquarters to Birmingham, Alabama. They then started playing against other teams, and McGraw's champions dominated them all. The Giants won every one of their preseason games, the only big league team to do so. Their final win was against Yale University, in what had now become the traditional windup game to the exhibition schedule.

The trip north had not been without incident, particularly for Dahlen. He made four errors in a game at Columbus, Ohio, as the Giants helped inaugurate Nell Park, the city's new 25,000-seat ball field.[2] A day later, at Wheeling, West Virginia, the bleachers caved in. Fortunately, it happened before the game, and no one was seriously hurt. Pitching for Wheeling that afternoon was Bill Kennedy, the onetime ace of the Brooklyn pitching staff. Kennedy, now 37, had been a teammate of Dahlen's on the National League champion Superbas of 1899–1900.

Dahlen's most serious episode of the trip home took place during a stopover in Nashville, where he had an infected hand lanced. The procedure went well; nevertheless, this was a worrisome operation in an era when cases of blood poisoning, often fatal, occurred far more often than they do today.

Because of the Giants' failure to prove themselves in a post-season series against the American League, there were those who believed that McGraw's team was not baseball's "true" world champions. However, on opening day 1905, no such people were visible at the Polo Grounds. Instead, there was a capacity crowd of delirious New Yorkers, who had packed the park to see their beloved Giants begin the defense of their championship.

The day had begun with an automobile parade through the streets of Manhattan. Autos, liberally decorated with yellow bunting with the words "Champion Giants" written in black, carried the Giants players. With flags flapping in the breeze all over the Polo Grounds, with the lively tunes from the Seventh Regiment band, with the general good nature of the attendees, and with the lovely spring weather, a holiday mood permeated the ballpark in particular and the city in general.

Mayor George McClellan, the son of the Civil War general, along with his police and fire commissioners, were there to represent the City of New York. Representing baseball were National League president Harry Pulliam and former Giants star John Montgomery Ward. Also, the great Cap Anson, recently elected Chicago's city clerk, and his wife, Dorothy. But the spectator who drew the most attention was Jim Jeffries, the popular undefeated heavyweight champion of the world.[3]

When the crowd spotted McGraw in the first of the autos carrying the Giants onto the field, they let out a thunderous roar that echoed throughout the stands. Manager McGraw, assisted by his players, raised the blue and gold championship pennant, which read "Giants, Champion Baseball Club of National League, 1904." The band struck up the *Star-Spangled Banner* and Mayor McClellan threw out the first ball.

Led by the stellar pitching of Joe McGinnity, the Giants made it a perfect day with an easy 10–1 victory over the visiting Boston Doves. They followed with an even more lopsided win, 15–0, behind Mathewson, and then took four of five from Philadelphia. By then the Giants were in first place, and they would hold the lead the rest of the way, eventually finishing nine games ahead of Pittsburgh.

In later years, McGraw would call his 1905 team the best one he ever managed. Basically, it was the same team that won the pennant in 1904, but with one major addition. This team had Mike Donlin for the entire season, and McGraw's best feat of managing may have been his ability to keep Donlin in check. The fast-living, hard-drinking "Turkey Mike" batted .356 for the season, the highest average on the team and the third highest in the National League.

Yet according to William F. H. Koelsch, who covered the Giants for *Sporting Life*, the major reason for the team's success, both this year and last, was McGraw's trade for Dahlen. Koelsch's descriptions of Dahlen's fielding prowess were cast in the same superlatives John Foster and Abe Yeager had used when they covered Dahlen in Brooklyn.

"It is doubtful if Bill Dahlen has ever shown more brilliantly than he did last week," Koelsch wrote in May. "In the games last week," he continued, "Dahlen's great work was exceptionally brilliant for even such a fast fielder as he has always been. Dahlen's accurate throwing and quick recovery after making difficult stops electrified the fans." Then, in an acknowledgment of Dahlen's durability, "Manager McGraw is fortunate in that his star shortstop is seldom out of the game from one end of the season to the other."[4]

The May 12 issue of the *New York Times* was similarly commendatory. This is how the *Times* described Dahlen's previous day's contribution to preserving Christy Mathewson's 4–0 shutout of St. Louis.[5] "Dahlen's work could not have been excelled, and most of his chances were stops of rather long and hard hits, which required fast and accurate throwing to first to catch the runners."[6] A day later, he was the middle man in a spectacular double play, and also singled and stole second to set up the winning run in a 6–5 victory over the Cardinals.

Dahlen was also instrumental in several other Mathewson victories. He provided most of the offense with two home runs off Orval Overall in a May 23 7–0 shutout of the Reds, the third and final time Dahlen homered twice in a game. Facing the Cubs again three weeks later, his ninth-inning single off Mordecai Brown drove in the game's only run in Mathewson's no-hitter at Chicago. And when Matty beat Brooklyn 3–2 on September 12, it was again a ninth-inning single by Dahlen that drove in the winning run.

However, there was also a negative side of the Dahlen-Mathewson connection. It was a Dahlen mental error in a September 23 game against the Cubs that led to the end of Matty's 11-game winning streak. Chicago had two on and two out in the bottom of the fifth inning when Dahlen, after fumbling a ground ball, recovered and stepped on second base for the force. Assuming it was the third out, he rolled the ball to the mound and headed to the Giants bench. But umpire Bob Emslie had called the runner safe, a ruling that allowed Johnny Evers, the runner on third base to score. Carl Lundgren made the run hold up, defeating the Giants, 1–0.

Correspondent Koelsch's praise of Dahlen would continue throughout the 1905 season. In July, he wrote that "Bill Dahlen continues to shine as the stellar light of the champions' infield. It is no longer 'Bad Bill,' but 'Bill the Wizard.'[7] However, Koelsch's suggested name change would never quite take hold. The press had tagged Dahlen with the "Bad Bill" designation in his early days in Chicago, and the sobriquet would stay with him throughout his life, and even beyond. Newspapermen would use the "Bad Bill" appellation in stories about him long after he retired, and it was even part of his obituaries. Dahlen's intensity, his unfriendly, hostile temperament, his many confrontations with umpires, and his readiness to start a fight at the slightest provocation had all contributed to the "Bad Bill" image.

After the Giants clinched the pennant, Koelsch again credited their success in winning this one, plus the one a year earlier, to McGraw's acquisition of Dahlen. "The cornerstone for the past two championship clubs was laid when he [McGraw] made the trade for Dahlen. Not only did he [Dahlen] round out the Giants infield, he was largely instrumental in the development of Devlin."[8] Conversely, the trade had not worked out well for Brooklyn. Other factors beyond the loss of Dahlen had no doubt contributed to the Superbas' decline; still, they had just suffered through the worst year in their history, losing 104 games.

Dahlen, now in his 15th major-league season, would bat just .242 in 1905. It was a new low for him, although the additional walks he drew this year had raised his on base percentage. And, as he always seemed to do, he was making count the hits he was getting. He drove in 81 runs, which was one more than his league-leading total of a year ago. At midseason,

Dahlen was actually leading the league in home runs, with five. He finished with seven, which tied him for third place with teammate Donlin and Brooklyn's Harry Lumley. Dahlen had not hit that many home runs in a season since he had nine for Chicago back in 1896.

Yet more than anything, even more than his spectacular fielding, it was Dahlen's aggressive play that made him so valuable to the Giants. He was "the straw that stirred the drink," to use a phrase that would be introduced three-quarters of a century later. For example, there was the game at Pittsburgh on June 10, where the Giants entered the ninth inning clinging to a 3–0 lead. Dahlen led off with a walk, but he was still at first two outs later when Dummy Taylor singled to center. Dahlen went tearing around second heading for third. As he neared the bag, he noticed that Pirates center fielder Ginger Beaumont was loafing on the ball. Dahlen never stopped running and scored all the way from first. Taylor later scored on another less-than-hustling play by the Pirates, putting the game safely away, as the Pittsburgh fans showered their hometown heroes with boos.

Dahlen also provided the spark in what may have been the Giants' most exciting win of the season, a 3–2 triumph over the Cubs. On July 14, New York was trailing Ed Reulbach 2–1 as it came to bat in the home ninth. The first two batters, McGann and Mertes, went down on fly balls, making Dahlen the Giants' last hope. When Bill got behind 0–2, those hopes looked slim. They revived a bit when he managed to get himself hit by a Reulbach pitch.

As the tying run, Dahlen was anxious to get to second base and made a few bluffs in that direction. Possibly unnerved by the feints, Reulbach proceeded to put him there with a wild pitch. By this time, Dahlen's antics had aroused the fans to such an extent that the *Times* commented that "a more excited crowd has never been seen at the Polo Grounds."[9] That excitement grew as Devlin singled Dahlen home to tie the score. Sammy Strang followed by doubling Devlin home with the winning run, setting the fans to cheer and hug one another in a communal celebration of their beloved heroes.

In spite of breezing along to another pennant, the Giants remained a belligerent bunch, always ready to argue or fight. Dahlen fit right in, although ascertaining what exactly were the necessary ingredients to set him off on one of his tirades is difficult. On July 3, the Giants were cruising to an easy win in Philadelphia. Their lead over Pittsburgh at the time was eight games, and Dahlen was enjoying a fine day. Going into the ninth inning, he had two hits, a stolen base, and had handled nine fielding chances flawlessly. Yet, while at-bat in the ninth inning, with the Giants enjoying a comfortable 9–1 lead, he protested a strike call so forcefully that umpire Emslie had no choice but to eject him.

Abusive as they must have been, Dahlen still used only words in his objection to the call. This contrasted sharply with one of his earlier run-ins with Emslie, in New York in 1897, when Bill was a member of the Colts. The trouble began when Emslie called him out for oversliding the bag after he had stolen third base. Dahlen got to his feet, charged the umpire, and "dragged him around by the collar." His ouster that day at the Polo Grounds led to one of the more vicious incidents of that all-round vicious decade.

The Colts were shorthanded that August afternoon, as they were so often during their injury-riddled 1897 season. Losing Dahlen left them with only one remaining position player—catcher Mal Kittridge. Manager Anson put Kittridge behind the plate and moved Tim Donahue, who had been catching, into Dahlen's place at shortstop. When the Giants' Jack Warner attempted to steal second base, Donahue moved over to cover the bag. Kittridge's throw was in plenty of time, but although clearly beaten, Warner jumped at Donahue with both spikes in a clear attempt to injure him.

Donahue got up swinging, as all his teammates rushed to get at Warner. After the usual pushing and shoving, order was restored, and Donahue went off to get his wounds bandaged. When he returned, Emslie sensing a riot was about to happen, called the game, though it was still tied. His decision set an already restless crowd even more on edge. They appeared primed to pour out of the stands, but for the first time that any of the locals could remember, the New York City police took control of the field to maintain order.

Nine days after Emslie tossed him out in Philadelphia, Dahlen was thrown out of a game against the Cubs at the Polo Grounds. His objection to a strike call by Jim Johnstone triggered another ejection in an August 23 game against Pittsburgh. Umpire Johnstone called a third strike on a full-count pitch in the fourth inning, then, after listening a while to the usual Dahlen invective, ordered him to leave.

Dahlen was also among the Giants players and fans who made life miserable for Johnstone and his partner, Bill Klem, in an earlier home game against Pittsburgh. While they threw out only two—Donlin and McGann, both by Klem—the two umpires underwent continual griping and revilement from the Giants bench. Nor did it stop with just the foul language. In the fifth inning of that July 19 game, Klem ruled that Pittsburgh's Tommy Leach had reached first base safely after his bunt. First baseman McGann showed his displeasure at the call by grabbing Klem by his coat.

Second baseman Billy Gilbert pulled his teammate away, but not before the rookie umpire, attempting to establish his authority, sent McGann to the showers.

Later in the inning, Klem called Honus Wagner safe on a steal of second. Several Giants disagreed vehemently, with the most vituperative protests coming from center fielder Mike Donlin. Having heard enough, Klem threw Donlin out too, but before Donlin left, Klem was cannonaded with a barrage of beer bottles from the stands. Most missed, but one did hit him in the back. Following the Pirates' 8–5 win, using the police to maintain order was again necessary. To protect the umpires from the New York fans, they needed a cordon of policemen to shepherd them off the field. Lost in all this squabbling and contentiousness was yet another spectacular play by Dahlen, one that turned a Wagner line drive into a double play. As described by the *New York Times*, Dahlen "jumped up and made a phenomenal one-handed catch, and throwing the ball to Devlin, caught (Otis) Clymer off third."[10]

Those fans whose baseball memories begin with the 1970s might find quaint the musings of one visiting writer covering a game at the Polo Grounds in 1905. Noting the applause given by the fans to good plays by the opposition, he wrote that it is only in New York that the crowds treat enemy players fairly. That, of course, did not necessarily make a visit to New York a pleasurable experience for opposing teams. Nor, in return, were the Giants welcomed graciously when they traveled to the league's other cities. Led by the vitriolic, umpire-baiting McGraw, whom umpires would eject a record 13 times this season, they had established a well-deserved reputation as the most contentious team in the league. Their truculence and bellicosity generated fan hatred for them in whatever city they visited. Things got so bad in Brooklyn, following a McGraw battle with Superbas owner Charles Ebbets, that Giants fans, fearing for their safety, stopped making the trip across the river to see their team play at Washington Park. Police protection for visiting Giants players had gotten to be a matter of course, but that protection did not necessarily extend to visiting Giants fans.

Hardly a game went by when the foulmouthed McGraw, along with many of his players, did not verbally, or in many cases physically, confront umpires, opposing players, and even fans. It was a season of many incredibly ugly incidents, which began during the season's first week. At Philadelphia, a mob infuriated by the Giants' antics that afternoon took out its frustrations by throwing rocks and bricks at the Giants' carriage following the game. As would happen with disturbing regularity throughout the remainder of the season, the police were required to restore peace.

The most serious of these "police rescues" came at Pittsburgh on August 5, when officers were needed to escort the Giants from Exposition Park to protect them from yet another enraged mob. After winning the opener of the four-game series, the Giants had lost the last two, reducing their lead over the Pirates to eight and a half games. With the score tied at 5–5 in the ninth inning of the finale, Pittsburgh's Claude Ritchey led off against Mathewson with a ground-rule double into the overflow crowd. On George Gibson's attempt to sacrifice Ritchey to third, Mathewson fielded the ball and threw to third baseman Devlin, who reached to tag Ritchey as he slid into the base. Unfortunately, neither plate umpire George Bausewine (in his only season in the league) nor base umpire Emslie was in good position to make the call. Bausewine called Ritchey safe, whereupon the Giants appealed to Emslie to overrule him. When Emslie declined to do so, they began swarming around Bausewine, who pulled out his watch and ordered them back to their positions. When the Giants refused, Bausewine allowed the allotted time to elapse, and then forfeited the game to the Pirates.

Hatred for the New Yorkers had been building in Pittsburgh for the past few years, and now it exploded. Spectators, numbering perhaps half the 18,000 who were there, rushed onto the field. They sought out McGraw and his players, who were huddled on their bench, and began taking punches at them. The rivalry between the Pirates and the Giants was a fierce one, but for neither team did it extend to tolerating fan assaults. Manager Fred Clarke and several of his players went into action. They helped shield their hated opponents from the angry fans until the police could lead them back to their horse-drawn carriages, which were parked behind the stands. And still it was not over. People began pulling the yellow blankets that read "New York Champions," off the horses, and as the carriages pulled away, they began throwing stones at them. Miraculously, no one was seriously hurt.

This was not the first incident between the Pirates and Giants this season. At the Polo Grounds, in May, McGraw had shouted such gross obscenities at Barney Dreyfuss that the Pirates owner felt compelled to report it to Harry Pulliam. The National League president fined McGraw $150 and suspended him for 15 days, but eventually rescinded both penalties. In June, Pittsburgh fans attacked the Giants players as they were leaving Exposition Park to return their hotel. Dennis and Jeanne Burke DeValeria wrote about this incident in their biography of Honus Wagner.

"The Giants carriage was bombarded by an assortment of fruits and vegetables as it passed the farmers' market en route to the team's quarters, the Monongahela House. Some players retaliated, others took whatever cover they could find. Shortstop Bill Dahlen was the only one hurt in the salvo when a well-aimed cantaloupe found his head."[11]

After clinching the pennant at St. Louis on September 30, the club returned home four days later to finish the season with five home games against the Phillies. A large crowd gathered at Grand Central Station to greet the train when it arrived at 6 p.m. The celebrants cheered all the players, with the largest ovations going, as always, to McGraw and Mathewson. Dahlen, who got his share of the fans' hurrahs, played in the double-header against Philadelphia the next day, but sat out the final three games of the season.

Giants team members had been extremely upset with the decision by McGraw and Brush to snub the American League champion Boston club and not play in a World's Series in 1904. Skipping the series had cost each of them a significant amount of money, and they had conveyed their objections in a variety of ways. They had voiced some of those objections with extreme indignation, which helped convince Brush and McGraw that they had been on the wrong side of history. They would not repeat their mistake this season. As early as August 16, with the Giants comfortably in the lead, McGraw had announced that he would be willing to play a post-season series against whomever the American League pennant winner might be. That, of course, included the New York team, should they win, added the "magnanimous" McGraw, aware that with the Yankees in fourth place, such a result was highly unlikely. He surely hoped so. McGraw, as everyone knew, did not like anything about the American League; however, the Yankees were now the team he hated most, and the one against which he least wanted to play.

While the Giants were coasting home in the National League, the American League race was an extremely heated one that did not get decided until the final week. The eventual pennant winners were Connie Mack's Philadelphia Athletics, who finished two games ahead of Fielder Jones's Chicago White Sox. In a year of overall weak hitting in the American League, the A's team average of .255 was good enough to lead. Philadelphia also had the individual runs batted in leader in first baseman Harry Davis, who had 83. Still, the Giants seemed the much stronger team offensively. Led by Donlin, McGann, and Bresnahan, their National League-leading batting average was 18 points higher than Philadelphia's. They were also first in the National League in runs scored, on base percentage, and slugging average.

Leading the two teams were a pair of Irishmen who could not have been more dissimilar. Connie Mack was the complete antithesis of John McGraw, both in physical appearance and in his behavior on the field. Yet he was just as capable a manager, and, like McGraw, he too realized that it was pitching and not hitting that won pennants. Five pitchers had combined for the 105 Giants victories: Mathewson (31–9), Red Ames (22–8), McGinnity (21–15), Taylor (16–9), and Hooks Wiltse (15–6). But Mack had put together a top-flight pitching staff of his own. His big four of Rube Waddell (27–10), Eddie Plank (24–10), Andy Coakley (18–8), and Chief Bender (18–11) was very much the equal of New York's. This figured to be especially so in a short series. And if Mathewson was the National League's outstanding pitcher, Waddell held that distinction in the American League.

"The Giants do not care to play minor leaguers," said Giants owner John T. Brush about the Yankees' offer of a postseason series in 1904.

Like Mathewson, who won 31 games, struck out 206 batters, and had an ERA of 1.28 to capture the pitching Triple Crown in his league, Waddell was the Triple Crown winner in his.[12] Rube won 27 games, had 287 strikeouts, and a 1.48 ERA. Unfortunately for the A's, Mack would not have his best pitcher available to face the National Leaguers. The erratic and unpredictable Waddell had injured his arm while engaged in some foolish "horseplay" with Coakley and was unable to pitch in the series.[13] Had the face-to-face duel between Triple Crown winners Mathewson and Waddell taken place, it would have been the only one in World Series history. Never since have two pennant winners also had Triple Crown-winning pitchers.

Brush, who apologized for his wrongheaded decision of 1904, had taken the lead in arranging the format for this year's post-season contests. The teams would play a best-of-seven series (not a best-of-nine as in 1903), with the site of the games alternating daily between the two participating cities. Financially, the teams would split 60 percent of the receipts from the first four games, with 75 percent going to the winners and 25 percent to the losers.

On Sunday night, October 8, a group of their loyal (and well-connected) supporters held a dinner in honor of the pennant-winning Giants at the Majestic Theater in Manhattan. With every member of the team in the audience, a myriad of Broadway performers feted and entertained them

into the night. The next morning, the entire Giants entourage boarded a
Pennsylvania Railroad train for Philadelphia. (Any notion of getting to
bed early before a big game must never have occurred to them.) They traveled in a special car, accompanied by a legion of followers, among whom
were celebrity Giants fans Jim Corbett, the former heavyweight champ,
and George M. Cohan, Broadway's biggest star. Arriving at 10 a.m., they
headed immediately for Columbia Park, the Athletics home field, where
they would open the series that afternoon.

The Giants had been wearing a new uniform this season, replacing
the block-lettered "New York" of recent years with a large blue "N" on the
right breast and a large blue "Y" on the left breast. But for the series, they
unveiled a dramatic change. Whether playing in New York or Philadelphia,
the Giants would take the field dressed in black uniforms, with the "N"
and "Y" lettering in white rather than blue. Their stockings were white,
as were their caps, which were set off with black visors. It was an interesting psychological ploy by McGraw, one that had his team looking
dynamic when contrasted with the A's, who were clad in their compara-
tively drab regular-season uniforms.

Minus Waddell, who would have been his likely choice, Mack chose
Plank to pitch the first game. McGraw, naturally, went with Mathewson,
who came through with a 3–0 win, allowing the A's just four widely scattered hits. For Matty, it was the first of what would be his three shutouts
in the series. Philadelphia's Bender was equally dominating the next day
in New York. He evened the series by besting McGinnity with his own
four-hit, 3–0, shutout. Bender's masterpiece had matched Mathewson's,
but it would be the only game the American Leaguers would win. In a
series where every game ended in a shutout, Giants pitchers chalked up
the next three.

Due to threatening weather in Philadelphia, a disappointingly small
crowd was on hand at Columbia Park for Game 3. Seeing so few people in
the stands, McGraw and A's captain Lave Cross suggested to umpires Hank
O'Day and Jack Sheridan that the game be postponed. Realizing that so
few fans had braved the weather, the umpires went along, citing "wet
grounds" as the reason. The teams then agreed to alter the original schedule of alternating cities for each game. They would play Game 3 in Philadelphia, as planned, but New York would be the home team for both Games
4 and 5, with Philadelphia hosting Games 6 and 7, if they were necessary.

The next day Matty beat Coakley 9–0 in the only game that was not
closely contested. In Game 4, McGinnity topped Plank 1–0, with the Giants
scoring the only run of the game in the fourth inning, and it was unearned.
Mertes reached on an error by shortstop Monte Cross and eventually

scored on a two-out single by Billy Gilbert. Philadelphia's best chance came in the eighth inning. With two out, Topsy Hartsel and Lave Cross were aboard with the possible tying and winning runs, but McGinnity struck out the dangerous Socks Seybold to end the threat. In the ninth, he got Danny Murphy on a fly ball and ended with a flourish, striking out Monte Cross and Danny Hoffman.

Then it was Matty again. New York's "Golden Boy" ended the series by outpitching Bender 2–0 before a huge Saturday assemblage at the Polo Grounds. After Dahlen executed the last out of the series by throwing out Lave Cross, the crowd poured out onto the field. Congregating in front of the

Chief Bender's 3–0 shutout of the Giants was the Athletics' only win of the 1905 World Series.

Giants clubhouse, they lingered for nearly an hour while cheering their heroes, especially Mathewson.

Commenting a few days later from the team's offices in the St. James Building at Broadway and 26th Street, McGraw continued to praise his ace. "I knew he would be too much for the Athletics," he said. "In all my baseball career, I never saw such pitching as Matty did in that Series, and I don't think anybody else ever did."[14] McGraw was correct. Nobody had before, and nobody has since. To this day, the 25-year-old Mathewson's effort against Philadelphia remains the most remarkable pitching performance in World Series history. In tossing three complete game shutouts, he allowed just 14 hits and one walk.

Bresnahan, Mathewson's batterymate, led all hitters with a .313-average. Hartsel (.294) was the only batter to have any success against Mathewson and McGinnity for a Philadelphia team that batted a feeble .161 for the series.[15] Each Giants player received a winner's share of $1,142, plus an additional $500 thanks to a generous gesture made by Brush. Back in May, Brush had directed club secretary Fred Knowles to set aside for the players the receipts for the many exhibition games the team played every year, money normally retained by the club itself. Several Giants, including Dahlen and McGraw, increased their earnings by collecting on bets they had made with Philadelphia backers. Additionally, each Giant received a commemorative button valued at $50 from the National Commission.

Yet while the series had been rewarding financially for Dahlen, it had not been so artistically. Although he fielded flawlessly, Philadelphia pitchers kept him hitless in 15 at-bats, making him the only regular on either side who failed to hit safely. Asked after one game what he thought of the American League ball used that day, Dahlen responded, "Don't know what to think. I haven't hit one yet." He did, however, achieve a series original by becoming the first player to steal home in a World Series game. The Giants had already scored four runs in the top of the fifth inning of Game 3 when Dahlen stole home on the front end of a double steal.

It was common practice in these times for big league teams to keep playing after the regular season ended as a way to pick up extra money. Thus, both the Giants and Athletics were in action the day after the series ended, each beginning a round of exhibition games in the East. In Paterson, New Jersey, Philadelphia dropped a 2–1 decision to the Paterson team of the Hudson River League. And out on Long Island, Vive Lindaman pitched the semi-pro Ridgewood team to a 5–2 win over the Giants. Lindaman had beaten the Yankees in an exhibition game a week earlier and would join the Boston Doves in 1906.

Christy Mathewson's three complete game shutouts against Philadelphia in the 1905 World Series remains the most remarkable piching performance in series history.

The new world champions can be forgiven somewhat for losing to the semi-pros. They had just barely finished celebrating their championship, and some, including Dahlen, Donlin, and Bresnahan just skipped the game. Dahlen did play in several other of these games, including one in Trenton on October 21 that ended the tour. The game itself was uneventful, but a banquet in that city the night before was not. In an incident symbolic of the pugnacious 1905 Giants, Mike Donlin concluded the evening's celebration by getting into a fistfight with a black waiter.

TWELVE

The Giants Fade,
and So Does Dahlen

While continuing to live in Brooklyn, Dahlen spent much of his time during the fall and winter of 1905–1906 in Manhattan and Queens, two of New York City's other boroughs. Manhattan was the site of a gym where he kept in shape playing "push ball" with other members of the Giants: John McGraw, Mike Donlin, Billy Gilbert, Art Devlin, and trainer Harry Tuthill. Queens was the home of the Aqueduct Race Track, a venue that Dahlen would visit regularly with Yankees outfielder Willie Keeler, his Brooklyn neighbor and friend. Bill would often run into McGraw at Aqueduct, as the Giants manager was an even more devoted horse player than he was. In fact, racetracks all across America were well-populated with all sorts of baseball people, in-season and out. McGraw, for one, would frequently attend the New York tracks, gathering information and making his bets with the bookmakers, before heading off to the Polo Grounds.[1]

Several of Dahlen's playmates had now become budding capitalists, although none had arrived at that status by betting on horses. Keeler was investing in real estate and already owned several properties in the city. McGraw, the recent recipient of a new three-year contract at $15,000 per year, had opened a billiards parlor at Broadway and 34th Street. His partner in this venture was jockey Tod Sloane, one of McGraw's many racetrack buddies. Gilbert and Donlin had recently opened a café at 125th Street, although not all of Donlin's offseason was spent so peacefully. Just four months after his assault on the waiter in Trenton, his hot temper and hard drinking landed him in trouble again. While on a New York Central train nearing Troy, New York, he punched a conductor in the face and threatened a porter with a gun. Train officials summoned the police, and Donlin ended up spending the night in an Albany jail.

Meanwhile, Dahlen seemed content investing his money at the race-track. As was his custom, he visited Nelliston for three weeks in February 1906, then a month taking the baths in Hot Springs. Teammates Donlin, Gilbert, and Dan McGann were also at Hot Springs before all headed to the Giants spring training camp at Memphis. Rainy weather in Memphis limited the number of practices the team could hold, forcing them to spend much of their time at their quarters in the Clarendon Hotel.

Though the Giants had led both major leagues in stolen bases for each of the past two seasons, McGraw devoted numerous sessions during training camp to teaching the art of base running. Led by Dahlen, Art Devlin, and Sam Mertes, the speedy New Yorkers had stolen 283 bases in 1904 and 291 in 1905. They would lead again in 1906, swiping 288, but it was more than just base stealing that McGraw was teaching. He was preaching the old Baltimore Orioles credo of taking the extra base through aggressive running and intimidation, which hardly seemed necessary in the wake of the persistent aggressiveness and intimidation shown by his club the past two seasons.

The Giants had dropped the "NY" from their uniforms this year and instead were wearing jerseys emblazoned with the words "WORLD'S CHAMPIONS" across the front. But as the weeks progressed it started to become obvious that they would not be wearing those uniforms again in 1907. The season got off to a bad start when Mathewson contracted diphtheria, an extremely deadly disease in the days before immunization. Diphtheria had killed McGraw's mother and four of his young siblings in the winter of 1884–85, and now it was threatening his friend and star pitcher.

Fortunately Mathewson recovered, but the illness forced him to miss the first three weeks of the season. Yet, to the surprise of everyone, the club played extremely well without him. They compiled a 15–4 record during his absence and led Chicago by two games on the day of his return. Matty lost to Boston in his first start of the season, and for the rest of the year would not be the almost unbeatable pitcher he had been in 1905. He pitched 72 fewer innings in '06; his win total dropped from 31 to 22; and his earned run average more than doubled, going from a league-low 1.28 to 2.97.

In all, the Giants won 96 games, a total that in most seasons would mean a pennant, but not in this one. In 1906, neither the Giants, nor any other National League team, would prove a match for the Chicago Cubs. Managed by first baseman Frank Chance, who had replaced Frank Selee as manager in mid-1905, the Cubs would set a still-existing league record for wins (116) and finish 20 games ahead of New York.[2] Second baseman Johnny Evers, shortstop Joe Tinker, and third baseman Harry Steinfeldt, joined Chance in giving the Cubs an outstanding infield. Frank "Wildfire" Schulte, Jimmy Slagle, and former Superba Jimmy Sheckard made up the outfield, with veteran Johnny Kling behind the plate. Mordecai Brown, Matty's successor as the league's top pitcher, led a staff that included Ed Reulbach, Carl Lundgren and Jack Pfiester.

Mathewson's illness, Donlin's broken ankle, Red Ames's twisted ankle, and the injuries to Bresnahan and McGann were all factors contributing to New York's second-place finish. So was second baseman Gilbert, who was overweight and played poorly all season. Nevertheless, imagining the Giants making up that 20-game deficit is difficult, even if they had been at full strength.

On June 12, the City of New York finally got around to honoring the club's 1905 world championship. New Yorkers traditionally love to celebrate joyous events with parades through Manhattan, and this celebration was no different. The procession began downtown at Union Square. A group of mounted police was out front, followed in order by the Sixty-ninth Regiment Band, a series of local amateur baseball teams, the Seventh Regiment Band, and finally an assemblage of automobiles. The autos carried players from both the Giants and their opponents that afternoon, the Cincinnati Reds. The entourage continued up Broadway, cheered along the entire way by huge crowds lining the street. Passing by City Hall they were greeted by Mayor George McClellan and a bevy of New York City officials.

After traveling the length of Manhattan, all reached the Polo Grounds, where the ground crew had decorated the baselines with little American flags, and also little Irish flags.[3] Following a display of fireworks the autos drove twice around the field. Seated in the last of the autos were the eminent stage performer De Wolf Hopper and the ubiquitous Jim Corbett, both longtime Giants fans. Several presentations followed, culminating in the conferral of the world championship flag. Reds owner Garry Herrmann, acting for the National Commission, presented the banner to Manhattan Borough president McGowan, who accepted on behalf of the mayor. Workmen then raised the large blue and gold championship banner on a pole above the grandstand for all to see.

However, once the ceremonies ended and the game began, the Giants looked like anything but champions. They committed seven errors, including one by Dahlen, in losing to Jake Weimer and the Reds 6–1. At that point, New York was in third place, but just three games behind the Cubs. Pittsburgh was a half game ahead of them in second. Most of the Giants players believed that the second-place Pirates, and not the league-leading Cubs, would be their most serious competitor. Dahlen, for one, had dismissed Chicago earlier in the month, predicting that the Giants' biggest threat would come from Pittsburgh. Similarly, Pirates manager Fred Clarke thought that the biggest threat to his club would come from New York. Apparently, it was not yet evident to even these veteran observers just how good this Chicago team was.

When the race was over, the Cubs, Giants, and third-place Pirates would be the only National League teams to finish with winning records. The absence of a close pennant race was in sharp contrast to what was happening in the American League. Chicago, New York, Cleveland, and Philadelphia staged a year-long battle for the lead before the White Sox edged the Yankees in the final week to win the flag. Fielder Jones's Sox then upset the heavily favored Cubs in the World's Series, boosting the prestige of the American League even higher. By being involved in two thrilling pennant races in three seasons, the Yankees had captured the devotion of a multitude of New York's baseball fans, including many who were once loyal to the Giants. The Yanks had been heavily outdrawn by the Giants in every year of their existence, but their 1906 attendance of 434,700 was more than 30,000 higher than the Giants. Late in the season, the Giants finally recognized and acknowledged New Yorkers' interest in the Yankees. Brush and McGraw, the two longtime Yankees disparagers, acceded to the demands of their patrons and began posting their neighborhood rival's scores on the Polo Grounds scoreboard.

But it was left to Yankees owner Frank Farrell to impose the ultimate humiliation on Brush and McGraw. Hoping to convert the Yankees' popularity into dollars for the Giants coffers, they proposed a post-season series between the two teams. Farrell, who had hoped the Yanks' post-season play would be against the Cubs in the World's Series, turned them down flat. Two years earlier, after Brush and McGraw had refused to meet the Boston Americans in the World's Series, Farrell had proposed they meet his team in a postseason series. Brush's refusal was brutally and mockingly short. "Who are these people?" he asked. "We do not know them at all. The Giants do not care to play minor leaguers, so this absurd challenge from a lot of nobodies will be ignored."[4] Now the "nobodies" were getting their revenge.

Another reason for the shift of favor to the Yankees was the "clean" brand of ball played by the American Leaguers. The rowdyism of the Giants had repulsed large numbers of local fans, who were especially disgusted with the antics of their leader, McGraw. His constant bullying and complaints that umpires were out "to get" the Giants, which had alienated fans in the league's seven other cities, was now beginning to alienate a significant number of New Yorkers.

An August 6 game against Chicago was a typical example of McGraw's ongoing attempts at intimidation. New York was still in striking distance of the Cubs when McGinnity faced Brown at the Polo Grounds that day. Chicago won, 3–1, with the key play of the game being an out call at the plate made by umpire Jimmy Johnstone on the Giants' Art Devlin. McGraw and Devlin's vociferous objections got them thrown out and incited the crowd to throw whatever objects they could find at the beleaguered Johnstone.

President Pulliam, who had suspended McGraw in May, suspended him again, along with Devlin. Yet still more was to come. When Johnstone reported for work the next day, gatekeepers told him that for security reasons they would not allow him to enter the park. However, the "security reasons" excuse was bogus; this was just another McGraw attempt at intimidation. Johnstone's partner, Bob Emslie, refused to umpire without him, and the game was eventually forfeited to Chicago.

Reds manager Ned Hanlon, McGraw's mentor in Baltimore, was one among many who spoke out against his former pupil's tactics. Hanlon warned that McGraw and the rest of the Giants would not get away with their "umpire intimidation" should they try it in Cincinnati. McGraw, meanwhile, continued to complain that the whole league was against him. Yet, in spite of their supposed animosity, some clubs seemed to be trying actually to help McGraw. In the middle of the race Hanlon sold him Cy Seymour, a onetime Giant and the league's defending batting champion. The 33-year-old Seymour was batting just .257 for the Reds, but the trade rejuvenated him. Following his July 13 return to the Giants, he batted .320 for the rest of the season. A day before getting Seymour, McGraw obtained outfielder Spike Shannon from the Cardinals in exchange for outfielder Sam Mertes and catcher/outfielder Doc Marshall.

Judged by the amount of ejections the Giants incurred this season, Dahlen was unusually well behaved. His only one came in the season's opening week. Brooklyn pitcher Mal Eason, who had picked him off second base in the fourth inning, did it again two innings later. Dahlen "went wild," said the *Brooklyn Daily Eagle*, and was quickly thrown out by umpire John Conway. Being thrown out of games was, of course, nothing new for Dahlen and never seemed to faze him. What did mortify him, though, was falling for baseball's timeworn ruse, the hidden-ball-trick.[5]

Honus Wagner victimized him by catching him off second base in a game at Pittsburgh on May 18. What made it even worse was that Dahlen's absentmindedness may have cost the Giants the game. When it happened, they were trailing 7–6, with two out in the eighth inning. Dahlen was on second with the potential tying run, and Gilbert was on first with the possible lead run. Mathewson was the due batter, but McGraw sent Sammy Strang up as a pinch hitter. Assuming pitcher Lefty Leifield had the ball, Dahlen started to take his lead when shortstop Wagner put the tag on him for the rally-ending third out.

After the game, Dahlen was disconsolate, upset and embarrassed that he, a 16-year veteran, could succumb to such an ancient maneuver. McGraw was simply angry. He hit Dahlen with a $100 fine, a substantial amount of money in 1906, but perhaps for that reason, he rescinded the fine the next day.

At 36, Dahlen continued to be a standout shortstop, but he had begun to shown signs of losing both power and speed this season. His .240 batting average was about the same as his .242 the year before, although overall he did get on base more often. Thanks to 76 walks, and being hit by pitches 10 times, his on base percentage rose 20 points.[6] Dahlen's power numbers dropped from seven home runs and 81 runs batted in in 1905 to just one home run and 49 RBI this year. His 16 stolen bases, down from 37 in 1905, was a new full-season low for him.

In December, Dahlen attended the National League meetings at New York's Hotel Victoria, where he hobnobbed with former teammates Willie Keeler and Joe Kelley. Keeler was now a fixture with the Yankees, while Kelley would spend the 1907 season managing the Toronto Maple Leafs of the Eastern League. McGraw, meanwhile, had spent part of his offseason in California, arranging for the Giants to hold spring training there. On February 24, 1907, team secretary Fred Knowles, along with Dahlen, Christy Mathewson, Cy Seymour, and a few other players, left on a Pennsylvania Railroad train for the trip to Los Angeles. They picked up Frank Bowerman, Dan McGann, Mike Donlin, and George Browne in Chicago, and then headed west via the Santa Fe Railroad. Dummy Taylor came aboard in Kansas City, and Joe McGinnity in Newton, Kansas, before the train finally arrived at Los Angeles's Santa Fe station on the first of March.

The complete spring training tour covered 8,000 miles from the time that first group left New York until the team returned shortly before opening day. After rain canceled many of the games scheduled for Los Angeles and San Francisco, the Giants played their way back east. Among their more notable stops was San Antonio, for a series against Jimmy McAleer's St. Louis Browns, and New Orleans, for one against Connie Mack's Philadelphia Athletics. The encounter with Philadelphia, billed as a replay of the 1905 World's Series, was a disaster. McGraw and his men got into a dispute with umpire Chief Zimmer that continued into the next day and resulted in the Giants forfeiting two of the games. McGraw made things even worse with a name-calling assault on A's owner Ben Shibe. "New York brawlers" and "hoodlums" were two of the terms New Orleans newspapers used to describe McGraw and his team.[7]

The Giants' unsuccessful 1906 season had led to bitter 1907 contract negotiations between McGraw and several of his players. Mike Donlin was so unhappy with his proposed cut in salary that he left the club to join his wife Mabel Hite on the vaudeville circuit. Donlin would miss the entire season. Dahlen held out for several weeks, before reluctantly agreeing to accept a $500 pay cut. He was also hoping to add some money from outside baseball. Dahlen and Keeler had invested in mining stocks, hoping to duplicate John McGraw's successful investment in a Nevada gold mine. Bill used the part of each winter he spent upstate ice skating with pitcher Hooks Wiltse as a way to get in shape for the upcoming season. Unfortunately, that did not help him avoid contracting a severe head cold during training camp, a malady that also hit Mathewson, Roger Bresnahan, and second-year pitcher Cecil Ferguson. Jack Hannifin, a rookie from the Connecticut League, played impressively as Dahlen's replacement during his illness.

Bill would have a new double-play partner this season. Unhappy with the 1906 performance of Billy Gilbert, McGraw sold him to Newark of the Eastern League. To take Gilbert's place playing alongside the 37-year-old Dahlen, he signed 38-year-old Tommy Corcoran. Corcoran, who had been a major leaguer since 1890, a year longer than Dahlen, was gone by late July, and young Larry Doyle had begun his long career as New York's second baseman.

Poised to begin his 17th major-league season, Dahlen would end it as the oldest position player in the league. Baseball, and indeed the country, had changed drastically since the day he broke in with Cap Anson's Chicago White Stockings back in 1891. He had played with and against many of the National League's earliest legends, a fact he reminisced about in a December 1906 interview with the *Sporting News*.

> "I've been in the big company since the spring of 1891, playing with only two clubs, Brooklyn and Chicago. Starting as young as I did, and lasting as long as I have, it gave me all the chance in the world to see the stars and watch them come and go. I wonder how many fellows are in the game today who were there when I arrived? Those that are still on deck are, as a rule, a bit decrepit compared with me, and all because I started young. Look at this Chicago bunch today. When I came it was Anson, (Fred) Pfeffer, (Tom) Burns, (Jimmy) Cooney, (Walt) Wilmot, (Cliff) Carroll, (Jimmy) Ryan, and (Elmer) Foster, besides myself; (Mal) Kittridge and (Tom) Nagle, catchers; old Hutch (Bill Hutchison), (Pat) Luby, (Ad) Gumbert, (Ed) Stein and maybe one or two others whom I've forgotten, pitchers. Cooney, Burns, and

Luby are dead. Kitt's at Montreal. The rest are doing the best they can
to make money away from the game. That year (Charley) Radbourn
was pitching his last in the big league, so I saw Rad go. Tim Keefe and
John Clarkson were just beginning to slide into has-been valley. Buck
Ewing was still a great man in the game."

Critics had long complained that starting a baseball season in mid-
April was too early. Frigid weather, common at that time of year in the
East and Midwest, made for too many postponements, they claimed.
Even when the games were not cancelled, charged the critics, far too
many of them were being played in conditions that both players and fans
found uncomfortable. A heavy snow that fell on New York City two days
before the scheduled April 11 opener only reinforced the calls of some
for a return to a May 1 start. Snow remained piled up all around the Polo
Grounds the day of the opener, but workmen managed to clear the field
and the game went on as scheduled, only to run into a different kind of
problem.

That morning, Police Commissioner Bingham had issued an order
that bore directly on opening day, and any other game that might draw a
large crowd. Bingham declared that he intended to enforce the New York
City law that prohibited the men of his force from policing private grounds.
"The police department is not going to help private corporations to make
money," said the commissioner. Bingham's directive left it up to the Giants
to decide whether they needed a security force to control the crowd at the

opener. If they did, it would be their
responsibility to provide that force.
The Giants chose not to do so, a
decision that would result in their
forfeiting the game.

With no championship flags to
raise, the pregame ceremonies were
not as tumultuous as the year
before. Still, a display of the national
colors rippled throughout the park,
and music was heard throughout,
including the playing of the *Star-
Spangled Banner* before the game.
Also on display for the first time at
the Polo Grounds were advertise-
ments that covered the outfield
walls. Those billboards hawking
such items as hats, shoes, or suits,

Hard-hitting (and hard-drinking) Mike
Donlin abandoned the 1907 Giants to
join his wife, Mabel Hite, on the vaudeville circuit.

announced that they would reward Giants players with their product for each home run hit.

Missing from the scene this day was McGraw, who had taken ill and was not at the park. First baseman and team captain Dan McGann ran the club in his absence. Both McGann and Billy Murray, the Phillies first-year manager, had two of their pitchers warm up before the game. Joe McGinnity and Red Ames warmed up for New York, while Frank Corridon and Bill Duggleby got ready for Philadelphia. This was not some lefty/righty type strategy, as all four pitchers were righthanders. Both managers were simply trying to decide which pitcher would be the best that day. McGann eventually chose McGinnity, and Murray opted for Corridon. Murray's choice was an excellent one. Corridon walked six, but he allowed only one hit, a third-inning single by Seymour, and had the Giants shut out 3–0 as Philadelphia prepared to bat in the ninth. But before they could, hordes of spectators poured onto the field. Without an adequate security force to stop them, they surrounded the players and prevented the game from continuing. After 15 minutes of unsuccessfully trying to get the boisterous fans off the field, umpire Bill Klem forfeited the game to Philadelphia.

Although the Giants lost, catcher Bresnahan made this game memorable by introducing shin guards into the baseball world. As the next day's *New York Times* described it, "Bresnahan created somewhat of a sensation when he appeared behind the bat for the start of play by donning cricket leg guards. As he displayed himself togged in mask, protector, and guards, he presented no vulnerable surface for a wild ball to strike."[8]

A pair of rainouts followed the opener, but then New York bounced back to win six of the next seven, including an April 22 game at Boston. Mathewson, in his first appearance of the season, gave up eight hits in defeating Patsy Flaherty 1–0. Flaherty was making his home debut after coming to the Doves in a big winter trade with Pittsburgh. Dahlen singled Bresnahan home with the winning run in the ninth, after Bresnahan had walked and moved to second when Flaherty hit McGann with a pitch.

Bill's early season showing made a favorable impression on veteran sportswriter William M. Rankin, who covered the Giants for the *Sporting News*. "Dahlen is far from a has-been yet," Rankin wrote in early May. "His work thus far shows that he is on the job and will try and stay on it for some time to come. When the weather settles down to summer business then Dahlen will be at his best."[9]

McGann, hit by Flaherty on April 22, was hit again on June 18, by Cincinnati's Andy Coakley. This blow was a lot more damaging, breaking McGann's arm and sidelining him for six weeks. Bresnahan suffered an even more severe injury that day when a Coakley pitch hit him in the head.

The blow was almost fatal, but during his 10-day hospital stay, the resource-ful Bresnahan continued his pioneering ways by designing a primitive bat-ting helmet.

Following Mathewson's shutout win at Boston and a loss at Philadel-phia, the Giants won their next 17 games. By the close of play on May 18, their record was a spectacular 24–3. Yet despite their phenomenal start, they were just one game ahead of the defending champion Cubs, who were 23–4. This would be the high point of New York's season. Three weeks later, after dropping 11-of-14, the Giants were five and a half games behind Chicago and sinking fast. Meanwhile, over in the American League, Clark Griffith's Yankees had also fallen out of the race early. Overall, it would be a long and disappointing season for local fans. Many had gone into the season hoping that 1907 would at last bring them an all-New York World's Series.

The Giants were in third place, two and a half games ahead of Philadel-phia with seven games to go, when they concluded this forgettable season by losing all seven. The final three were to Philadelphia, giving the Phillies a season-ending seven-game win streak, and allowing them to pass the Giants in the standings. New York's fourth-place finish was its first full-season finish other than first or second for a McGraw-led Giants team and revived rumors that he was about to resign. For Dahlen personally, his overall performance was mixed. Defensively, he continued to make the plays at shortstop. At least he made them most days, although August 22 was not one of them.

Filling in for the suspended John McGraw, Dahlen managed the Giants to an August 8, 1907, doubleheader sweep of the Pirates. It no doubt turned his mind toward even-tually managing a team of his own.

Playing at home against Pittsburgh, Dahlen had one of his worst defensive games ever. He contributed three errors in a game in which the Pirates used 21 hits (but none by Honus Wagner) to defeat Mathewson 20–5. His per-formance elicited boos from the fans, along with calls for McGraw to replace him with Danny Shay, a little-used utility player. Of course, many of those booing fans were likely the same people who had been on their feet cheering Bill's defensive genius in the Giants' previous series, against Chicago. His play in the final game, a day before the Pittsburgh debacle, had been particularly brilliant. "Dahlen was a mountain of strength at short, and his playing and fine stops evoked considerable applause," said the *New York Times*.[10]

Bill had experienced a much more pleasant afternoon against the Pirates two weeks before that three-error game. With Pulliam having suspended McGraw yet again, Dahlen managed the club in an August 8 doubleheader at Exposition Park. The Giants won both games: 4–3 behind Mathewson, and 7–0 behind Hooks Wiltse, in a game called after seven innings. His managerial success no doubt focused Bill's thoughts on a managerial career when his playing days were over.

Although Dahlen was hardly finished as a player, his advancing age and reduced production made him aware that the end of his long career was in sight. While he was still an outstanding shortstop, his batting and base-stealing totals declined for the third year in a row. He batted a lowly .207, with 34 runs batted in and just 11 steals. And though Dahlen's 20 doubles were 10th highest in the league, for the only season of his playing career he failed to hit a home run.

Of course, no season would be complete without a series of confrontations between Bill and the National League's umpiring staff. Despite his many years of experience, and the accumulated wisdom we all assume accompanies that experience, 1907 was no different. Four of the confrontations ended with Dahlen being told to leave the premises, with Klem responsible for three of the ejections. Then again, there were those, Christy Mathewson among them, who believed Dahlen would often try to get himself dismissed early so that he could take in that afternoon's racing card.

THIRTEEN

Banished to Boston

Well before their disheartening 1907 season ended, everyone formally connected to the Giants suspected that the club would be making post-season personnel changes. No matter how those changes would come, whether in one big trade or as a series of smaller deals, it appeared inevitable that several veteran Giants would not be with the club in 1908. With the addition of a young infielder high on John McGraw's list of priorities, Dahlen figured to be one of those who would be leaving. The trade speculation proved to be accurate, with the changes coming in one block-buster deal with the Boston Doves. On December 13, the closing day of the National League meeting at New York's Waldorf Astoria Hotel, the Giants and Doves made a five-players-for-three trade, and Dahlen was a major part of it. Accompanying him to Boston were catcher Frank Bowerman, first baseman Dan McGann, outfielder George Browne, and pitcher Cecil Ferguson. Going from Boston to New York were recently fired Doves manager Fred Tenney, a first baseman; Tom Needham, a catcher; and Al Bridwell, a 23-year-old shortstop who would replace Dahlen.

McGraw had devoted most of his offseason efforts in trying to put together a different deal, one for Cincinnati's Hans Lobert. When that failed, he turned to Joe Kelley, his old friend and the newly named replacement for Tenney as manager of the Doves. After conferring on and off for several hours, the two old Orioles pulled off the biggest trade the National League had seen in years. McGraw opened the negotiations by offering Roger Bresnahan, his disgruntled catcher, for Tenney. Kelley accepted, but he wanted McGraw to throw in McGann, whom he would use to replace Tenney at first base. McGraw did not feel Tenney was worth both Bresnahan and McGann and suggested Boston take Bowerman, his other catcher, instead of Bresnahan. Because the friction between them that began during the 1905 World's Series had continued to grow, McGraw knew that he had to get rid of one of his two catchers.

160

When Kelley countered by making Bridwell available, McGraw added Browne and Ferguson to the deal and requested that the Doves add Needham to take Bowerman's place. Offered the choice of either Dahlen, his former Superba teammate, or Jack Hannifin, a 23-year-old utility player, Kelley chose Dahlen.[1] (He eventually got them both when the Doves purchased Hannifin a few months later.) After McGraw and Kelley shook hands on the deal, Kelley took it to George B. Dovey, the owner of the Doves, for his approval. However, Dovey balked at the idea of sending Tenney to New York, having told his former manager that he would try to honor his request to be traded to Pittsburgh. Only after Kelley threatened to resign if Dovey canceled the trade, did the owner agree

Boston first baseman, and former manager, Fred Tenney was foremost among those coming to the Giants in the trade for Dahlen.

to let it stand. Kelley was pleased, but Tenney was not. Besides preferring to go to Pittsburgh, Tenney's second choice would have been Cincinnati. Ned Hanlon was retiring as the manager of the Reds, and Tenney thought he had a chance to replace him.[2]

Despite the bickering over Tenney, the consensus among baseball people was that the trade would improve both teams. Replacing Dahlen and McGann with Bridwell and Tenney, and adding them to holdovers Larry Doyle and Art Devlin, would give the Giants the fast infield that McGraw had coveted. Meanwhile, they expected the addition of veterans Dahlen, Bowerman, McGann, and Browne to strengthen the Doves chances of climbing above their second-division finishes of the past five seasons.

Kelley's club began its formal spring training on March 15, a week or more later than most of the other big league clubs. Three players were missing from the group that assembled at Augusta, Georgia: Bowerman was late; Dahlen, per usual, was getting himself in shape at Hot Springs; and Dave Brain, their English-born third baseman, was a holdout. Brain had slugged a National League-leading 10 home runs in 1907, and was asking for an $800 raise over the $3,000 Boston had paid him a year ago. Additionally, he wanted the Doves to pay his expenses for traveling to his Chicago home after the season, and to offer some concessions in the purchase of his uniforms.

The three players might have been missing that first day of practice, but George Dovey was not. The Doves owner was on the field and in uniform. The 46-year-old Dovey was routinely slugging batting-practice pitches from both sides of the plate. He even jokingly suggesting that if Brain did not sign, perhaps he would be the Doves third baseman in 1908. As it turned out, neither Brain nor Dovey would play third base for the 1908 Doves. In mid-May, when Brain approached Kelley about rejoining the team, the manager told him that second-year man Bill Sweeney had won the job. To emphasize the finality of Kelley's selection, Dovey sold Brain to Cincinnati. Brain appeared in just 27 games in 1908, 16 for the Reds and 11 for the Giants, in what would be his final big league season.

Dahlen reported to Augusta three days after the rest of the squad had gathered, looking fit after his work at Hot Springs. He had, of course, been to Augusta before. Back before the turn of the century, when he was a member of Ned Hanlon's Superbas, the Brooklyn club had used it as its spring training site. Even earlier than that, he had played in exhibition games there as a member of Cap Anson's Chicago Colts.

In his first spring meeting with the Boston press, Bill made the usual comments about how glad he was to be there, and how much better he expected the team to be. Declaring that he had grown tired of playing for McGraw, he stated that Brooklyn and Boston had topped the list of places where he hoped to be traded. And while he did not go as far as to forecast a pennant for his new club, he did offer to wager that the Cubs, the two-time defending National League champions, would not win again.

The always ungracious McGraw had his own take on Dahlen's departure. "Mark my words," he said, speaking from the Giants training camp at Marlin Springs, Texas, "Bridwell is going to make them forget about Dahlen. Bill was all right, but he started to slow up, especially on balls hit to his right."[3]

Dahlen entered the 1908 season in the midst of a long homerless streak, after having failed for the first time to hit any the season before. The streak was now almost two years old, dating from May 4, 1906, when he had his only home run of that season against Boston rookie Jim Moroney. But in just his second home game with the Doves, Dahlen ended the drought and he did so with a vengeance. His second-inning blast off Philadelphia's Lew Moren landed on the railroad tracks that ran behind Boston's South End Grounds. He would hit two more this season, off Brooklyn's Harry McIntire and Pittsburgh's Lefty Leifield, both in May and both at home.

A visit to any city by a McGraw-led club always carried with it a potential for violence, but the chance of an outbreak seemed more likely than usual when the Giants traveled to Boston on April 27. Yet despite lots of ferocious bench-jockeying in this first game between the two teams since the big trade, the only "incident" was a spat between McGraw and McGann, and that occurred in a hotel. The fans were civil, and particularly welcoming to Tenney, the Doves now-former manager, who received a very warm greeting. The cheers for Tenney continued during his acceptance of a leather traveling bag, given in recognition of his 14 years of service with the Boston club. For Tenney, it was an indication that the fans forgave him for wearing the uniform of the hated New Yorkers.

The game itself was an excellent pitching duel between the great Christy Mathewson and Boston's Irv Young. Mathewson prevailed 2–0 over Young, a 23-game loser the year before. Dahlen went hitless against his former teammate, but it was one of the few early season games in which he failed to get at least one hit. His batting average was .312 after 10 games, and exactly .300 after 19.

Nor had he show any signs of slowing in the field. A report in the June 6 *Boston Globe* marveled at his handling of 15 of 16 chances in two games against the Cubs. "Nothing finer has been seen in Boston in many moons than the fielding of Bill Dahlen in the last two games."[4] He was even more spectacular later that month, registering 13 of 14 successful chances in a June 27 game against Philadelphia. In addition to his physical skills, Dahlen put on display daily all the wily, heads-up tactics and baseball knowledge he had acquired over his 18-year career. The *Globe* continued to marvel at what a truly fine player he was. "No finer shortstopping work has been seen here than this player has been doing," wrote their *Sporting Life* correspondent, J. C. Morse.[5]

Between those two spectacular exhibitions of how to play shortstop, Dahlen experienced his first ejection as a Dove. It came as a result of a fair /foul dispute with umpire Cy Rigler, allowing Rigler entrance to that long list of National League umpires who had given Dahlen the thumb. Bill later received a letter from league president Harry Pulliam tactfully suggesting that he start paying less attention to the umpiring calls he sees. Dahlen would have a much more serious encounter with Rigler four years later, when he was managing the Dodgers.

Manager Kelley had been batting Dahlen sixth in the order, but in July he moved him up to second for several games, before again dropping him back to sixth. It was also Dahlen that Kelley called upon to manage the club whenever he was unavailable. But Bill's most memorable afternoon of the season may have come in an August 6 home encounter with Pittsburgh. Having taken the day off to battle the touch of malaria that had put him in a weakened condition, he was on the bench when umpire

Jim Johnstone ousted Kelley and Browne, two-thirds of the Doves outfield. Hannifin, who had been playing short, had to fill one of those spots, leaving Dahlen the only man available to play shortstop. The Pirates won easily, 9–1, and Dahlen did not get a hit in his two at-bats. Yet despite his weakened condition, he put on such a fine defensive show, the appreciative crowd at the South End Grounds gave him several long, loud ovations.

The preseason remarks by McGraw, about Bridwell making New York a better team, and by Dahlen, about the Cubs not repeating, would come together in a fateful way late in the 1908 season. It was Bridwell who got the "game-winning" single against the Cubs on September 23, the game that ended 1–1 when Fred Merkle memorably forgot to touch second base. With the teams tied for first place after 153 games, the Giants and Cubs would have to replay that September 23 game to decide the pennant winner. However, in the week leading up to that playoff game, the Giants had stumbled, losing three times to Philadelphia's Harry Coveleski. For the New Yorkers to keep pace with Chicago, they had to win their final three games.

All were at home, against Boston, and the Giants swept all three, which is not surprising. The Giants were battling for a pennant and Boston was a weak team playing out the string. Nor was it surprising that the Giants won so easily, by scores of 8–1, 4–1, and 7–2. Nevertheless, the series raised suspicions that not all the Doves were doing their best to win these games. The charges centered specifically on the ones who had come over from the Giants in the winter. According to the rumors, McGraw had told Dahlen and Browne that if they played poorly he would bring them back to New York for the 1909 season. Dahlen went 1–12 in the series, and Browne 1–11. Nevertheless, both fielded flawlessly, and their poor hitting was more likely due to the pitching of Red Ames, Hooks Wiltse, and Joe McGinnity than to any *quid pro quo* with McGraw. If the rumors were true, and they were totally unsubstantiated then, the plan went for nought. Mordecai Brown beat Mathewson in the makeup game, and Chicago had its third consecutive pennant.

The Doves, cellar-dwellers in 1906 and seventh in 1907, moved up another notch in the standings this season. Yet, Dovey had expected more after the big trade, and the sixth-place finish cost Kelley his job. Dovey and Kelley had been engaged in a long-running verbal battle anyway. Their quarrel was over the owner's dissatisfaction with what he perceived as his manager's weak work ethic. Eventually, Dovey arranged to have Kelley return to his former managerial position at Toronto, in the Eastern League, and named Bowerman his replacement.

McGraw had predicted that Boston would let Kelley go after the season ended, a prediction that greatly upset Dovey. For along with his forecast that they would fire Kelley, the Giants skipper had also spread word that Dahlen and McGann, two of the men he had traded to Boston a year ago, were going to be released. McGraw was right about McGann. Boston did release him after the season, and two years later, at the age of 39, McGann committed suicide in a Louisville hotel.

However, while Boston claimed that it did not plan to release Dahlen, it may have been considering it. The Doves had used an untried youngster named Walt Thomas at short for five late season games. When Thomas proved unready for the major leagues, they quickly reinstated Dahlen, and the five

Manager Joe Kelley of the Boston Doves had Dahlen substitute for him when he was unavailable.

games Thomas played would be his only big league appearances. In all, Dahlen played in 144 games in 1908, a goodly amount for someone who was now 38 years old. And he was doing more than just showing up. His offensive numbers were up in every significant category, and J. C. Morse credited him with playing "great ball for the locals this season."

Although Boston's sixth-place finish was a disappointing one, it still finished a comfortable 10 games ahead of the seventh-place Superbas. The Brooklyn club had gone steadily downhill since the Ned Hanlon-led championship teams that Dahlen shortstopped in 1899–1900, finally hitting bottom in 1905. Following his last-place finish that year, Hanlon, unhappy that control of the club was now in Charlie Ebbets's hands, left for Cincinnati. Ebbets named onetime National League outfielder Patsy Donovan to succeed Hanlon. Donovan was the younger brother of Bill Donovan, the former Brooklyn pitcher and future manager of the Yankees.

Donovan came to the Superbas with managerial experience, having previously led the Pirates, Cardinals, and Washington Senators, all of whom were largely unsuccessful under his command. The Superbas moved up from last place to fifth in 1906, but after another fifth-place finish in 1907, came the drop to seventh in '08. Sensing that Donovan was not tough enough for the job, Ebbets was ready to make a change, and Dahlen was his choice. However, his attempts to secure him from Boston were made "on the cheap" and doomed to fail. He first offered Boston Phil Lewis, his own weak-hitting shortstop, in exchange for Dahlen. Dovey not only refused, he scolded Ebbets for the Brooklyn president's assumption that Dahlen could be had so easily. "I see by the New York and Brooklyn newspapers that Charlie Ebbets has had several conferences with Dahlen in regard to the management of the Brooklyn club next season. I have figured that Dahlen will be back at his old place at the South End Grounds next year, as I can't see anyone in sight that would fill the bill for my club."[6]

Dovey went on to give his thoughts on Ebbets's proposed Lewis-for-Dahlen deal. "I wouldn't have Lewis on my team. I think the Boston public is entitled to the best that I can give it, and I would consider the trade of Dahlen for Lewis a big joke. Perhaps Dahlen would like to return to the Great White Way, and Mr. Ebbets would like to give the player the opportunity, but I presume that I shall have to be consulted before the change is brought about."[7] In return for Dahlen, Dovey wanted cash or a player of comparable value. He did not want to stand in the way of his player's advance, he said, but "I am not going to let Dahlen go for a bat bag, and I will not consider Lewis."[8]

Meanwhile Ebbets claimed that he and Dovey had reached an agreement shortly after the season ended that would allow Dahlen go to Brooklyn. However, it had been strictly a verbal agreement and he had no written proof that the conversation had ever taken place. Suggesting that Dovey now wanted the exorbitant price of $7,000 for Dahlen's release, Ebbets expressed his dissatisfaction with the tactics of the Boston owner.

"It looks as if I have to go elsewhere for a manager," he said. "When I talked with Mr. Dovey, first, regarding Dahlen, he assured me that the only thing involved was a money consideration, the usual amount of $1,500 fixed in ordinary transfer of players. Now, I take it, he wants one of the Brooklyn stars and a bunch of money, besides, for a man whose usefulness as a player is about ended. Dahlen's coming to Brooklyn as a manager is entirely in the nature of an experiment, and I'm willing to try the experiment but not at an impossible equivalent. I'm willing to pay a reasonable sum for Dahlen and will leave it to a disinterested party to name the amount, but I don't intend to be held up."[9]

Undismayed, Ebbets continued his pursuit of Dahlen, approaching new manager Bowerman with a three-way deal that would bring Bill to Brooklyn. The first step in Ebbets's plan would have Boston trade Dahlen to Cincinnati for the Reds shortstop, Rudy Hulswitt. Cincinnati would then send Dahlen and third baseman Mike Mowrey to the Superbas for outfielder John Hummel. The deal needed approval from Clark Griffith, who had recently replaced John Ganzel as the Reds manager, but it never came. Nor did another rumored three-way trade involving Brooklyn,

Boston, and New York ever reach fruition. That one would have had Dahlen going from Boston to Brooklyn, third baseman Buck Herzog from New York to Boston, outfielder Cy Seymour and veteran pitcher Joe McGinnity from the Giants to the Superbas, and Hummel and pitcher Harry McIntire from the Superbas to the Giants.

Unable to get Dahlen, a frustrated Ebbets named one of his own players, Harry Lumley, to replace Donovan. Lumley, a 28-year-old outfielder, had enjoyed three fine seasons with the Superbas (1904–06), but had slipped badly the last two. The Brooklyn fans, who liked Donovan and were sorry to see him leave, were not pleased with the decision. Yet while they were unhappy with the choice of Lumley, they were nevertheless relieved

Brooklyn's visionary president, Charles Ebbets, was stymied in his attempts to have Dahlen manage the Dodgers in 1909.

that it was he and not Roger Bresnahan who would be managing the Dodgers in 1909. Not that they had anything in particular against Bresnahan, but when Ebbets expressed interest in the Giants catcher, McGraw had asked for left-hander Nap Rucker in return. Ebbets wisely refused to give up his best pitcher, and McGraw traded Bresnahan to St. Louis where he became manager of the Cardinals.

During all the negotiations involving him, Dahlen mostly kept quiet. He did say he preferred to start his managerial career in the minors, but would gladly take the Brooklyn job if Ebbets offered it to him. In reality, Dahlen had set his heart on getting the job at Brooklyn, and he was bitterly disappointed when the negotiations to bring him there fell through. Although Ebbets had made what appeared to be every reasonable effort to bring him to Brooklyn, Dahlen still wondered aloud if the Dodgers had really wanted him. Yet, Dahlen's doubts aside, it was clear that they did. After the Dodgers hired Lumley, Ebbets revealed that beyond the trade proposals he had made, he had informed Dovey that he was willing to pay as much as $5,000 for Bill's release. When Dovey refused, Ebbets said he finally realized that because Dahlen had played so well in 1908, Boston just did not want to let him go.

Dovey may have been acting in what he saw as his team's best interests; nevertheless, his stance did engender some criticism. John Foster, writing in *Sporting Life*, faulted him for not allowing Dahlen to do what he so wanted, the chance to manage a major league team. The National League owed Dahlen a debt of gratitude, Foster argued. He recalled that when the league was trying to recover from its battle with the Players League, it was Dahlen who had done so much to bring the fans in Chicago back to the ballpark. Foster reminded his readers that back then Bill was the best young player in the league, and Chicagoans made their way to West Side Park to see the new star.

His managerial career temporarily on hold, Dahlen was back in Boston for the 1909 season, where both he and the Doves suffered through a bleak and mostly joyless year. For the Doves, the season was an artistic debacle, compounded by personal tragedy. On June 19, owner George Dovey died suddenly while riding a train in Ohio en route to Cincinnati. He succumbed after being stricken with what the *New York Times* called a "hemorrhage of the lungs." Ownership of the Boston franchise passed to his brother, John. Less than six weeks after Dovey's death, all of baseball suffered a calamity when a depressed Harry Pulliam, the president of the National League, committed suicide in his room at the New York Athletic Club.

On the field, the last-place Doves lost 108 games and finished a laughable 65½ games behind the champion Pirates. Their combined record against Pittsburgh and second-place Chicago was a jaw-dropping two wins and 41 losses. A fed-up Bowerman left in mid-July, with the cellar-dwelling Doves already 33 games behind. He resigned his managerial post in protest when the new owner traded away outfielder Johnny Bates, his best player. Bates and infielder Charlie Starr were sent to Philadelphia for pitchers Lew Ritchie and Buster Brown and infielder Dave Shean.

Other than his home run and three hits on opening day, and an overall solid April, Dahlen's final season as an active player was a dismal one. Clearly unhappy at Boston's blocking his managerial path, he played in only 69 games (just 49 at shortstop), batting .234 in 197 at-bats. Harry Smith, who replaced Bowerman as manager, used rookie Jack Coffey at shortstop, while Dahlen spent the second half of July and the month of August as a pinch batter and (even at age 39) a pinch runner. His playing days ended when Smith released him with a month still left in the season.

However, there was some good news for Bill in this generally dispiriting season. Under the leadership of manager Lumley, Brooklyn had not done much better than Boston. After he brought the Dodgers home sixth, 55½ games behind Pittsburgh, Ebbets wasted no time in firing him. Among those who were supposedly considered as Lumley's successor were Willie Keeler, released by the Yankees; John Ganzel, who had managed the Reds in 1908; Billy Murray, let go as manager by the Phillies; and catcher Johnny Kling, of the Cubs. However, Dahlen remained Ebbets's first choice, and in November he got his man, naming Bill to manage the Dodgers in 1910.

Between time spent searching for a house in Brooklyn, a jubilant Bill and Jeannette made their usual post-season jaunt to Nelliston. As he always did on these trips, he spent time visiting with his mother and boyhood chums, but mostly hunting and fishing. And as he also always did at this time of year, Bill generously arranged for some poorer people in the area to have turkeys for their Thanksgiving dinner.[10] He almost made another contribution on his visit upstate, although this one would have been most unwilling. While dressing to go out to dinner with friends one evening, Jeannette noticed that she had lost a two-caret diamond ring that Bill had given her. Both she and Bill thought it was lost forever, and went ahead with their plans to meet their friends at Nelliston's Elms Hotel. Later that night, to their surprise and relief, they found the ring in the crop of a guinea hen.[11]

FOURTEEN

Managing the Dodgers

The press had greeted Dahlen's managerial appointment as a positive step for Brooklyn baseball. They cited his experience, pugnacity, and tactical knowledge of the game in predicting a long and successful managerial career for him. Noting that he had played under Cap Anson, Ned Hanlon, and John McGraw, the *Brooklyn Daily Eagle* credited him with "the plugging propensities of the first, the craftiness of the second, and the aggressiveness of the third." People in Brooklyn also reacted positively to the appointment. Most had fond memories of Dahlen from his years with the club when it was known as the Superbas, and they were solidly behind him. The local fans believed he had more baseball knowledge than Patsy Donovan and Harry Lumley, his two recent predecessors, yet they were realistic enough not to expect too much too soon. No one expected Dahlen to produce a pennant-winner in 1910; they did, however, expect him to make the Brooklyn team respectable.

Upon getting the job, Bill had tried to convince Willie Keeler to sign on with the Dodgers, following his best pal's recent release by the Yankees. The two were friends again after a brief falling out following Ebbets's selection of Dahlen as his manager. Bill had taken offense at Keeler's suggestion that while Dahlen was officially the manager, Ebbets would be the one running the team. Despite Bill's resentment, it was not an unfair suggestion. Ebbets had a well-deserved reputation for meddling and wanting to run the whole show. Aware that the Giants were also interested in signing Keeler, Dahlen offered him several thousand dollars more than McGraw did, but despite the higher offer, Keeler eventually chose to sign with New York.

The Dodgers had been using Jacksonville, Florida, as their spring training headquarters the past three years, but Dahlen moved them to his favorite preseason location, Hot Springs. Exuding enthusiasm, he got to work right away. On the day the players were to report, the new manager greeted them at the train station at 10:00 a.m. After making sure they had a good lunch, he got them into uniform and by 2:00 p.m. had them working out at their Whittington Park facility. Manager Dahlen conducted an intensely run training camp, spending long hours attempting to impart to his players all he had learned in his long career. One change was obvious immediately. His men were running the bases in a daredevil style that had long been absent from Brooklyn baseball.

While not given to making long speeches, Dahlen had a keen eye for everything that was going

Dodger left fielder Zack Wheat immediately impressed all who saw him.

on, and he was also an excellent teacher. The highlight of the trip north came just before its end, in Washington. Rained out of their game with the Senators, Dahlen and his players visited the White House and got to meet President William Howard Taft, a devoted baseball fan. A few days later, Taft would throw out the first ball at the Senators' opener, setting a precedent that every future president was expected to follow.

One of Dahlen's spring projects was to convert George Hunter, a 23-year-old left-handed pitcher, into an outfielder. It would have been a perfect role for Keeler, but having been unable to sign him, Dahlen, a career infielder, worked on the conversion himself. The experiment proved unsuccessful, and he released Hunter in May. Knowing he needed another outfielder, Dahlen had traded pitcher Harry McIntire to the Cubs for rookie Bill Davidson shortly before opening day. Also coming to Brooklyn in the McIntire deal were a pair of Smiths: Tony, who would be the team's shortstop, and Happy, a throw-in outfielder. Around the same time he released Hunter, Dahlen made other moves, all directed at making his club younger. He sold his opening-day shortstop, Tommy McMillan, to Cincinnati, and released Harry Lumley, his predecessor, and first baseman Tim Jordan, a two-time National League home-run champion. Dahlen replaced Jordan with Jake Daubert, a rookie who had won the job in spring training. Daubert not only outhit Jordan, his skills at the position had players and press comparing him to the Yankees peerless first baseman, Hal Chase.

Daubert was just one of many rookies and young players Dahlen would use during the 1910 season. Rounding out the infield were veteran John Hummel at second base, Smith, the newcomer at shortstop, and second-year man Ed Lennox at third. The outfield was incredibly raw, having entered the 1910 season with a combined total major league experience of 28 games. Right fielder Jack Dalton, purchased from Des Moines of the Western League in June, was completely new to the big leagues. Center fielder Davidson had played two games for the Cubs in 1909, and left fielder Zack Wheat left had played in 26 for Brooklyn. The 21-year-old Wheat had come up the previous September and immediately impressed all who saw him. He batted .304, and though he had just 102 big-league at-bats, experts around the league were already calling him the Dodgers' best player.

Dahlen used veteran Al Burch as a fill-in at both the right and center field positions, often platooning him with Dalton. He would play the left-handed hitting Burch against righthanders, and the right-handed hitting Dalton against lefthanders. Behind the plate was yet another rookie, Tex Erwin, who shared the catching duties with the notoriously weak-hitting Bill Bergen. Dahlen's top pitchers were veterans Doc Scanlan and George Bell and rookie Cy Barger, all righthanders, and Nap Rucker, the only lefthander and the best of the lot. Veteran Kaiser Wilhelm, and rookies Elmer Knetzer and Rube Desseau spot-started and did most of the relief work.

The man directing it all was, of course, a rookie himself, at least as a manager. A rookie manager was also in the opposing dugout on opening day in Philadelphia. Red Dooin, the Phillies veteran catcher, had taken over for Billy Murray, and like Dahlen was making his managerial debut. Only one of those debuts could be successful, and it was Bill's. Brooklyn won 2–0 behind Rucker, who allowed only two hits and struck out seven. The Dodgers scored in the third against Phillies pitcher George McQuillan on Bergen's triple and Burch's single, and in the ninth on doubles by Wheat and Lennox.

Characteristically, Dahlen had little to say to the press after the game. He admitted that he was thrilled at the victory, but gave all the credit for it to the players. Sadly, for all concerned with Brooklyn baseball, this would be the only time all season that the Dodgers had a winning record. They dropped the next four, eight of the next nine, and quickly sank to the bottom of the league standings. Among the losses was the twice-postponed (by rain) home-opener, also with the Phillies. Following the usual festivities, which included fan and civic groups presenting the new manager with gifts and bouquets of flowers, McQuillan avenged his earlier defeat by besting Rucker, 6–2.

Brooklyn was still last a week later when they headed to Pittsburgh to begin their first swing through the West. "I'd like to win about half of the games on the first Western trip," Dahlen said upon departing. And despite enduring a six-game losing streak in the middle of the trip, they almost did. Brooklyn's 6–8 record was far from spectacular. Still, it was the best that any Eastern team had done on this first Western trip. On returning home, the team ran off a seven-game winning streak, thanks to some great pitching. The streak ended when Bell pitched a six-hitter, but lost a 1–0 heartbreaker to Cincinnati's Jack Rowan, who allowed only two hits.

In all, they won 11 of 20 on the homestand, including a memorable performance by Barger in a June 15 win against the first-place Cubs. The rookie not only pitched all 14 innings in outlasting Chicago's Lewis "King" Cole 3–2, he was also the hitting star of the game. Barger had four hits, including two doubles, the second of which drove Erwin home with the winning run. He had barely reached second base on his hit when a group of happy fans hoisted him on their shoulders and carried him off the field. Beating "King" Cole was no easy task in 1910. Cole, also a rookie, had come into this game having won his last eight decisions. For the season, he won 20, lost only four, and led the league with a 1.80 earned run average. Ebbets showed his appreciation for Barger's efforts by rewarding him with a credit slip for a new suit of clothes.

Brooklynites, who had not seen winning baseball for several years, responded to the Dodgers' winning streak by coming out to Washington Park in large numbers. But it was not only the winning that drew them to the games. The laxity and indecision the players had shown under Lumley had driven them away; the energy and intelligence they were showing under Dahlen had drawn them back. Credit for the turnaround belonged to the new manager, said *Sporting Life's* John Foster.

"Dahlen has impressed them with the fact that they must play ball, and play up to date baseball if they want to stay with him, and he is out with them every day instructing them in the many little things that go to make a good baseball team."[1] Back in spring training, Dahlen confessed that he did not know how good a club he had, but promised that "they would keep playing ball until the ninth inning is over or they will go somewhere else to play."[2]

With money flowing into his till, the sartorial-minded Ebbets was so pleased he presented Dahlen and all his players with new Panama hats. He even tried to silence the grumbling about what they perceived as inadequate salaries, by promising bonuses to all his players if they finished in the first division.

The winning streak brought the Dodgers up to sixth place, but if Ebbets or the fans had any illusions of them being a winning team, they were only temporary. Brooklyn would remain sixth for a good part of the rest of the season, ultimately ending in that position. With a final record of 64–90, they finished a half game ahead of seventh-place St. Louis, but 40 games behind the champion Cubs.

Although they were mired in the second division, Dahlen's young club won over both the fans and the press. In July, with the Dodgers struggling along at 33–38, the *Eagle* reprinted this item that had appeared earlier in the *Pittsburgh Press*. "Hand it to William Dahlen and Larry Sutton, manager and scout for the Dodgers. All the teams yelping for young blood should read this list: Daubert, Erwin, Wheat, Davidson, Dalton, Tony Smith. That's class from first to last."[3]

Brooklyn did have the best fielding team in the league, and the pitching, led by Rucker, was adequate. Bell had a fine 2.68 earned run average, but lack of run support doomed him to an atrocious 10–27 won-lost record.

Barger was 15–15 in his rookie season, while Rucker won 17 and lost 18. Rucker, Brooklyn's most valuable commodity, was among the league's best pitchers and Dahlen used him to the utmost. The 25-year-old Georgian led or tied for the league lead in games started (39), complete games (27), innings pitched (320.1), and shutouts (six). Dahlen, of course, was well aware of Rucker's ability from having faced him the last three years. Bill had also been in the Boston lineup the day in 1908 that Rucker no-hit the Doves.

Left-hander Nap Rucker was among the best pitchers in the National League, but he was the only reliable one Dahlen had.

Offensively, the Dodgers had been woefully weak. Twenty-seven of their losses were by one run, and in spite of respectable first full seasons by Wheat and Daubert, their hitting was by far the worst in the National League. Brooklyn finished at the bottom in batting average (.229), on base percentage (.294), and slugging average (.305). The Dodgers' hitting early in the season was so poor it even had their manager contemplating a return to active duty. At age 40, Bill had been on the major league scene for a long, long time. The only man still playing big league baseball from his rookie year in 1891 was Cy Young, who debuted a year earlier. Young, who was pitching for Cleveland in the 12-team National League then, was currently pitching for Cleveland in the then undreamed-of American League.

Nevertheless, Dahlen felt he was in good enough shape to take up his position at shortstop at any time. He never did, though. Apart from a pinch-hitting appearance in April and two more in June, he confined his time on the field to his third

Legendary umpire Bill Klem, who ejected Dahlen from many games when Dahlen was a player and also after he became a manager.

base coaching duties. He did, however, try to aid the offense in other ways. When his players complained about the poor hitting background at Washington Park, he asked concessionaire Harry Stevens to change the background on his outfield wall sign from white to a darker color.

Dahlen got through the first month of his managerial tenure without being ejected. The first one came on May 15, in the third inning of his 25th game at the helm. Cy Rigler asked him to depart after he left the bench to claim that a double hit by Cincinnati's Dick Egan had gone foul. Nine more invitations to exit early would follow, including one that was not so early. On September 18, Bill Klem tossed him in the 10th inning of the second game of a double-header against Chicago. Klem had called Wheat, who was carrying the potential winning run, out on a play at the plate. Wheat thought that Cubs catcher Johnny Kling had missed the tag, as did many Brooklyn players and fans. Dahlen and Burch left the bench to protest the decision as pop bottles rained down on Klem from the Wash-

ington Park stands. Klem ejected both of them. Each then took the allotted 60 seconds to leave following the umpire's pulling his watch on them.
After they restored order and cleared the pop bottles, third baseman Pryor
McElveen singled Hummel home with the winning run. Even that 10th-
inning ejection was not the latest of the season for Dahlen. In July, Klem
tossed him in the 13th inning of a 14-inning loss at Cincinnati.

With more than six weeks left in the season, Brooklyn re-signed
Dahlen to manage the club in 1911. "Dahlen has more than made good this
season and will lead the Dodgers next year," said President Ebbets.[4] Foster applauded the move, praising the manager for molding a group of
young players and demoralized veterans into a creditable and entertain-
ing team. He had accomplished this, said Foster, by making trades, getting rid of "deadwood," and moving players in and out until he found
those that suited his style of play. Foster noted that many of those who
began the 1910 season with the Dodgers were long gone when it ended. "A
manager who can make something of a record out of a state of affairs like
that shows that he has ability to do something more than the ordinary,"
he said.[5]

Hopes in Brooklyn were high for 1911, yet Dahlen immediately began
cautioning against too much optimism about his second season. He began
doing this shortly after the end of his first. Using the language of the racetrack, he intimated that his club was similar to a two-year-old racehorse.
"We may have a pretty fair team, and I hope that we've got one that will be
making a fight in the first
division, but when some
of these well-meaning
chaps begin to talk about
Brooklyn winning the
championship, I wish they
would back up a little, for
there are plenty of young
players on the team, and
you never can tell whether
those young players are
going to take the bit well
and get away to a flying
start, or whether they will
fret at the post and lose so
much that they can't overcome the handicap before
the end of the race."[6]

"He will be better than Hal Chase next season," said
Dahlen about Brooklyn's sophomore first baseman
Jake Daubert.

Nevertheless, the significant improvement shown by the 1910 team, with most of the credit for that improvement being attributed to his leadership, made for a pleasant offseason for Dahlen. Living quietly in Brooklyn, he attended the winter meetings with an eye on improving his club, but was unable to make any deals. Pittsburgh's Fred Clarke offered him pitcher Howie Camnitz, but asked for Nap Rucker or Cy Barger in return. Dahlen said no, as he would when faced with comparable requests all season.

Whenever discussing trades, the other teams invariably would ask Brooklyn to include one of its three best players in the deal: Rucker, arguably the best lefthander in the league, or either Zack Wheat or Jake Daubert, both clearly on their way to stardom. Dahlen was particularly high on Daubert. As a rookie, his young first baseman had been compared defensively to the great Hal Chase. Now Dahlen was taking that comparison a step further. "Keep your eye on Jake Daubert," he said in January. "He will be better than Hal Chase next season."[7]

Alert to any way of improving his young team, Dahlen wrote letters to several of his veterans, including pitchers Rucker and George Bell, asking them to report to Hot Springs early. His plan was to have these veterans work themselves into shape before the youngsters reported, and then to serve as mentors to them. Despite the turnaround in attitude he had instilled a year ago, Dahlen still believed there was a bit too much selfishness on the 1910 club. His intention was to root out that selfishness using whatever means necessary. He saw the mentoring of the young by the veterans as a step in that direction.

Another was to crack down on and eventually get rid of the "high livers" on the club. Some Brooklyn players, it appeared, were not always as circumspect in their demeanor on road trips as they should have been. "One or two of our home-grown young men were in the habit of celebrating one good afternoon in the field with two or three good evenings in the neighborhood of a rathskeller," said Brooklyn's *Sporting Life* correspondent.[8]

"They don't do that on me this year," vowed Dahlen. "It's not a season of festivity. We are going in for the real thing in baseball. I think that I have a start, and these estimable young men who are associated with me must come to the front and help me out. We want Brooklyn lingering around the first division," he continued, "and not bothered with trying to keep out of the way of Boston and St. Louis."[9]

As usual, Bill was among the first to report to camp, taking a steamer to New Orleans and then traveling by rail to Hot Springs. Wife Jeannette, catcher Tex Erwin, and trainer Dan Comerford accompanied him on his journey. Others, including Rucker, Bell, and Daubert, arrived via the same route. For Daubert, a Pennsylvanian, this was his first look at the Atlantic Ocean.

In reviewing his 1911 roster, Dahlen could not help pointing out the club's progress. "Three years ago they were saying that there was only one player on the Brooklyn club worth having, and that was Rucker. Don't hear that now, do you? The other day one of the baseball men called attention to the fact that we had one of the best first basemen in the league (Daubert), one of the best outfielders (Wheat), and a second baseman (Hummel) who would fit in pretty well with any one of four or five teams because of his hitting and his ability to act as an all-around player. Shows that we have made a little impression in the baseball world, even if we have been unable to win any pennant or annex a position in that much desired first division."[10]

A position in "that much desired first division" was Dahlen's goal, and one he thought the Dodgers had an excellent chance of reaching this season. "I think we can carry the fight to some of these first division chaps this year," he said before departing for the South, "and if we do there will be a lot of groaning in two cities I can name. The first name of one of them is Cincinnati and the other would run like a hungry calf for milk if you happened to call Philadelphia. I'll stack my youngsters against the youngsters in both those clubs and make a little wager on the side."[11]

As he had done the year before, Bill worked his young club very hard in spring training. He had always begun a new season in the best of shape as a player. Now that he was a manager, he was determined that those in his charge would do the same. Two-a-day workouts were a standard part of the regimen, as was mountain climbing. Dahlen, who stayed in shape during the winter by strolling around his Bay Ridge Neighborhood, believed that climbing mountains was the best thing a player could do to improve his wind.

His denials and protestations aside, Ebbets had meddled in the running of the club in 1910. This year would be different, he said, promising to let Dahlen run it as he saw fit. Knowing he had Ebbets's approval, Dahlen continued the make-over of the Dodgers he had begun in 1910. Based on their impressive play during training camp, two rookies took over the left side of the Brooklyn infield. Bert Tooley replaced Tony Smith at short-stop, and the highly touted Eddie Zimmerman, who had starred at Newark in 1910, won the third base job from Ed Lennox. Another youngster, Bob Coulson, won the right field position, with Jack Dalton returning to the minor leagues. Bill Schardt, a rookie righthander up from the Milwaukee Brewers of the American Association, was added to the starting rotation.

Brooklyn had another promising rookie in camp: outfielder Larry LeJeune, winner of the Central League's 1910 batting and home run titles. The Dodgers expected that LeJeune would be their center fielder this year and on into the future. Unfortunately, he was injured in a car accident during training camp, and his career would consist of six games with Brooklyn in 1911 and 18 with Pittsburgh in 1915. Never able to make it as a big leaguer, LeJeune did however, win five minor league batting titles. With LeJeune out of the picture, Dahlen platooned Al Burch and Bill Davidson in center until early August, when he released Burch.

After breaking camp and heading north, bad weather plagued the club all the way. A fed-up Dahlen suggested that for the 1912 season, the club stay in Hot Springs until just before the season starts. It was an interesting suggestion, but one that had no chance of being implemented. Ebbets may have given his manager the go-ahead to run the club on the field, but as president, he would remain in charge of the business end. The exhibition games played by the Dodgers and other big league clubs on their way back to their home cities brought money into the team's treasuries. Neither Ebbets nor any of the other owners were going to give them up.

Barger opened Brooklyn's 1911 season by losing 2–1 to the Rustlers at Boston. Newspapers were now calling the Boston club the "Rustlers" in honor of their new owner, W. Hepburn Russell. Barger got the opening-day start, only because Rucker had injured an ankle in his final preseason tune-up and was unavailable. Rucker would not make his first appearance until April 27, Brooklyn's 12th game. By then, the club was already 3–8 and in last place, thanks primarily to losing four straight to the Giants at Hilltop Park, the home park of the New York Yankees.

McGraw's club had opened its season with two losses at home to the Phillies. A day later, on April 14, a fire destroyed the Polo Grounds' stands, making it impossible for them to continue playing there. Ebbets offered to share Washington Park with his bitter rivals, while co-owners Frank Farrell and Bill Devery of the Yankees invited them to play their home games at Hilltop Park. The many conflicting home dates for the Giants and Dodgers made the sharing of Washington Park impractical. Instead, owner John Brush and manager McGraw accepted the offer of Farrell and Devery. The Giants would eventually play their home games at Hilltop Park for 11 weeks while workmen rebuilt the Polo Grounds.

New York's four-game sweep of the Dodgers, which began the day after the fire, was extremely upsetting to the Brooklyn faithful. Even more so, in a way, was losing their home opener to the lowly Rustlers, and then being shut out by them a day later. Dahlen had warned the fans about getting too enthusiastic over his young team, but that did little to ease their disappointment. The Dodgers would struggle all season, and though they won the same number of games as the year before, and lost four fewer, they still slipped from sixth place to seventh. And, though they finished 33½ games behind the pennant-winning Giants, they were actually six and a half games closer than they had been to the pennant-winning Cubs of 1910. That New York had displaced Chicago at the top of the National League was due in no small part to the Brooklyn club. Dahlen's Dodgers finished 13–9 against Frank Chance's Cubs, and just 5–16–1 against McGraw's Giants. The seven and a half-game disparity was the exact amount by which New York finished ahead of Chicago.

His team's dreadful record against the Giants, the team Dodgers fans most wanted to beat, surely did not help Dahlen's popularity in Brooklyn. The Dodgers lost their first nine to McGraw's band before Rucker finally posted a win against the New Yorkers, edging Hooks Wiltse 1–0. Only by winning the final three games of the season did the Dodgers get their win total against New York up to five. While these games were mainly meaningless, they did prevent the Giants from gaining their highly sought-after 100th victory, something they had not achieved since 1905. McGraw and his men had to settle for 99 wins and a 99–54–1 record.

Among Dahlen's many frustrating experiences during Brooklyn's battles with the Giants were two that occurred at Hilltop Park during both games of the morning-afternoon Decoration Day double-header. His problem in both involved the pitching mound, and they began early. In the second inning of the morning game, after Giants pitcher Rube Marquard had fanned John Hummel, Dahlen started complaining about Marquard's feet in relation to the pitching rubber. Umpire Hank O'Day listened patiently for several minutes, but when Bill continued complaining, he ordered him to leave.

Marquard, meanwhile, continued pitching as before in defeating Brooklyn's Doc Scanlan, 4–1, and leaving Dahlen hoping for a split. With his ace, Rucker, ready to face fellow left-hander Bugs Raymond, it was surely a reasonable hope. But before the afternoon contest even began, Dahlen noticed something amiss. The Giants ground crew had obviously elevated the height of the mound. Now Raymond was a tragic alcoholic, but he was, when sober, a terrific pitcher. His best pitch was a screwball, a pitch made even more effective when its trajectory was coming down at a batter, as it would be from the illegally heightened mound.

Knowing that McGraw would try anything he thought he could get away with, Dahlen reported the chicanery to umpire Bill Brennan. He pointed out that since the end of the morning game a mini-mountain had grown in the center of the diamond. Brennan agreed, but said he was not a surveyor, and even if he were, he had no tools to measure the mound's height. (The *Eagle* agreed that Brennan was not a surveyor, adding that they did not think he was much of an umpire either.) Brennan allowed Dahlen to protest the Giants' 3–0 victory, but the league allowed the result to stand.

Getting shut out, as they did that afternoon by Raymond, was a regular occurrence for this Dodgers squad. Though Daubert and Wheat continued to fulfill their promise, the Dodgers were again the worst offensive team in the league. They finished a distant last in batting average (.237), on base percentage

Hank O'Day, another longtime National League umpire who tossed Dahlen out of games both when he was a player and a manager.

(.301), and slugging average (.311). The newcomers were of little help with the bat: Coulson batted .234, Tooley .206, and Zimmerman an atrocious .185.

Brooklyn's major bright spot was Rucker, who at 22–18 was sensational. He missed the first two weeks of the season, and then lost his first six decisions, but ended up winning more than a third of the team's 64 victories. He also finished third in the league in strikeouts and per game hits allowed.[12] However, Rucker was mostly a one-man show. The next two biggest winners behind him had only 11 each — Barger at 11–15, and Knetzer at 11–12. Schardt was 5–15, while Bell was 5–6 and Scanlan, 3–10. For both Bell, who was 36, and Scanlan, who would return to being a full-time medical doctor, 1911 was their final major league season.

Inevitably, most managers get criticized over the way they handle their pitchers, and Dahlen was no different. The "problem," said the critics, was that the feisty "Bad Bill" was just too softhearted with his starters, that he just did not have it in him to remove them soon enough. Of course, convincing any of President Thomas Lynch's National League umpires of the Brooklyn manager's "softheartedness" would have been extremely difficult. Blithely continuing his career-long battle with the men in blue, Dahlen this year exceeded his 10 early dismissals of 1910 by one. After Mal Eason tossed him at Pittsburgh on June 13, his fourth ejection in a week, the *Brooklyn Daily Eagle* gave him a gentle reminder that his job as manager of the Dodgers was to manage, not to argue.

"At the rate he is going," wrote the *Eagle*, "Manager Dahlen is managing about two and one-third innings per game. The rest of the game he is in the clubhouse, or under the stand, or somewhere else, far from active participation in the strife, where his giant intellect might be supposed to guide his henchmen to victory. A scrappy manager is a great comfort, but that it is necessary for a manager to scrap himself into obscurity every day is not a part of the generally accepted philosophy of the sport. It is therefore gently hinted to Br'er Dahlen that he let the umpirical aeroplanes sail for a few days without trying to sharpshoot them."[13]

Naturally, Dahlen completely ignored the warning. Several weeks later, Lynch suspended him for three days following umpire Bill Finneran's ejection of him and pitcher Scanlan for arguing balls and strikes. He had barely returned when on July 8 he was involved in Washington Park's ugliest incident of the season. Brooklyn's Schardt and Pittsburgh's Lefty Leifield were tied 1–1 with the Pirates batting in the ninth inning when the trouble erupted. With the count 2–2 on Honus Wagner, Schardt threw a pitch that looked to everyone on the Dodgers side to be a strike. Catcher Bill Bergen fired the ball to third baseman Zimmerman in the traditional post-strikeout gesture, when rookie umpire Ralph Frary called, "Ball Three." Frary, it should be mentioned, had already made several questionable calls during the game, most of which had gone against the Dodgers.

Given another chance, Wagner then singled, stole second, and scored the lead run on Newt Hunter's single. Seeing Wagner, whom they thought should have been called out, scoring the potential winning run set off both the Brooklyn bench and the Brooklyn crowd. Fans started tossing bottles on the field, many of them dangerously close to Frary, which motivated Washington Park's small private police contingent to rush

Dahlen chose the final game of the 1911 season to make his final appearance as an active player.

onto the field. (A law still forbade any city police personnel from patrolling at any of the New York baseball parks.) Simultaneously, those on the Dodgers bench began screaming denunciations at Frary, who reacted by dismissing them all. Tossed out were Dahlen, just returned from a three-day suspension, pitchers Pat Ragan and Sandy Burk, catcher Tex Erwin, and outfielder Al Burch. Frankie Deery, the team's young mascot, had also been seated on the bench, and Frary ordered him to leave as well. The police finally quieted the crowd, and Pittsburgh added another run to win 3–1.

Dahlen used the final game of the season, the second game of the October 12 double-header at the Polo Grounds, to make his last active appearance as a player. Bert Tooley, the regular shortstop, wanted to get a head start on traveling home to Michigan, and Bill granted his request. He played errorlessly in the field, with four assists and two putouts, but showed his rustiness at the plate. In his three at-bats, Giant starter Louis Drucke struck him out twice and reliever Bert Maxwell fanned him once. When it was Dahlen's turn to bat in the eighth inning, he sent Bob Higgins, a rookie catcher, in to pinch-hit.[14]

FIFTEEN

Building a Contender
— for Someone Else

With Ebbets's blessing, Dahlen was back to lead the 1912 Dodgers in what would be their final season at Washington Park. Charlie Ebbets had long nurtured a dream to build a new baseball park in Brooklyn, and now that dream was nearing reality. By 1913, the Dodgers would be playing in a magnificent new structure, one that would bear Ebbets's name. After choosing a site in Brooklyn's "Pigtown" area, between the Bedford and Flatbush sections of the borough, Ebbets secretly began buying up the necessary parcels of land. He picked a spot at the southeast corner of Prospect Park for his new baseball palace, and to make it as accessible as possible, located it adjacent to the tracks of nine separate trolley car lines.

Construction of Ebbets Field, an edifice that was to become one of Brooklyn's most recognizable landmarks, began in March 1912. Ebbets had hoped to have it ready by August 27, the anniversary of the 1776 battle of Long Island, fought not far from where the park would stand. To complete it by then called for a very tight schedule, one that needed everything to go exactly as planned. But because large building projects almost never go "exactly as planned," the August 27 date was never a realistic one. The inevitable weather and construction problems delayed the opening until the start of the 1913 season.

Along the way, Ebbets added two major stockholders to the Brooklyn organization. With construction costs approaching $750,000, he made brothers Ed and Steve McKeever, who owned the construction company that was building Ebbets Field, half partners in the club. Dahlen did not realize it at the time, but the addition of the McKeevers would eventually lead to his dismissal.

The Dodgers reported for spring training to Hot Springs in late February. The early arrival would allow them to get two and a half weeks of work in before they had to turn Whittington Park over to Fred Clarke's Pirates. Spring 1912 was a particularly rainy season, and the club's trip back north was again beset with cancellations. Upset at his team's haphazard training schedule, Dahlen vowed to find a new site to conduct his preseason preparations in 1913. Hot Springs was a wonderful place to shake any added winter weight, but he and his team needed a full-time facility to prepare adequately for the regular season.

As the Dodgers made ready for the new campaign, manager Dahlen seemed especially pleased with his rebuilt pitching staff. His new lineup of pitchers included three rookies: righthander Maury Kent, a baseball and football star from the University of Iowa; and lefthanders Earl Yingling and Frank Allen. Dahlen was particularly high on Allen, a 22-year-old Alabamian whom he envisioned as another Nap Rucker. "Allen made the Washingtons look like Indian cigar signs the other day," he said after Allen's final exhibition appearance against the Senators. A fourth addition was Eddie Stack, obtained in a trade with the Phillies for Doc Scanlan.[1]

Dahlen felt certain that with young Otto Miller taking over as his number one catcher he had upgraded that position as well. Miller, who had been a substitute the past two seasons, would be an important part of Brooklyn teams for the next 10 years. Veterans Tex Erwin and newly acquired Eddie Phelps would serve as Miller's backups. The departure of Bill Bergen, the club's longtime backstop, to Newark of the International League, left John Hummel as the only remaining regular from the 1909 team Dahlen had inherited.[2]

James "Red" Smith, called up the previous September, replaced Zimmerman at third base. Elsewhere, the infield remained the same. Hummel, who could play almost anywhere, was back at second. Also back was Bert Tooley, to play shortstop, although rookie Bob Fisher would soon win that job. At first base was Jake Daubert, the team's captain and, based on a vote by the fans, its most popular player. Daubert and the Yankees' Hal Chase continued to inspire arguments among New York baseball fans about which was the better first baseman. When someone asked Giants manager John McGraw his opinion, the always loyal McGraw responded that he would not trade his first baseman, Fred Merkle, for either one of them.

Zack Wheat was a permanent fixture in left field, with a pair of 28-year-olds, Hub Northen and Herbie Moran, rotating between center and right. Both Northen and Moran were left-handed batters, like Wheat, giving Brooklyn an all left-handed-hitting outfield.

The potential of this team to challenge for the first division had so galvanized the borough of Brooklyn that a record number of fans showed up for the opener against the hated Giants. In fact, so many came out that they turned Washington Park's final opening day into a mockery of the game of baseball. The park's capacity was listed at 18,000. Occasionally 20,000 or more had squeezed their way in. However, the estimated attendance for this game ranged as high as 30,000. Those fans that could not find seats began to find standing room in the outfield. They continued lining up on the freshly planted grass until they had occupied an area that stretched almost all the way to the skin of the infield.

Ebbets, watching all this, and frantic to prevent the umpires from calling a forfeit against his team, appealed for help to New York City's mayor, William Gaynor. The mayor, there to throw out the first ball, could see that the park's security contingent was completely overwhelmed. Overriding the law about city police not being used at a private facility, Gaynor made a special request to have a contingent of them enter the park to restore order. When the police arrived, they managed to clear enough of the crowd to allow the game to be played. Nevertheless, it was a farce, from its beginning until the umpires called it in the sixth inning because of darkness.

Fly balls that outfielders would have easily caught under normal circumstances, landed in among the standees and became ground-rule doubles. New York took better advantage of these circumstances than did

Brooklyn. The Giants had 10 "doubles" in piling up 18 runs against Rucker, Cy Barger, and Eddie Dent. Meanwhile, Rube Marquard limited the Dodgers to seven hits and just three runs.

A day later, about 25,000 fewer fans watched Brooklyn even its record, and Bill Klem give Dahlen his first early ouster of the new season. Dahlen had argued that Klem's awarding first base to Fred Merkle, after Bill Schardt hit him with a pitch, was a mistake. According to Dahlen,

Manager Dahlen leading his Dodgers through a pregame practice.

who was familiar with the maneuver, Merkle had moved his body in the way of the ball. Klem listened patiently, but his patience soon ran out, and he asked Dahlen to leave.

Four days later, Bill was kicked out again, after a nasty encounter with Cy Rigler over an interference call. This latest dismissal earned Dahlen a three-day suspension, which kept him out until an April 20 game at the Polo Grounds. When he returned, he became involved in the worst umpire confrontation of his career.

Now Dahlen's reputation for battling umpires was well deserved; the men in blue ejected him close to 70 times in his career. But most of his invitations to leave early had come after word-of-mouth battles. Some had been venomously vitriolic, and some merely full of pungent sarcasm, but for the most part, they had not progressed beyond words.

Of course, there had been a few exceptions, cases where the partici- pants had seen fit to employ more than ver- bal expressions of disagreement. Most notable among these exceptions was the fracas with Ed Swartwood in July of 1900, which, coincidentally, had also occurred at the Polo Grounds. Yet even there, the punch that Swartwood aimed at Dahlen had missed its target. However there were no misses in this incident, which saw man- ager Dahlen and umpire Rigler slugging it out toe-to-toe at home plate.

The brawl began after the Dodgers had scored three runs in the top of the ninth to take a 3–2 lead. Having pinch-hit for starting pitcher Eddie Stack, Dahlen brought in his ace, Rucker, to face the Giants in the home ninth. Rucker retired leadoff batter Buck Herzog, but Heinie Groh followed with a single to left. That brought to the plate Art Wilson, the Giants second-string catcher. Wilson was in the game only because Rigler had tossed out regular catcher Chief Meyers in the top of the inning for disputing his ball and strike calls. In fact, it was Wilson's error that had contributed to Brooklyn's taking the lead.

After missing Rucker's first pitch,

Two-hundred and forty pound umpire Cy Rigler claimed he punched Dahlen in self-defense.

Wilson connected with the second, launching a high towering fly directly down the right field line that came down in the upper deck. Rigler called it a fair ball, although each of the Dodgers fielders in the line of vision thought it was foul. Apparently Wilson did too, because he made no motion to run to first base until Rigler had signaled that it was a fair ball. Coming with Groh on base, the blast turned Brooklyn's 3–2 lead into a 4–3 Giants victory.

Wilson had barely begun to move when an enraged Dahlen was at home plate screaming in Rigler's face that the ball had landed foul. He was yelling and waving his arms about, when Rigler, who later said he thought Dahlen was getting ready to hit him, struck first. He smashed the Brooklyn manager full in the face, the punch landing under Dahlen's left eye. Dahlen retaliated with a punch of his own, and before Wilson had reached second base, the two men were standing at home plate exchanging blows.

Tex Erwin, the big Dodgers catcher, tried to jump between them, but the two combatants kept on swinging, over and around Erwin as needed. Meanwhile, the fans, already in a feisty mood over Rigler's ejections of Meyers, and his earlier one of Art Fletcher, rushed toward the melee. So did the players off both benches, along with the contingent of Pinkerton security men. Erwin was finally able to pull Dahlen away, while Giants coach Wilbert Robinson did the same with Rigler. Actually, Coach Robinson was acting as the Giants manager today, running the team while John McGraw served a five-day suspension for his clash with umpire Bill Finneran. As the entire assemblage of intermingled players and fans headed toward the center field clubhouse, the Pinkertons struggled to get the fans separated out and headed toward the exits.

Most observers judged the Dahlen-Rigler bout a draw, which is surprising in that Rigler was a huge man for his day, more than six feet tall and weighing around 240 pounds. As recently as 1903 he had played right tackle for the original Massillon Tigers professional football team.

Dahlen stuck by his protest during post-game comments to the press. "The ball was way foul, and I knew it, and maybe the umpire did," he said. "It could not have been less than six feet foul, and some said it was a great deal more."[3] First baseman Daubert, who had an excellent view, was even surer. He thought the ball was at least five yards foul. Capturing the fighting spirit of the day, rarely used Dolly Stark, playing shortstop that afternoon, said with bluster that "it was foul, and I can lick the man who says it wasn't."[4]

Chiming in too was President Ebbets, who had been a spectator at the game. "The ball was distinctly foul," claimed the Dodgers chief executive. "I was sitting in a seat that allowed me to look right down the right field foul line. The markers on the New York grandstand should be continued all the way up and five feet above, so that the umpires and public will have a better guide."[5]

That night, Ebbets sent a note to National League president Tom Lynch asking that Rigler be "punished for his unwarranted assault upon Dahlen."[6] Lynch obliged. On April 23, he fined Rigler $100. He also fined Dahlen $100, and in addition suspended the Brooklyn manager for two weeks. Lynch claimed that after investigating the incident, he was unable to figure out who struck the first blow, as each man had accused the other of swinging first.

Willie Keeler, whom Dahlen had gotten to coach for him this year, managed the club in his friend's absence. Keeler's main duty with Brooklyn was to help educate the young players in the art of hitting. John McGraw had begun the practice of hiring former players to coach his men in particular phases of the game. In addition to Robinson, a former catcher who was there to coach the pitchers, McGraw had on his staff Arlie Latham, a top base stealer from the 19th century, to tutor his runners.

Ebbets, who believed the entire fault for the melee lay with Rigler, was outraged at what he considered an unjust punishment for Dahlen. He issued a long statement defending his manager, which included these excerpts:[7]

"Dahlen will never pay that fine, for I will pay it for him, one way or another. I do not think he deserved the fine, and as it was incurred in the course of his duty to the club, there is no reason why he should pay it...

"Dahlen has taken the whole matter to heart very much, especially that part of the finding which says he 'grabbed' the umpire, which is not true. He feels that he has been put in the class of roughhouse managers and he has no desire for a reputation of that kind...

"The penalty was especially severe on Dahlen on the ground that he was protesting after the game was over. It was not over. Neither Groh, who was on first, nor Wilson, who hit the ball into the stand, had crossed the plate before Dahlen made the protest...

"I am game, and the players and myself take our medicine, but there has undoubtedly appeared to have been discrimination against Dahlen and the Brooklyn team in the two series with New York and with this decision. Dahlen has not been able to go to the front with the slightest protest without having the watch pulled on him."

There is an interesting and historically significant side note to this game. Jeff Tesreau, the Giants' starting pitcher, left with nobody out in the ninth and was charged with all three runs Brooklyn scored that inning. Rube Marquard relieved Tesreau and got the side out without any runs being charged to him. Under today's scoring rules, when the Giants scored two in the last of the ninth to win the game, the scorer would credit Marquard with the victory. However, the custom of the time was to award the decision in cases like that to the starter, in this case, Tesreau. Marquard had already beaten the Dodgers in the season opener and had won his next start at Boston. He would then go on to win his next seventeen decisions, giving him nineteen straight wins and tying Tim Keefe's major league record set with the 1888 Giants. Had he gotten credit for the April 20 win, Marquard would have had 20 consecutive wins, and the record would have been his alone.

Marquard's streak had reached 18 when he faced Brooklyn in the first game of a July 3 doubleheader at the Polo Grounds. His opponent in this face-to-face matchup between the league's two best left-handers was Rucker, who had a seven-game winning streak of his own. Although Rucker was the better pitcher that afternoon, allowing only four hits and one walk while Marquard yielded nine hits and walked five, the Giants won the game. Each team scored an unearned run, but the Giants also pushed across an earned one to raise Marquard's consecutive games-won streak to 19.[8] New York also won the second game, 10–9, extending the team's winning streak to 16, which the Dodgers broke the next day by sweeping the July 4 morning-afternoon double-header.

Dahlen had promised after the suspension resulting from the Rigler fight that he would now be on his best behavior. He would speak only in a whisper and would do his best to avoid using foul language. Of course, no one who had followed Dahlen's career expected him to live up to those pronouncements. Therefore, it surprised no one when he almost immediately went back to battling both the umpires and with the opposition. He did, however, manage to keep from getting ejected post-Rigler until the second game of the July 3 double-header — a period of more than two months.

After having lost the opener to Marquard, Brooklyn was leading that second game 9–8 in the bottom of the eighth. With Maury Kent on the mound for the Dodgers, the Giants had Art Fletcher at second, Josh Devore at third, and Fred Snodgrass at bat. While working on Snodgrass, one of Kent's pitches got away from Erwin. Devore raced home to tie the score, and when Erwin's throw to Kent covering the plate hit Snodgrass, Fletcher also scored to put New York ahead 10–9.

Dahlen protested loudly and vigorously to umpire Bill Brennan that Snodgrass had interfered with Erwin's throw. He argued that not only should Fletcher not be allowed to score, Snodgrass should be called out for interference. Virtually the entire Brooklyn team joined their manager in his animated objections, though Brennan settled for putting just Dahlen and outfielder Hub Northen out of the game. Two days later, following a fifth game in New York, the teams concluded the six-game series with one at Washington Park. Dahlen's kick over a strike called on Otto Miller in the ninth inning led to Brennan tossing him out yet again.

After winning two of three from the Giants to open the season, the Dodgers had gone into a tailspin. By Decoration Day they had endured four-, five-, and six-game losing streaks, and were in the cellar, 16½ games behind New York. The Brooklyn fans had not expected a pennant-winner this season, but they had

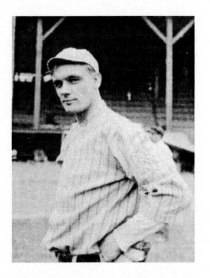

Rube Marquard's 19-game winning streak in 1912 began and ended with wins against Dahlen's Dodgers.

expected a team that would at least contend for a spot in the first division. The club's dismal start soured not only the fans but also the press. Abe Yager in the *Eagle* began criticizing both Dahlen's lineup choices and his strategic moves. By midsummer rumors began surfacing that Dahlen was on his way out as manager. One story making the rounds had the Dodgers trading Hummel to the St. Louis Cardinals for second baseman Miller Huggins, to make Huggins the club's player/manager in 1913.[9]

In all, it had been another disappointing season for everyone connected with Brooklyn baseball: another seventh-place finish, six wins fewer than the season before, and the third consecutive year of falling attendance. Rucker (18–21) led the league with six shutouts and finished with a third-best 2.21 earned run average, but he was Dahlen's only reliable pitcher. The offense again scored the fewest runs in the league, though both Ebbets and Dahlen were cheered by what they perceived to be bright signs for the future.

Both Daubert and Wheat had continued along their paths to stardom, while two promising rookies emerged. One was George Cutshaw, who batted .280 for the season and replaced Hummel as the club's everyday second baseman. The other was outfielder Charles "Casey" Stengel, whom Dahlen brought to Brooklyn from Montgomery of the Southern Association. Signed on the recommendation of his boyhood pal Zack Wheat, Stengel became an instant favorite with the Brooklyn fans. He played his first major league game on September 17, batting second and playing center field. The Dodgers were hosting the Pirates, possessors of a 12-game winning streak, but Stengel's sensational debut helped Brooklyn end that streak. He had four singles— three against starter Claude Hendrix and one off reliever Jack Ferry — and drew a walk, stole two bases, and drove in two runs in the Dodgers' 7–3 victory. Thoroughly impressed by the brash young rookie, Dahlen made him the regular center fielder for the season's final three weeks, and Stengel responded with a .316 batting average. With the addition of Stengel and Cutshaw, Dahlen was continuing to put together an excellent team in Brooklyn. Unfortunately, it would never fulfill its potential under his leadership.

On October 5, the last day of the season, the Dodgers played their final game at Washington Park. Fittingly, Tesreau of the Giants shut them out, 1–0. Dahlen's double duty as both manager and third base coach gave the fans and the press the freedom to criticize his abilities in both roles. His work on the coaching lines came in for its share of second-guessing, at least from the fans. The "experts" in the stands always seemed to know best when to hold runners and when to send them. So whenever Dahlen's choices did not agree with theirs, they felt at liberty to let him know about it. After several of these critiques, writers covering the team would point out information about the runners (such as an injury) or about the fielders (such as their having a particularly strong or weak arm) that Dahlen was aware of but that the fans probably were not. These items of information were seldom, if ever, followed by letters of apology from the censuring fans.

Dahlen's managerial skills also came in for their share of criticism from both the press and the fans, but he continued to have the backing of Ebbets. Although Ebbets had devoted the major portion of the 1912 season to the construction of his new park, he still found the time to issue announcements defending his manager. He had faith in Dahlen and he was not contemplating a change, Ebbets said on more than one occasion. "I can't blame Dahlen for the injuries to our best men, can I?" he asked in June. Ebbets also had another explanation for why he believed the Dodgers had played so poorly. He blamed it on the club's seven players who were recently married. Like most owners and managers at the time, Ebbets did not consider being a newlywed advantageous to a player's performance.

Ebbets's ongoing defense of Dahlen aside, once the season ended the speculation about who would manage the Brooklyn club in 1913 started up again. According to some, Daubert was the leading candidate, but he denied even wanting the job. Then, when Roger Bresnahan and Frank Chance became available after being fired by the Cardinals and Cubs respectively, their names jumped to the top of the Dodgers managerial sweepstakes. Ebbets ended all the conjecture by announcing in November that Dahlen would be back to manage the Brooklyn club in 1913.

"Dahlen is a better manager than Roger Bresnahan, and as good a leader as Frank Chance under existing conditions," said Ebbets in making the announcement. "Dahlen made the New York team for McGraw in 1905. He has a thorough knowledge of inside ball and is honest and conscientious."

Bill had taken in all the speculation surrounding his future with great equanimity. "I'm at peace with the world," he said, as the rumors flew around him. "If I believed everything that I read I couldn't very well believe anything, and I'm disposed to drift right along and catch fish whenever they bite."[10]

Assured now of his position, Dahlen headed south to look for a spring training site to replace Hot Springs, eventually selecting Augusta, Georgia. He had used previous training camps to weed out veterans and work in newcomers, but planned a different approach for this year. Dahlen expected that the players reporting to Augusta's Albion Hotel would, for the most part, be the ones with which he would open the season. "I haven't got to rebuild more than half the team this year," he said in January. "I've had to do that in the past. If you will look back — and I am making neither apology or criticizing anybody for criticizing me — it has been the first effort of every year in spring training to try to patch up an infield or string an outfield so that it might work well. On the face of things, we've got players this season who are good enough not to make all of that necessary."[11]

When the Dodgers returned to Brooklyn, they baptized their new home, Ebbets Field, with a game against the New York Yankees. It was an interesting choice of opponents. A few years earlier, during the early days of the American League, Charlie Ebbets had been among the most hostile of the National League owners to the new league, with good reason. Defections to the Americans by such stars as Lave Cross, Bill Donovan, Fielder Jones, Willie Keeler, Joe Kelley, and Frank Kitson had devastated his championship clubs of 1899–1900. But hostilities had mostly ceased by 1913, and peace between the leagues now reigned. An unmistakably clear indication of that peace was Ebbets's invitation to the Yankees to help him open his new park. On April 5, a crowd estimated at somewhere between 25,000–30,000 watched Nap Rucker defeat new manager Frank Chance's American Leaguers, 3–2. It was a day full of ceremony: Shannon's 23rd Regiment band serenaded the crowd with the triumphal march from *Aida*, Mrs. Ed McKeever raised Old Glory, and Genevieve Ebbets, Charlie's sister threw out the first ball. But for everyone who was there, the major

Dahlen and New York Yankees manager Frank Chance before the first game at Ebbets Field.

topic of conversation was Ebbets Field itself. The magnificent new state-of-the-art baseball palace was described as follows:

> At the corner of Sullivan and Cedar Streets was a curved brick façade highlighted by classical arched windows. Inside was an ornate lobby rotunda with a baseball-themed terrazzo floor. The double-tiered stands ran along the foul lines from the right field corner to a bit beyond third base, where a single double-deck bleacher section extended to the left field corner.[12]

Ebbets, with a background in architecture, had eschewed wood, mandating that the building be constructed with concrete and steel. His purpose was to protect against the fires that had destroyed several wooden ballparks in the past, most recently the Polo Grounds in 1911. Upon completion, Ebbets Field was a "quintessentially urban ballpark" built on a "very tight site," whose dimensions were dictated by the layout of the surrounding streets.[13] The distance to left field from home plate was 419 feet; to straightaway center it was 476 feet; and to right center, 500 feet. However, because of the configuration of Bedford Avenue, which ran behind right field, the distance down the right field line was only 300 feet. The vast dimensions were responsible for the first two home runs at the new park: inside-the-parkers by Casey Stengel and Jake Daubert.

Four days after beating the Yankees, Rucker was back on the mound for the official opening of Ebbets Field. A disappointingly small crowd of approximately 10,000 witnessed the inaugural on a bright but bitterly cold day. They saw the Phillies win 1–0, scoring the game's only run, an unearned one, during a wild top half of the first inning.

Over the next 45 years there would be countless numbers of daffy innings at Ebbets Field. This was the first one, an inning that saw Dodgers right fielder Benny Meyer drop two fly balls, and the Phillies have two runners thrown out stretching. Dahlen had acquired Meyer from Toronto of the International League in exchange for Hub Northen, a player he felt lacked the speed to play in his outfield.

Dode Paskert began the game by hitting Rucker's first pitch sharply past shortstop Bob Fisher. He tried to stretch it into a double, but was out on a throw from left fielder Wheat to second baseman Cutshaw. After Otto Knabe doubled to right, Hans Lobert hit a foul fly ball that right fielder Meyer lost in the sun and dropped. Given another chance, Lobert flied out to center fielder Stengel, with Knabe taking third after the catch. Next was Sherry Magee, Philadelphia's best hitter, who lifted a fly ball to right. Meyer, still battling the sun, dropped it for a two-base error as Knabe scored easily. Albert "Cozy" Dolan then ripped a single to center, but when Magee tried to score, Stengel's throw to catcher Otto Miller nailed him for the third out. Despite three hits and two Brooklyn errors, the Phillies managed only one run in the inning.

Philadelphia righthander Tom Seaton made the run stand up, making for a tough loss for Rucker and a forgettable major league debut for Meyer. Dahlen never said much to the press, but when a reporter asked about Meyer after the game, he absolved the youngster from blame. "Meyer is human, and the wind was strong," said the disheartened manager.

The Dodgers bounced back to win their next two games, on the road, but when they returned home Seaton beat Rucker again, by the same 1–0 score. Next day, different pitchers, same results. Ad Brennan of the Phillies beat Pat Ragan, 1–0. Brooklyn finally scored its first Ebbets Field run a day later during Frank Allen's 2–1 loss to Erskine Mayer. The win was the first as a big-leaguer for Mayer, who allowed Brooklyn just two questionable hits and one unearned run.

One of the Dodgers hits was a double by Stengel on a fly ball that Phillies right fielder Sherry Magee lost in the sun. This "gift" aside, Stengel had begun the season with the same solid hitting he had shown in September. By the end of April his batting average was up to .352, and he celebrated

May Day by hitting two inside the park home runs off Boston's Otto Hess. He tailed off some after that, but he was still in the .290s going into July. Then on July 4, Stengel injured his ankle in a game against the Giants and was forced to miss almost a month of play. When he struggled after returning, Dahlen began sitting him down when the opposing pitcher was left-handed. Dahlen had noticed that the left-handed hitting Stengel had done much better against right-handers than he had against lefties. During his September call-up his overall batting average was .316, but it was .351 with 11 runs batted in against right-handers, and only .250 with two runs batted in against left-handers. Thirty-five years later Stengel would use this concept of platooning left- and right-handed batters in managing the Yankees to 10 American League pennants and seven world championships.

Brooklyn's 1913 season mirrored, in many ways, Stengel's ups and downs. Between May 8 and June 3, they occupied the lofty position of second place, and all were hailing Dahlen as a marvelous manager. Some New

York newspapermen, while praising his genius, paid him the ultimate compliment a manager in the city could get; they compared him favorably to John McGraw. One even claimed that he was "out-McGrawing McGraw" in aggressiveness, brains, and leadership. A month later, the Dodgers had slipped a notch to third, behind New York and Philadelphia, but were still very much in the thick of the race. Dahlen, who was always extremely cautious about predicting success, went as far as to say that this team had a chance to win the pennant. This from a man who rarely spoke to the press, and when he did usually limited himself to yes and no answers. However, Brooklyn's winning ways during the first half of the 1913 season would be the high point of Dahlen's managerial career, and it would be short lived.

Dahlen platooned the young Casey Stengel in Brooklyn, a tactic that Stengel would later use with great success as manager of the Yankees.

On Friday, July 4, the first-place Giants were at Ebbets Field for a morning-afternoon double-header. Big crowds, eagerly anticipating Brooklyn closing the gap on the New Yorkers, attended both games. To their discontent, they saw a Giants team that was much too strong for Dahlen's youngsters. Yet again, the Dodgers were unable to cope with the pitching of Tesreau and Marquard and lost both ends of the double-header. They also dropped the two single games that followed. A 17–4 loss to the Braves, on the day before the Giants series began, had initiated a terrible stretch for Dahlen and his club. They lost 10 consecutive games, all at Ebbets

Dahlen as the manager of the 1912 Dodgers. Owner Charles Ebbets never blamed him for the losing seasons.

Field. By the time it ended, the Dodgers had fallen to fifth place, 15 games behind the Giants, and any dreams of a pennant were gone.

Injuries to several players, including Stengel's sprained ankle on July 4, were largely responsible for the losing streak. Hummel, Fisher, and George Cutshaw had, like Stengel, also suffered ankle injuries, and, coincidentally, all four had occurred while they were sliding into second base. Meanwhile, Rucker, long the ace of the staff, had struggled all season with a sore arm. At one point it had gotten so bad that he arranged to visit the celebrated baseball healer, Dr. John "Bonesetter" Reese of Youngstown, Ohio. Nevertheless, most fans never allow for things like player injuries when judging managers, and those who had loved Dahlen in May were now calling for his ouster. Some sportswriters continued to support Dahlen, believing he was getting the most possible out of the club. But another group existed that was hostile to him, and they were quick to revive their calls for Daubert to manage the team in 1914.

Going into the final day of the season, the Dodgers were in sixth place, one game behind the Braves. They would finish with a double-header at Boston and if Brooklyn could win both games they would pass the Braves and finish fifth. Perhaps knowing his job depended on the result, Dahlen went with his two hottest pitchers. He used Rucker in the first game and Ed Reulbach in the second. The Dodgers had picked up the veteran Reulbach from the Cubs in an August trade for Eddie Stack. Finishing fifth might have saved Dahlen's job, but Boston won both games and now his dismissal seemed inevitable.

Speculation about Dahlen's successor began anew the day after the season ended, with Daubert continuing as the leading contender. Besides being Brooklyn's most popular player, he had just won the first of his two consecutive batting titles. Daubert had also won the Chalmers Award, an early version of the Most Valuable Player award. The Dodgers would be leaving in late November to play 12 games in Cuba, and Daubert would help lead the tour.

Also prominently mentioned was Harry Smith, the former manager of the Doves. Smith had led the Brooklyn-controlled Newark Indians to the International League championship this past season. However, bringing Smith to Brooklyn seemed unlikely, as Ebbets had already upset the people in Newark with his past personnel moves. Last August, with the Indians fighting for the pennant, he had called up three of their best players: outfielder Bill Collins, catcher Lew McCarty, and left-hander Raleigh Aitchison, the league's best pitcher. He had no intention of alienating them any further and would leave Smith in Newark.

Throughout Dahlen's four years in Brooklyn, Ebbets had never blamed him for the Dodgers failure to win. The club had experienced a terrible run of injuries and bad luck during his entire tenure, and this year was the worst of all. At one time or other, Erwin, Wheat, Miller, Stengel, Daubert and Red Smith had all been disabled. His manager "couldn't keep the team in the first division with a lot of subs in the lineup," reasoned Ebbets.

Dahlen had invoked the fear of what injuries could do to his team even before the season started. "There's only one thing to be dreaded," he said while assessing the Dodgers' chances. "All baseball men are afraid of it, and I am no exception. If two or three men get hurt then we'll have to hang back a little until they are fit. But I do hope that the Lord will be good to us this year and let us get away with the team intact. We never have been able to do it, for some reason, in the last four years, and it seems to me it is about time the old luck broke and remained broken for good."[14]

Ebbets also reminded all those clamoring for Dahlen's discharge that early in the season, before the injuries started piling up, the Dodgers had been among the league leaders. That as late as June 1, they were in second place, just two and a half games behind Philadelphia. Meanwhile, with his job hanging in the balance, Dahlen went off on a hunting trip with pitcher Reulbach.

SIXTEEN

The End of the Line

The long-rumored end came on November 17, 1913, with President Ebbets's announcement that "William Dahlen has been unconditionally released as the manager of the Brooklyn baseball club." While the news surprised no one, and pleased many, Ebbets called Dahlen's firing "the most unpleasant moment" of his career in baseball. The owner had always been appreciative of Dahlen's services, first as the shortstop on Brooklyn's championship teams of 1899–1900, and then of his four years of work as a manager. He remained a staunch defender to the end, believing that injuries more than anything else had been responsible for the team's four second division finishes under Dahlen's leadership. Excerpts from the text of Ebbets's full statement are an indication of how highly he thought of the man who was now his ex-manager:

> "Mr. Dahlen has been with the Brooklyn club as manager for four years. During that time he has discharged his duties honestly, impartially, and without fear or favor, using at all times rare judgment. To be sure, he had made mistakes on the ball field....
> "There are errors aplenty in baseball. If there were not, baseball would not be the great attraction it is. But Mr. Dahlen has not, in my opinion, made as many mistakes as his critics believe. His judgment in handling the players under contract of the Brooklyn Club has been wonderful. During his first three years as manager, he dispensed with the services of many players who were either incompetent, misbehaving, or troublesome, rarely misjudging a player, as is evidenced by the fact that all the men he passed up, only one was of major league caliber....
> "By reason of his keen judgment, he leaves behind a body of men who as players and gentlemen, on and off the field, are a credit and honor to the Borough of Brooklyn, a team which, with the addition of two or three first-class men will be a championship contender in 1914....
> "In building up the team, Manager Dahlen has been unfortunate in

finishing in a low position each year in the championship race, but I will say, without fear of contradiction, that he has been a good manager."[1]

Most of the Dodgers players and many of the more knowledgeable people in baseball agreed with Ebbets, but that was not enough. His co-owners, the McKeever brothers, had been actively campaigning for a change of managers for more than a year, believing that Dahlen was not getting enough out of the talent he had. Ebbets had finally given in to them. The change was also well received by the many Brooklyn fans who had been calling for Dahlen's dismissal. Their unhappiness was with the manager's style of play, which they felt was too conservative. As an active player, Dahlen had played the game with daring and flamboyance, but he had not displayed those traits as a manager.

In announcing Dahlen's dismissal, Ebbets also revealed that he had chosen a replacement, and that the club would introduce the new manager in a few days. He was, said Ebbets, a man well known to followers of baseball. Conjecture over whom the new man might be began immediately, with first baseman and captain Jake Daubert still the clear favorite. A cablegram announcing the Dodgers' trip to Cuba, which Daubert was leading, had suddenly ended seemed to confirm that it indeed was Daubert.

However, newspapermen covering the club continued to discuss other names, some old and some new. Mentioned most prominently were Cubs catcher and former Cardinals manager Roger Bresnahan; former White Sox manager Fielder Jones; current Tigers manager Hugh Jennings; former Red Sox manager Jake Stahl; longtime Pirates outfielder Tommy Leach, now with the Cubs; and recently released Giants coach Wilbert Robinson.

Expecting that he was about to be fired as manager of the Dodgers did not prevent Dahlen from his postseason hunting trip with pitcher Ed Reulbach.

Some seemed a more likely choice than others, but while newspapers in New York handicapped the different contenders, those in Baltimore, where Robinson lived, were announcing that he had already been chosen. They were, of course, correct. Robinson, who had been hunting in North Carolina, headed to Brooklyn where on November 20, Ebbets introduced him as the Dodgers' new manager.

Although Dahlen had not produced a winning team in his four years at the helm, he had completely revamped the Dodgers roster. He rid the club of many of its old-timers, those he felt had been strictly "going through the motions," along with its cadre of "midnight carousers." Only Zack Wheat, then a rookie, Nap Rucker, and John Hummel remained from the team he inherited in 1910. Robinson would take the basic lineup of players assembled by Dahlen, add some pitching, and in three years bring Brooklyn a pennant.

The genial, outgoing "Uncle Robbie," as he would come to be known, would also become the most beloved manager in Dodgers history. His personality, which made him so popular with fans and press, was in sharp contrast to the dour and uncommunicative Dahlen. The press had been mostly fair to Dahlen, criticizing him no more or less than they would any manager; nevertheless, Bill had been distrustful of them. He felt the newspapers often misquoted him, and he could best solve that problem by not saying anything at all to them.

Along with the fans and the newspapermen, the umpires too were no doubt glad to see Dahlen go. He had been an obnoxious antagonist of theirs for more than 20 years, never abandoning the rough and tumble manner prevalent in the game when he broke in.

Yet, as loud and abrasive as Dahlen had always been on the field, he had unceasingly been quiet and taciturn off it. His firing changed nothing. He remained silent both about it and about two rumored managerial jobs in the high minors for which he was supposedly being considered. One report said the job with the Jersey City Skeeters of the International League was his if he wanted it, while another had him replacing Herman Bronkie as manager of the Toledo Mud Hens of the American Association.[2]

But he would get neither one, as Bronkie retained his position, and Rudy Hulswitt got the Jersey City job. Instead, when spring training 1914 rolled around, Dahlen was back in the employ of the Brooklyn organization. The newspapers reported that he had signed on as a scout, but Ebbets, in announcing the appointment, made it sound like much more. After again praising Dahlen for his work in building a strong Dodgers team, Ebbets said his new job would be as his "assistant in securing material for the Brooklyn club." While that sounded like the classic job description for a scout, Ebbets insisted that Dahlen was not a scout.

"I would not term it a scout," he said. "He will be more than that; he will be an assistant, where his keen knowledge of baseball players will be more than that of a scout. I want to impress upon you that, recognizing his ability, he will be of great benefit to us; he is placed in this position by reason of his loyalty to organized baseball."[3] What all the rhetoric amounted to was that Dahlen was now Brooklyn's *chief* scout, reporting directly to Ebbets.

Bill spent the late winter of 1914 where he spent almost every late winter, in Hot Springs. Only this time the goal was not necessarily to get into shape; it was, instead, a vacation with Jeannette. From Hot Springs he reported to Augusta, where he watched the new manager get his former players ready for the season. Those players had one more tribute planned for their old leader, a banquet at the Albion Hotel. Robinson, Daubert, and Ed Reulbach were the organizers of the event, which 80 people attended and deemed a huge success. All the Dodgers were there, including Ebbets, plus the reporters covering the club, along with several well-connected local fans. Also attending were members of the Brooklyn-owned Newark Indians, many of whom had played under Dahlen with the Dodgers.

Daubert had been collecting money for a gift since late last season, a gift the club presented at the banquet. It was a silver service for seven, which was sitting on a table, covered by an American flag. The flag had a series of ribbons attached, and at the appointed time, several Dodgers veterans simultaneously yanked on their assigned ribbons to uncover the gift.

In 1914, Robinson's first year, Brooklyn moved up to fifth place, but the season was a disastrous one financially. Competition from the Brooklyn Tip-Tops of the new Federal League caused Ebbets Field attendance to drop from 347,000 to less than 123,000. Among the first casualties of the reduced revenues coming into the Ebbets-McKeever cash registers was Dahlen. The Dodgers let him go as part of their organizational revamping and financial belt-tightening. When he first heard they might cut him loose Dahlen made the case to the team's leadership for his retention. He reminded the club that in 1913, to stay loyal to Brooklyn and the National League, he had turned down a two-year offer to manage in the Federal League. His answer from one Dodgers official was, "Well, why don't you go over to the Feds now?"

So much for loyalty going both ways, though Ebbets, always a Dahlen supporter, did attempt to explain the reason for his discharge. Ebbets blamed the release of his chief scout on the cut down of player roster size from 25 to 21. "The 21 player limit has lessened the need of a scout. Managers in the smaller leagues will act as our agents and there is no need of employing a man to go combing the bushes for players," he said. He further announced that Bill had been a loyal member of the team and that the Brooklyn organization would take care of him by trying to get him a minor league managerial job.

Whether or not Ebbets actually tried, and he probably did, no minor league managerial job for Dahlen ever materialized. Several friends suggested that he become an umpire, but Dahlen, perhaps recalling his own many jousts with the men in blue, chose not to try that path. Living in Brooklyn, he could often be seen at sandlot and semi-pro games or just tending to his flower and vegetable garden. He was also a frequent visitor to the local big league parks, and occasionally a participant.

Wilbert Robinson would take the team Dahlen built and win a pennant with it in 1916.

On September 30, 1921, Dahlen played in a benefit game at the Polo Grounds for Christy Mathewson, who was battling tuberculosis in a sanatorium at Saranac Lake. Dahlen played shortstop on a squad made up of Mathewson's former teammates in a game against the current Giants. The old-timers defeated the National League champs 2–0, although the soon-to-be World Series winners hardly gave it their best. In a game shortened to five innings by rain, Dahlen singled and hit into a double play against rookie right-hander Rosy Ryan. Defensively, he had three assists and three putouts, and combined with second baseman Billy Gilbert and first baseman Fred Merkle for a double play.

In May 1933, Dahlen attended a ceremony at Ebbets Field marking 50 years of professional baseball in Brooklyn. Often he would go out to the local parks just to watch a ballgame. He was so impressed with the heads-up style of play of the visiting Phillies after watching one May 1937 game at Ebbets Field that he compared them with the champion Superbas teams on which he had played. "Why this team's playing the kind of game we used to play. Those fellows are doing something more than walking up there, getting on base, and then standing around to wait for someone to hit a home run. They're playing the smartest baseball I've seen in years—using the squeeze play, the double steal, and all that."[4]

The '37 Phillies may have been playing smart baseball in May, but for Dahlen to compare them with the 1899–1900 Superbas, one of the great teams of all time, was laughable. Philadelphia was in the midst of 16 consecutive years in the second division, and was on its way to yet another seventh-place finish.

Dahlen attended but did not play in a Dodgers old-timers game at Ebbets Field on September 22, 1940. Many of those who did play had been members of Brooklyn's 1916 and 1920 pennant-winners, but the now 70-year-old Dahlen was the only one there who had played on the 1899 and 1900 pennant-winners.

While Dahlen lived his post-baseball life mostly in obscurity, occasionally his name would surface. A report by Philadelphia correspondent James Isaminger in the October 8, 1936, issue of the *Sporting News* stated that Dahlen was no longer with us. "Members of the 1905 victorious Giants who are now dead are Christy Mathewson, Mike Donlin, Bill Dahlen, and perhaps one or two more," claimed Isaminger.[5]

Yet in J. G. Taylor Spinks's column in that same issue, Spinks noted that Dahlen had worked as a gate watcher at the Eighth Avenue entrance to the Polo Grounds during the recent Giants-Yankees World Series. He reported that Dahlen was happily running a gas station in Brooklyn, although quoted him as saying wistfully that "It must be great to be young and a Giant or a Yankee."[6]

At age 68, Dahlen worked as an usher for the two 1938 World Series games in Yankee Stadium. Also working as an usher for the Cubs-Yankees games at the stadium was 78 year old Arlie Latham, a fine third baseman in the 1880s and 1890s, and later a coach under John McGraw. Latham was a special officer assigned to the press box, while Dahlen directed fans to the $3.30 unreserved grandstand ticket booths. He would also find employment as a ticket taker at Ebbets Field in the mid-1940s.

During the summer of 1941, as Joe DiMaggio was compiling his record 56-game hitting streak, Dahlen was working as a Yankee Stadium bullpen attendant. On July 1, he watched from that distant venue as DiMaggio's streak reached 44, tying the record of his old pal, Willie Keeler. A few days earlier, DiMaggio had passed his own streak total of 42. "That was so long ago that I had forgotten it until DiMaggio's stunt began to get a lot of publicity," Dahlen said. "In the 'nineties nobody paid any attention to a thing like that." For that matter, reading and hearing about Dahlen during DiMaggio's pursuit of the record was likely the first time many modern fans had ever heard of his streak, or of him.

Dahlen talked some more about the streaks in a 1943 interview with writer Harold Burr, in what Burr called his "snug Brooklyn apartment."

Although he thought very highly of DiMaggio, Dahlen said, he was nevertheless sorry to see Keeler's streak broken. "I didn't care about myself. But I kind of hated to see anybody break Keeler's mark. Wee Willie — we always called him Bill — and I were pals. We went everywhere together — Bill and I and Bill's cigars. He smoked more cigars than General Grant," said Dahlen, whom Burr described as constantly puffing on a cigarette.[7]

Over the years, Dahlen told Burr, he had worked at various jobs. "I punched a clock in a shipyard during the First World War, worked on the docks, ran a filling station in Brooklyn, and had a fling on the side managing the Morse Drydock and Repair Company semi pros."[8] He was also a part-time scout for several big league clubs, worked at the Polo Grounds, and as a night clerk at Brooklyn's main post office.

Dahlen was living in Brooklyn at the home of his niece, Harriet Bartels, when he died at Kings County Hospital on December 5, 1950, exactly a month short of his 81st birthday. Jeannette had passed away 18 months earlier. His daughter, Corrine; his brother, Harry; and several nieces and nephews survived him. They buried him in Brooklyn's Evergreen Cemetery, not very far from where he once spent his glory days.

SEVENTEEN

From Nelliston to Cooperstown

Late in 1913, shortly after the Dodgers fired Bill Dahlen as their manager, the *New York World* wrote this about him. "Dahlen was a credit to the game, although at times he queered himself by the objectionable way he chose to nag umpires and uselessly delay games." Then, in a statement that proved entirely mistaken, they predicted that "He will, however, go down in the history of the sport as one of its most famous players and characters."

Of course, just the opposite has happened. In the more than 90 years since that was written, Dahlen's brilliant career has all but faded from baseball's collective memory. Yet there is new hope that current and future generations will come to appreciate that brilliance. In the last few decades, baseball historians and statisticians began taking a fresh look at player performances, not only the current generation, but also those of the past. Foremost among these sabermetric analysts has been Bill James, who has pioneered several methods of judging players performance and value. His latest contribution is called "win shares," which purports to measure each player's contributions, offensively and defensively, to his team's wins.

According to James's compilations, there are 30 position players in baseball history who had 400 or more win shares and are now eligible for the Hall of Fame. All 30 are in the hall. Additionally, there are 12 position players in history who had 375 to 399 win shares and are eligible for the Hall of Fame. Eleven of the 12 are in the hall. The lone exception in the 375–399 win share category is Bill Dahlen. Tommy McCarthy, with 170 win shares, is in the Hall of Fame; Bill Dahlen, with 394 win shares, is not.

James has also suggested that one Hall of Fame criterion should be whether the player was, in any season, the best in the game at his position.

Dahlen meets that test in multiple seasons. James gives Dahlen his highest rating for defensive wins as a shortstop, an A+, the same as Honus Wagner, Ozzie Smith, Mark Belanger, and Dave Concepcion. Dahlen ranks in the top 10 in nine of 11 fielding categories (Ozzie Smith is in seven).

John McGraw called him a "brilliant fielder, a good batter, a great thrower, and a splendid base runner." And in his overall rankings, James rates him the seventh-best position player of the decade of the 1890s. Sadly, he might have been even better. "If he had greater ambition, I do not doubt but that he would be the acknowledged star of the baseball world," said Jim Hart, who often clashed with Dahlen when he owned the Chicago club of the 1890s.

Detroit Tigers manager Hughie Jennings, who played with and against Dahlen, may have summed it up best. In 1912, Jennings was putting a group of rookies through their paces while admonishing them on the importance eating, sleeping, and living baseball.

"I have known but one really good player who could place baseball second to other things. That man is Bill Dahlen, now Brooklyn manager. Dahlen played the ponies and indulged in other outside activities. He never practiced. He never gave the game a thought when off the field and he always reached the clubhouse two or three minutes before starting time. Sometimes the game had to wait till Bill took his place at shortstop. If Dahlen had devoted his entire time to baseball, he'd have been the greatest infielder of all time."[1]

Remember, when Dahlen's active career ended, in 1909, he had played in more games (2,444) than anyone in major league history, a record he held until Wagner passed it in 1915. He also stood second in walks and in total plate appearances, and in the top 10 in runs batted in, extra base hits, singles, and stolen bases. Dahlen stole at least 20 bases in 15 seasons, including a high of 60 in 1892. Additionally, he ranked 11th in runs, hits, doubles, and total bases, and 13th in triples and home runs. Dahlen was first man to play 2,000 games at shortstop and the first to compile 2,000 hits at the position.

Dahlen's total player rating, as judged by *Total Baseball VII*, is 51.1, a score that is 31st among all major leaguers and 24th among non-pitchers. It is the highest rating for anyone not in the Hall of Fame, and obviously higher than some who are already members. Among those position players whom Dahlen ranks ahead of are Joe DiMaggio, Carl Yastrzemski, Robin Yount, Roberto Clemente, Charlie Gehringer, Ed Delahanty, and Reggie Jackson.

Granted, Dahlen does not compare with any of these men offensively. A good portion of his high ranking is due to his superb abilities at shortstop. As mentioned earlier, only one shortstop from any era — Rabbit Maranville — has exceeded Dahlen's total putouts, and just two — Ozzie Smith and Luis Aparico– have topped him in total assists. By *Total Baseball's* measurements of fielding runs, Dahlen prevented more runs from scoring than any shortstop ever, and more than anyone at any position, except Nap Lajoie and Bill Mazeroski.

Writer Bob Carroll included Dahlen among the dozen players he considered deserving of enshrinement in a 1985 article called "For The Hall of Fame: Twelve Good Men."[2] Carroll particularly stressed Dahlen's defensive contributions as a "grounder-gobbling shortstop on four National League pennant winners between 1899 and 1905." Since then, the hall has inducted seven of the men on Carroll's list: Mazeroski, Richie Ashburn, Bobby Doerr, William Hulbert, Ernie Lombardi, Bid McPhee, and Hal Newhouser.

Dahlen "is not only one of the best players not in the Hall of Fame, but he's certainly better than at least fifty players already in it," said John Thorn, the co-author with Pete Palmer of the first seven editions of *Total Baseball.* That was in 1994, the year the Veterans Committee voted former Yankee shortstop Phil Rizzuto into Cooperstown. Like many of us, Thorn believed that admitting Rizzuto while denying admission to Dahlen was a gross injustice. "The problem with the veterans committee is that their knowledge of the game's history only coincides with their own connection with the game. There's not anyone alive who remembers when Dahlen played," reasoned Thorn.

Yet despite all of his qualifications, and despite all the knowledgeable endorsements he has received, the Hall of Fame has completely ignored Dahlen. He received one vote in 1936, the first year of voting, and one in 1938. It is less than an hour's drive, a little more than 20 miles, from Nelliston to Cooperstown. It is time that Bill Dahlen makes that symbolic journey.

APPENDIX A

Bill Dahlen and His Hall of Fame Contemporaries

Players who began their careers within three years, plus or minus, of Dahlen's start in 1891.

GAMES PLAYED

BILL DAHLEN	**2,444**	Jesse Burkett	2,067
Jake Beckley	2,389	Joe Kelley	1,853
Bobby Wallace	2,383	Ed Delahanty	1,837
George Davis	2,372	Hugh Duffy	1,738
Fred Clarke	2,246	Billy Hamilton	1,594
Willie Keeler	2,123	Hugh Jennings	1,283

AT-BATS

Jake Beckley	9,538	Jesse Burkett	8,426
George Davis	9,045	Ed Delahanty	7,511
BILL DAHLEN	**9,036**	Hugh Duffy	7,044
Bobby Wallace	8,618	Joe Kelley	7,006
Willie Keeler	8,591	Billy Hamilton	6,283
Fred Clarke	8,584	Hugh Jennings	4,895

RUNS SCORED

Jesse Burkett	1,720	**BILL DAHLEN**	**1,590**
Willie Keeler	1,719	Hugh Duffy	1,554
Billy Hamilton	1,697	George Davis	1,545
Fred Clarke	1,622	Joe Kelley	1,421
Jake Beckley	1,602	Bobby Wallace	1,057
Ed Delahanty	1,600	Hugh Jennings	992

HITS

Jake Beckley	2,934		**BILL DAHLEN**	**2,461**
Willie Keeler	2,932		Bobby Wallace	2,309
Jesse Burkett	2,850		Hugh Duffy	2,283
Fred Clarke	2,678		Joe Kelley	2,220
George Davis	2,665		Billy Hamilton	2,164
Ed Delahanty	2,597		Hugh Jennings	1,526

DOUBLES

Ed Delahanty	522		Joe Kelley	358
Jake Beckley	473		Hugh Duffy	325
George Davis	453		Jesse Burkett	320
BILL DAHLEN	**413**		Billy Hamilton	242
Bobby Wallace	391		Willie Keeler	241
Fred Clarke	361		Hugh Jennings	232

TRIPLES

Jake Beckley	244		George Davis	163
Fred Clarke	220		Willie Keeler	145
Joe Kelley	194		Bobby Wallace	143
Ed Delahanty	186		Hugh Duffy	119
Jesse Burkett	182		Billy Hamilton	95
BILL DAHLEN	**163**		Hugh Jennings	88

HOME RUNS

Hugh Duffy	106		Fred Clarke	67
Ed Delahanty	101		Joe Kelley	65
Jake Beckley	87		Billy Hamilton	40
BILL DAHLEN	**84**		Bobby Wallace	34
Jesse Burkett	75		Willie Keeler	33
George Davis	73		Hugh Jennings	18

RUNS BATTED IN

Jake Beckley	1,577		Bobby Wallace	1,121
Ed Delahanty	1,466		Fred Clarke	1,015
George Davis	1,439		Jesse Burkett	952
Hugh Duffy	1,302		Hugh Jennings	840
BILL DAHLEN	**1,234**		Willie Keeler	810
Joe Kelley	1,194		Billy Hamilton	742

BASES ON BALLS

Billy Hamilton	1,189		Bobby Wallace	774
BILL DAHLEN	**1,064**		Ed Delahanty	741
Jesse Burkett	1,029		Hugh Duffy	664
Joe Kelley	911		Jake Beckley	616
Fred Clarke	875		Willie Keeler	524
George Davis	874		Hugh Jennings	347

STOLEN BASES

Billy Hamilton	914		Ed Delahanty	455
George Davis	619		Joe Kelley	443
Hugh Duffy	574		Jesse Burkett	389
BILL DAHLEN	**547**		Hugh Jennings	359
Fred Clarke	509		Jake Beckley	315
Willie Keeler	495		Bobby Wallace	201

BATTING AVERAGE

Ed Delahanty	.346		Fred Clarke	.312
Billy Hamilton	.344		Hugh Jennings	.312
Willie Keeler	.341		Jake Beckley	.308
Jesse Burkett	.338		George Davis	.295
Hugh Duffy	.324		**BILL DAHLEN**	**.272**
Joe Kelley	.317		Bobby Wallace	.268

TOTAL PLAYER RATING

George Davis	51.4		Fred Clarke	26.7
BILL DAHLEN	**51.1**		Hugh Jennings	26.3
Ed Delahanty	42.9		Jake Beckley	22.6
Bobby Wallace	35.7		Joe Kelley	19.6
Billy Hamilton	27.4		Willie Keeler	13.2
Jesse Burkett	27.0		Hugh Duffy	5.8

APPENDIX B

Bill Dahlen and Hall of Fame Shortstops

A comparison of Dahlen and current Hall of Famers who played the majority of their games at shortstop. All numbers reflect the players' entire career, not just those as a shortstop.

GAMES PLAYED

Robin Yount	2,856	Joe Cronin	2,124
Honus Wagner	2,794	Dave Bancroft	1,913
Rabbit Maranville	2,670	Joe Sewell	1,903
Luis Aparicio	2,599	John M. Ward	1,827
Ozzie Smith	2,573	Arky Vaughan	1,817
Ernie Banks	2,528	Joe Tinker	1,806
BILL DAHLEN	**2,444**	Phil Rizzuto	1,661
Luke Appling	2,422	Travis Jackson	1,656
Bobby Wallace	2,383	Lou Boudreau	1,646
George Davis	2,372	Hugh Jennings	1,283
Pee Wee Reese	2,166		

AT-BATS

Robin Yount	11,008	John M. Ward	7,685
Honus Wagner	10,439	Joe Cronin	7,579
Luis Aparicio	10,230	Dave Bancroft	7,182
Rabbit Maranville	10,078	Joe Sewell	7,132
Ernie Banks	9,421	Arky Vaughan	6,622
Ozzie Smith	9,396	Joe Tinker	6,441
George Davis	9,045	Travis Jackson	6,086
BILL DAHLEN	**9,036**	Lou Boudreau	6,029

Luke Appling	8,856		Phil Rizzuto	5,816
Bobby Wallace	8,618		Hugh Jennings	4,895
Pee Wee Reese	8,058			

RUNS SCORED

Honus Wagner	1,739		Joe Cronin	1,233
Robin Yount	1,632		Arky Vaughan	1,173
BILL DAHLEN	**1,590**		Joe Sewell	1,141
George Davis	1,545		Bobby Wallace	1,057
John M. Ward	1,410		Dave Bancroft	1,048
Pee Wee Reese	1,338		Hugh Jennings	992
Luis Aparicio	1,335		Phil Rizzuto	877
Luke Appling	1,319		Lou Boudreau	861
Ernie Banks	1,305		Travis Jackson	833
Ozzie Smith	1,257		Joe Tinker	774
Rabbit Maranville	1,255			

HITS

Honus Wagner	3,420		Joe Sewell	2,226
Robin Yount	3,142		Pee Wee Reese	2,170
Luke Appling	2,749		John M. Ward	2,136
Luis Aparicio	2,677		Arky Vaughan	2,103
George Davis	2,665		Dave Bancroft	2,004
Rabbit Maranville	2,605		Lou Boudreau	1,779
Ernie Banks	2,583		Travis Jackson	1,768
BILL DAHLEN	**2,461**		Joe Tinker	1,690
Ozzie Smith	2,460		Phil Rizzuto	1,588
Bobby Wallace	2,309		Hugh Jennings	1,526
Joe Cronin	2,285			

DOUBLES

Honus Wagner	643		Lou Boudreau	385
Robin Yount	583		Rabbit Maranville	380
Joe Cronin	515		Arky Vaughan	356
George Davis	453		Pee Wee Reese	330
Luke Appling	440		Dave Bancroft	320
Joe Sewell	436		Travis Jackson	291
BILL DAHLEN	**413**		Joe Tinker	263
Ernie Banks	407		Phil Rizzuto	239
Ozzie Smith	402		Hugh Jennings	232
Luis Aparicio	394		John M. Ward	231
Bobby Wallace	391			

TRIPLES

Honus Wagner	252		Luis Aparicio	92
Rabbit Maranville	177		Ernie Banks	90
BILL DAHLEN	**163**		Hugh Jennings	88
George Davis	163		Travis Jackson	86
Bobby Wallace	143		Pee Wee Reese	80
Arky Vaughan	128		Dave Bancroft	77
Robin Yount	126		Ozzie Smith	69
Joe Cronin	118		Joe Sewell	68
Joe Tinker	114		Lou Boudreau	66
Luke Appling	102		Phil Rizzuto	62
John M. Ward	96			

HOME RUNS

Ernie Banks	512		Joe Sewell	49
Robin Yount	251		Luke Appling	45
Joe Cronin	170		Phil Rizzuto	38
Travis Jackson	135		Bobby Wallace	34
Pee Wee Reese	126		Dave Bancroft	32
Honus Wagner	101		Joe Tinker	31
Arky Vaughan	96		Rabbit Maranville	28
BILL DAHLEN	**84**		Ozzie Smith	28
Luis Aparicio	83		John M. Ward	26
George Davis	73		Hugh Jennings	18
Lou Boudreau	68			

RUNS BATTED IN

Honus Wagner	1,733		Pee Wee Reese	885
Ernie Banks	1,636		Rabbit Maranville	884
George Davis	1,439		John M. Ward	869
Joe Cronin	1,424		Hugh Jennings	840
Robin Yount	1,406		Ozzie Smith	793
BILL DAHLEN	**1,234**		Luis Aparicio	791
Bobby Wallace	1,121		Lou Boudreau	789
Luke Appling	1,116		Joe Tinker	782
Joe Sewell	1,055		Dave Bancroft	591
Travis Jackson	929		Phil Rizzuto	563
Arky Vaughan	926			

BASES ON BALLS

Luke Appling	1,302	Dave Bancroft	827
Pee Wee Reese	1,210	Lou Boudreau	796
Ozzie Smith	1,072	Bobby Wallace	774
BILL DAHLEN	**1,064**	Ernie Banks	763
Joe Cronin	1,059	Luis Aparicio	736
Robin Yount	966	Phil Rizzuto	651
Honus Wagner	963	John M. Ward	421
Arky Vaughan	937	Joe Tinker	416
George Davis	874	Travis Jackson	412
Joe Sewell	842	Hugh Jennings	347
Rabbit Maranville	839		

STOLEN BASES

Honus Wagner	723	Bobby Wallace	201
George Davis	619	Luke Appling	179
Ozzie Smith	580	Phil Rizzuto	149
BILL DAHLEN	**547**	Dave Bancroft	145
John M. Ward	540*	Arky Vaughan	118
Luis Aparicio	506	Joe Cronin	87
Hugh Jennings	359	Joe Sewell	74
Joe Tinker	336	Travis Jackson	71
Rabbit Maranville	291	Lou Boudreau	51
Robin Yount	271	Ernie Banks	50
Pee Wee Reese	232		

*Ward began his career in 1878, but stolen bases were not tallied until 1886.

BATTING AVERAGE

Honus Wagner	.328	John M. Ward	.278
Arky Vaughan	.318	Ernie Banks	.274
Hugh Jennings	.312	Phil Rizzuto	.273
Joe Sewell	.312	**BILL DAHLEN**	**.272**
Luke Appling	.310	Pee Wee Reese	.269
Joe Cronin	.301	Bobby Wallace	.268
George Davis	.295	Joe Tinker	.262
Lou Boudreau	.295	Luis Aparicio	.262
Travis Jackson	.291	Ozzie Smith	.262
Robin Yount	.285	Rabbit Maranville	.258
Dave Bancroft	.279		

Total Player Rating

Honus Wagner	81.8		Joe Sewell	35.5
George Davis	51.4		Ernie Banks	26.9
BILL DAHLEN	**51.1**		Hugh Jennings	26.3
Robin Yount	46.0		Travis Jackson	23.7
Lou Boudreau	42.5		Joe Tinker	23.4
Luke Appling	42.4		Phil Rizzuto	16.1
Ozzie Smith	42.4		Pee Wee Reese	14.7
Joe Cronin	39.9		Rabbit Maranville	14.0
Arky Vaughan	39.7		Luis Aparicio	11.3
Dave Bancroft	37.5		John M. Ward	8.4
Bobby Wallace	35.7			

APPENDIX C

Bill Dahlen's Lifetime Batting Statistics

	G	AB	R	H	2B	3B	HR	RBI	SB	BB	HBP	BAV	OBP	SLG	TB
1891 CHI	135	549	114	143	18	13	9	76	21	67	7	.260	.348	.390	214
1892 CHI	143	581	114	170	23	19	5	58	60	45	5	.291	.347	.422	246
1893 CHI	116	485	113	146	28	15	5	64	31	58	5	.301	.381	.452	219
1894 CHI	122	507	150	182	32	14	15	108	42	76	3	.359	.445	.566	287
1895 CHI	129	516	106	131	19	10	7	62	38	61	10	.254	.344	.370	191
1896 CHI	125	474	137	167	30	19	9	74	51	64	8	.352	.438	.553	262
1897 CHI	75	276	67	80	18	8	6	40	15	43	7	.290	.399	.478	132
1898 CHI	142	521	96	151	35	8	1	79	27	58	23	.290	.385	.393	205
1899 BKL	121	428	87	121	22	7	4	76	29	67	15	.283	.398	.395	169
1900 BKL	133	483	87	125	16	11	1	69	31	73	7	.259	.364	.344	166
1901 BKL	131	511	69	136	17	9	4	82	23	30	5	.266	.313	.358	183
1902 BKL	138	527	67	139	25	8	2	74	20	43	8	.264	.329	.353	186
1903 BKL	138	474	71	124	17	9	1	64	34	82	2	.262	.373	.342	162
1904 NY	145	523	70	140	26	2	2	80	47	44	1	.268	.326	.337	176
1905 NY	148	520	67	126	20	4	7	81	37	62	12	.242	.337	.337	175
1906 NY	143	471	63	113	18	3	1	49	16	76	10	.240	.357	.297	140
1907 NY	143	464	40	96	20	1	0	34	11	51	4	.207	.291	.254	118
1908 BOS	144	524	50	125	23	2	3	48	10	35	8	.239	.296	.307	161
1909 BOS	69	197	22	46	6	1	2	16	4	29	0	.234	.332	.305	60
1910 BKL	3	2	0	0	0	0	0	0	0	0	0	.000	.000	.000	0
1911 BKL	1	3	0	0	0	0	0	0	0	0	3	.000	.000	.000	0

Games: 2,444

At Bats: 9,036

Runs: 1,590

Hits: 2,461

Doubles: 413

Triples: 163

Home Runs: 84

Runs Batted In: 1,234

Stolen Bases: 547   On Base Percentage .358
Bases On Balls: 1,064   Slugging Average: .382
Hit By Pitch: 140   Total Bases: 3,452
Batting Average: .272

APPENDIX D

Bill Dahlen's Lifetime Fielding Statistics

Year			G	PO	A	E	DP	PCT	LGPCT
1891	CHI	3B	84	120	211	42	13	.887	.881
		OF	37	69	7	6	4	.927	.912
		SS	15	28	46	16	4	.822	.889
1892	CHI	SS	72	178	232	41	29	.909	.897
		3B	68	113	189	19	14	.941	.879
		OF	2	3	0	0	0	1.000	.912
		2B	1	3	2	1	0	.833	.929
1893	CHI	SS	88	229	306	65	33	.892	.897
		OF	17	27	2	2	1	.935	.915
		2B	10	27	24	4	1	.927	.933
		3B	3	3	5	1	0	.889	.893
1894	CHI	SS	67	192	258	50	43	.900	.898
		3B	55	96	129	25	10	.900	.879
1895	CHI	SS	129	281	527	86	70	.904	.899
		OF	1	1	0	0	0	1.000	.917
1896	CHI	SS	125	310	456	71	66	.915	.903
1897	CHI	SS	75	215	291	38	48	.930	.908
1898	CHI	SS	142	369	511	76	77	.921	.913
1899	BKL	SS	110	256	377	40	48	.941	.910
		3B	11	19	41	2	5	.968	.903
1900	BKL	SS	133	321	517	55	59	.938	.922
1901	BKL	SS	129	301	450	57	49	.929	.925
		2B	2	3	7	0	0	1.000	.941
1902	BKL	SS	138	278	440	66	34	.916	.913
1903	BKL	SS	138	296	477	42	48	.948	.911

Year			G	PO	A	E	DP	PCT	LGPCT
1904	NY	SS	145	316	494	61	61	.930	.920
1905	NY	SS	147	313	501	45	58	.948	.931
		OF	1	1	0	0	0	1.000	.955
1906	NY	SS	143	287	454	49	36	.938	.933
1907	NY	SS	143	292	426	45	39	.941	.932
1908	BOS	SS	144	291	553	43	58	.952	.930
1909	BOS	SS	49	101	184	29	20	.908	.926
		2B	6	14	11	3	1	.893	.938
		3B	2	4	5	0	0	1.000	.930
1911	BKL	SS	1	2	5	0	1	1.000	.925
Total		SS	2133	4856	7505	975	881	.927	.916
		3B	223	355	580	89	42	.913	.882
		OF	58	101	9	8	5	.932	.913
		2B	19	47	44	8	2	.919	.935

Notes

INTRODUCTION

1. Although Dahlen's active career ended in 1909, he did appear in three games in 1910 and one in 1911 while managing Brooklyn.

2. Dahlen played 2,133 of his 2,444 major-league games at shortstop.

3. *Reach's Official 1924 Baseball Guide.*

ONE: FROM NELLISTON TO CHICAGO

1. From an address by Ambassador Sean G. Ronan to the German-Irish Society at the House of the Rhineland-Palatinate Representation in Bonn, February 8, 1973.

2. From "The Revolution of 1848" Website, administered by Professor Gerhard Rempel of Western New England College.

3. Washington Frothingham, *History of Montgomery County, New York* (Nelliston, NY: Nelliston Community Group, 1978) p. 174.

4. Ibid.

5. Ruth V. Lupo, *Waymarks In Nelliston, New York* (Nelliston, NY: Nelliston Community Group, 1978) p. 152.

6. Ibid.

7. From an oral interview with Terry Collins conducted by Kathryn McGowan for the Mohawk Valley Library Association's "I Spy" project.

8. *Sporting News*, January 16, 1943.

9. Almost all the good young players that made their way to Chicago were not discovered directly by Anson. He had a network of friends and former teammates all over the country who would find promising young players and send them to him.

10. Chicago's population had doubled in the past 10 years to over a million, allowing it to pass Brooklyn and Philadelphia and now trail only New York City.

11. *Brooklyn Daily Eagle*, July 30, 1896.

TWO: THE BEST YOUNG PLAYER IN THE GAME

1. More than a century and a quarter later, Chicago is the only one whose membership has remained continuous.

2. Dubbed Anson's "Colts" in 1890 because of all the young players he had recruited, that name was quickly replacing White Stockings as the team's nickname.

3. Hutchison remains the only pitcher to lead his league in wins for three consecutive seasons and not be elected to the Hall of Fame.

4. *Chicago Tribune*, April 23, 1891.

5. *Chicago Tribune*, April 26, 1891.

6. *Sporting News*, May 16, 1891.

7. *Chicago Inter Ocean*, June 8, 1891.

8. *Chicago Inter Ocean*, June 6, 1891.

9. *Chicago Inter Ocean*, July 29, 1891.

10. *Chicago Tribune*, September 16, 1891.

11. *New York Evening Telegram*, September 30, 1891.

12. *Chicago Tribune*, November 12, 1891.

13. Day was allowed to be present at the entire meeting, while Hart was allowed in only to testify.

14. For a full discussion of Boston's winning streak and the controversy it engendered, see Robert L. Tiemann's "The Forgotten Winning Streak of 1891" in the 1989 *Baseball Research Journal*, pp. 2–5.

15. All of Dahlen's rookie records for Chicago have since been broken.

16. *Sporting News*, March 14, 1896.

17. *Sporting Life*, September 24, 1904.

18. *Leslie's Illustrated Weekly*, March 18, 1915.

19. *Sporting News*, October 17, 1896.

20. The Players League disbanded in January 1891 after just one season.

21. The other eliminated American Association franchises were Boston, Cincinnati, Columbus (OH), and Philadelphia.

22. *Mohawk Valley Register*, October 23, 1891.

23. *Sporting News*, October 31, 1891.

24. Defined as the sum of a player's adjusted batting runs, fielding runs, and base stealing runs, minus his positional adjustment, all divided by the runs per win factor for that year.

25. *New York Clipper*, January 28, 1893.

THREE: A RECORD-BREAKING HITTING STREAK

1. Robert L Tiemann, "The National League in 1893," *Baseball Research Journal*, 1993, p. 18.

2. *Reach's Official 1893 Base Ball Guide.*

3. Al Kermisch "Researcher's Notebook Unravels More Mysteries" *Baseball Research Journal*, 1986, pp. 32–33.

4. According to Chicago baseball historian Edward Hartig, Spalding, ever the businessman, realized that playing on his own property made more sense than leasing. So in 1894 he moved all the team's games to the West Side Grounds where they played until 1915. The move left the city's south side without a ball club, opening the way for the American League to fill the void in 1901.

5. *Nineteenth Century Stars*, p.74.

6. *Brooklyn Daily Eagle*, June 4, 1893.

7. *Sporting Life*, September 16, 1893.

8. *Louisville Courier-Journal*, July 23, 1978.

9. *Sporting News*, December 31, 1892.

10. *Sporting Life*, June 24, 1893.

11. *Sporting News*, November 25, 1893.

12. On August 6, a week after the Louisville incident, Ryan was involved in a near-fatal accident. He was seriously injured and three people were killed in a train wreck at Toledo, as the team traveled from Cleveland to Louisville. The injury was severe enough to force him to miss the last seven weeks of the season.

13. Curiously, the only team to make a southern swing this year was the Baltimore Orioles, who won their first three regular season games and the pennant.

14. David Voight, "1894!" *Baseball Research Journal*, 1994, p. 82.

15. Two American Leaguers have done it since: Mel Almada of Washington in 1937 and Mark McGwire of Oakland in 1987.

16. *Sporting News*, May 19, 1894.

17. *Brooklyn Daily Eagle*, May 9, 1894.

18. The *Chicago Tribune* explained that the reason for the barbed wire fence, which management claimed was "horse high," "pig tight," and bull strong," was to keep the fans from attacking the umpires, thereby causing the home team to lose by forfeit.

19. *Reach's Official 1895 Base Ball Guide*, p. 82.

20. *Chicago Tribune*, August 6, 1894.

21. Chicago baseball historian Edward Hartig says that while several sources claim the Colts moved their games to South Side Park at 35th and Wentworth he is sure they continued to play their games at West Side Park. He says the day after the fire the *Chicago Tribune* mentioned that the game was being played despite a section of the stands being closed due to the fire. Similar references were made several more times over the next week, along with references to the cleanup, fans being able to see the progress of the renovation, etc.

22. *Chicago Inter Ocean*, August 8, 1894.

23. *Total Baseball* rated three pitchers ahead of Dahlen: Amos Rusie and Jouett Meekin of New York and Cy Young of Cleveland.

24. The measure of runs saved *beyond* what a league-average player at that position might have saved, a number which is defined as zero.

FOUR: "A DISORDERLY ELEMENT,"
BUT ANOTHER MARVELOUS SEASON

1. *Sporting News*, December 9, 1909.

2. In May 1896, Pfeffer came back to the Colts after being released by the Giants. He batted only .244, and the Colts finished fifth.

3. *Sporting News*, March 9, 1895.

4. Burt Solomon, *The Baseball Timeline* (New York: Avon Books, 1997), p. 83.

5. Bill James, *The New Bill James Historical Abstract* (New York: Free Press, 2003), p. 52.

6. Everitt's .358 average is still the team record for a rookie.

7. *Sporting Life*, June 22, 1895.

8. Camp, who'd pitched in three games for the 1894 Colts, died in March 1895 at age 25.

9. Mark Armour. "Jiggs Parrott." Biography Project of the Society for American Baseball Research. www.sabr.org

10. *Leslie's Illustrated Weekly*, April 1, 1909.

11. The 1894 Colts lost their first six games and 11 of their first 13.

12. *Total Baseball* rated him the fourth best position player in the league in 1896, as compared to the best in 1894.

13. His 19 triples tied his own club record set in 1892 and since broken.

14. On Chicago's last visit to Washington, Dahlen's fans there presented him a walking stick.

15. *Sporting News*, October 3, 1896.

16. *Brooklyn Daily Eagle*, October 2, 1896.

17. *Chicago Tribune*, September 30, 1896.

18. *Brooklyn Daily Eagle*, October 2, 1896.

19. *Sporting Life*, October 31, 1896.

FIVE: THE CAPTAIN BECOMES EXPENDABLE

1. Meanwhile, Willie Keeler of Baltimore was compiling a 44-game streak dating from opening day. That broke Dahlen's record consecutive-game hitting streak of 42, set just three years earlier. Unlike Dahlen's midseason streak, which received almost no notice, Keeler's streak drew some.

2. *Sporting Life*, May 15, 1897.

3. *Sporting Life*, March 20, 1897.

4. *Chicago Tribune*, May 31, 1897.

5. Dahlen played at Boston on June 17, a 19–7 loss in which he went hitless in five at-bats.

6. This was the last season in which the official scorer had the option to credit a player with a stolen base in such a situation.

7. Cubs researcher Edward Hartig says that during this time each newspaper would use its own nickname for the club. Among those used in addition to Orphans and Colts were Ex-Colts, Rainmakers, Cowboys, Rough Riders, Remnants, Recruits, Panamas, and Zephyrs. Although the name Cubs first appeared in a *Chicago Daily News* article in late March 1902, Colts was still the preferred name for most of the papers. The team was also called the Nationals (1905–07) and the Spuds (1906). Prior to the 1907 season, manager Frank Chance made it known that he liked Cubs. Owner Charles Murphy approved and the nickname became official.

8. *Sporting News*, March 8, 1980.

9. *Sporting Life*, December 11, 1897.

10. When manager Tom Burns was asked to pick a name for the team to replace the Colts, he chose the Maroons.

11. Pretzel was a nickname attached to many players of German descent in these years.

12. This would be John Heydler's only season as an umpire, but two decades later he would become the president of the National League.

13. *Brooklyn Daily Eagle*, June 3, 1898.

14. Brooklyn team president Charles Ebbets had replaced Billy Barnie with Griffin, but after four games he took over the managerial duties himself.

15. *Sporting News*, May 7, 1898.

16. *Sporting News*, July 16, 1898.

17. *Sporting News*, July 2, 1898.

18. Attendance figures are from *Nineteenth Century Major League Attendance*, a monograph by Robert L. Tiemann.

19. *Sporting Life*, September 24, 1898.

20. *Sporting Life*, December 10, 1898.

21. *Sporting Life*, December 17, 1898.

Six: A Trade to
Brooklyn Brings a Championship

1. *Brooklyn Daily Eagle*, January 23, 1899.
2. *Sporting News*, January 7, 1899.
3. *Chicago Tribune*, January 23, 1899.
4. *Chicago Tribune*, January 24, 1899.
5. *Chicago Tribune*, January 26, 1899.
6. *Sporting News*, February 4, 1899.
7. *New York Times*, January 29, 1899.
8. *Chicago Tribune*, January 26, 1899.
9. *Chicago Tribune*, January 23, 1899.
10. *Ibid.*
11. *Baltimore Sun,* January 26, 1899.
12. *Chicago Tribune*, January 23, 1899.
13. Mark Armour and Daniel Levitt devote a chapter to the building, success, and tribulations of the 1899 Superbas in their book, *Paths of Glory* (New York: Brasseys, 2003).
14. *Brooklyn Daily Eagle*, February 12, 1899.
15. Ruth V. Lupo, *Waymarks In Nelliston, New York* (Nelliston, NY: Nelliston Community Group, 1978) pp. 81–82.
16. Philip J. Lowry, *Green Cathedrals* (Manhattan, KS: Ag Press, 1986) pp. 39–40.
17. *Brooklyn Daily Eagle*, April 16, 1899.
18. *Brooklyn Daily Eagle*, April 18, 1899.
19. *Brooklyn Daily Eagle*, June 10, 1899. John C. Heenan, a native of Troy, NY, was generally recognized as the heavyweight champion circa 1860.
20. It was actually 92 of 99 victories, as two of the wins were by forfeit.
21. Andy McCue, "A History of Dodger Ownership," *The National Pastime*, 1993, p. 37.
22. The Superbas' home record in 1899 was 61–16.
23. *Sporting Life*, October 28, 1899.
24. *Sporting Life*, May 5, 1900.

Seven: One of the
Great Teams of All Time

1. *Brooklyn Eagle*, April 20, 1900.
2. *Sporting Life*, April 21, 1900.
3. *Brooklyn Daily Eagle*, April 28, 1900.
4. *Sporting Life*, July 21, 1900.
5. James, *The Politics of Glory*, (New York: Macmillan, 1994), p. 244.
6. *Brooklyn Daily Eagle*, May 5, 1900.
7. *Brooklyn Daily Eagle*, September 23, 1900.
8. *Sporting Life*, August 11, 1900.
9. *New York Times*, July 17, 1900.
10. *Brooklyn Daily Eagle*, October 10, 1900.
11. *Sporting Life*, June 30, 1900.
12. *Ibid.*
13. *Ibid.*
14. *Ibid.*

15. The measure of runs saved *beyond* what a league-average player at that position might have saved, a number which is defined as zero.

16. *Sporting Life*, November 17, 1900.

17. A rumor had it that the whole incident was staged by Cap Anson and the other Chicago players as a practical joke on Dahlen.

18. *Brooklyn Daily Eagle*, May 27, 1900.

19. *Brooklyn Daily Eagle*, May 27, 1900.

20. *Sporting Life*, October 13, 1900.

21. B. B. C. stood for Brooklyn Baseball Club. In 1900, baseball was still considered to be two words.

22. *Brooklyn Daily Eagle*, October 29, 1900.

23. *Sporting Life*, November 10, 1900.

24. *Sporting Life*, December 8, 1900.

25. *Sporting Life*, December 8, 1900.

26. *Sporting Life*, December 8, 1900.

27. *Sporting Life*, December 8, 1900.

28. *Sporting Life*, December 8, 1900.

29. *Sporting Life*, December 15, 1900.

30. *Sporting Life*, December 15, 1900.

EIGHT: THE AMERICAN LEAGUE COMES CALLING

1. Among his teammates, Dahlen was also often referred to as "Rube the Ranger," because of his rural roots.

2. The American League adopted the foul-strike rule in 1903.

3. *Brooklyn Daily Eagle*, April 27, 1901.

4. *Brooklyn Daily Eagle*, May 2, 1901.

5. *Brooklyn Daily Eagle*, May 3, 1901.

6. *Brooklyn Daily Eagle*, June 20, 1901.

7. For the full details of this game, see pp. 23–24 of Joseph J. Dittmar's *Baseball Records Registry* (Jefferson, NC: McFarland & Company, 1997).

8. *New York Times*, May 14, 1901.

9. *Sporting Life*, September 21, 1901.

10. Pittsburgh's reputation as the league city where the most betting took place suffered this season. The Pirates lost so infrequently that betting on their games decreased sharply.

11. The largest since the advent of division play is Cleveland's 1995 30-game margin over Kansas City in the American League Central Division.

12. Warren McLaughlin won the other three, the only three wins of his seven-game major-league career.

13. Chesbro was 6–0 vs Brooklyn including three straight shutouts.

14. Bill Duggleby was one of five Philadelphia Phillies players who had jumped to the American League, but whose contracts were nullified in April 1902 by a ruling of the Pennsylvania Supreme Court. Duggleby had returned to the Phillies after just two games with the Philadelphia Athletics.

15. *Brooklyn Daily Eagle*, August 16, 1901.

16. *Ibid.*

17. *Brooklyn Daily Eagle*, October 8, 1901.

18. Hanlon, who lived in Baltimore, would have preferred to move the team there.

19. *Sporting Life*, September 7, 1901.

20. *Ibid.*

21. *Sporting Life*, November 16, 1901.

22. *Brooklyn Daily Eagle*, May 19, 1901.

23. The Board of Discipline of the National Baseball League was set up in 1898. Its goal was to suppress rowdy ballplaying.

24. *Brooklyn Daily Eagle*, July 22, 1901.

25. *Sporting Life*, October 25, 1901.

26. *Sporting News*, October 18, 1902.

27. Attendance fell from 234,937 in 1901 to 112,066 in 1902 in Philadelphia, and from 379,988 in 1901 to 226,417 in 1902 in St. Louis.

28. Mark Armour and Daniel Levitt, *Paths of Glory* (New York: Brasseys, 2003), p. 20.

NINE: "IT HAS ALWAYS BEEN MY AMBITION TO PLAY IN NEW YORK CITY"

1. *Sporting Life*, June 28, 1902.

2. *Sporting Life*, July 5, 1902.

3. John Devaney, *Sport Magazine*, October 1963.

4. *Sporting Life*, July 5, 1902.

5. *Sporting News*, February 10, 1910.

6. *Sporting News*, May 30, 1903.

7. *Sporting News*, June 6, 1903.

8. *Sporting Life*, June 13, 1903.

9. By midseason, the club's scrappy play brought the fans back and final attendance would be up by 25,000 over 1902.

10. Chesbro's record would last only until 1908, when Chicago's Ed Reulbach broke it by pitching 44 consecutive scoreless innings.

11. *Sporting Life*, January 16, 1936.

12. *Brooklyn Daily Eagle*, December 14, 1903.

13. John J. McGraw, *My Thirty Years in Baseball* (New York: Boni and Livingston, 1923).

14. Noel Hynd, *The Giants of the Polo Grounds* (New York: Doubleday, 1988), p. 122.

15. *New York World*, December 14, 1903.

16. *Brooklyn Daily Eagle*, December 15, 1903.

17. *New York Times*, December 14, 1903.

18. Curiously, when the Giants tried to trade for Dahlen to play shortstop following the 1893 season George Davis was already on the team as a third baseman. His switch to shortstop would not come until 1897.

19. For more detail, see Bill Lamb's comparison of Dahlen's and Davis's offensive statistics in the 1999 *Baseball Research Journal*, p. 61.

20. McGraw thought he had both Elberfeld and Ed Delahanty signed to play for the Giants in 1903 but lost them both to the American League as part of the peace agreement.

21. Hynd, *The Giants of the Polo Grounds*, p. 122.

22. *Brooklyn Daily Eagle*, December 23, 1903.

TEN: THE MOST HATED TEAM IN BASEBALL

1. On October 7, a day before the season ended, the 1904 champion Giants played an exhibition game against the champion Giants of 1889. In a contest marked more by clowning than serious play, the current champions won, 10–8.

2. *New York Times*, April 3, 1904.

3. *Sporting Life*, April 2, 1904.

4. *New York Times*, April 22, 1904.

5. The American League adopted the rule in 1903 as part of the general peace agreement. The AL's batting average, which was .277 in 1901 and .275 in 1902, was just .256 in 1903.

6. *Sporting Life*, August 6, 1904.

7. *Sporting Life* said that the name Giants was not a misnomer for this year's club, which averaged 5'10½" and 171 pounds.

8. The modern term "World Series," without the apostrophe "s" after "World," did not come into general use until the 1930s.

9. Shortly after McGraw's announcement, Chicago Cubs president Jim Hart announced that should his team win the pennant, they too would refuse to play against the American League in a World's Series.

10. Hynd, *The Giants of the Polo Grounds*, pp. 125–126.

11. David Hinckley, "Whip Hand: John McGraw and the Series That Wasn't, 1904", *New York Daily News*, May 30, 2003.

12. Ibid.

13. Ibid.

14. *Sporting Life*, September 24, 1904.

15. The Giants were 20–2 against Boston, 19–3 against Brooklyn, and 17–4 against Philadelphia.

16. The schedule had increased to 154 games this year.

17. *Total Baseball's* total player rating for the National League in 1904 rates Wagner first, with a 4.9, followed by Roy Thomas of Philadelphia, Tommy Leach of Pittsburgh, and Frank Chance of Chicago, and then Dahlen with a 3.4.

Eleven: From "Bad Bill" to "Bill the Wizard"

1. *Sporting Life*, August 6, 1904.

2. The Giants had a total of 11 errors in this game, including six by third baseman Art Devlin.

3. Exactly four weeks later, Jeffries retired undefeated. He would come back in 1910 to fight then heavyweight champion Jack Johnson, who knocked him out in the 15th round.

4. *Sporting Life*, May 20, 1905.

5. Christy Mathewson was in the midst of a major league record 24 consecutive wins against St. Louis.

6. *New York Times*, May 12, 1905.

7. *Sporting Life*, July 8, 1905.

8. *Sporting Life*, November 11, 1905.

9. *New York Times*, July 15, 1905.

10. *New York Times*, July 20, 1905.

11. Dennis DeValeria and Jeanne Burke DeValeria, *Honus Wagner: A Biography* (Pittsburgh: University of Pittsburgh Press, 1998), pp. 154–155.

12. For a pitcher to win the Triple Crown requires that he lead the league in wins, strikeouts, and earned run average. But earned run averages for pitchers did not become an official statistic in the National League until 1912 and in the American League until

1913. Thus Mathewson and Waddell were not recognized as Triple Crown winners in 1905.

13. There were rumors that gamblers had paid Waddell to fake the injury, but there has never been any proof of these charges.

14. *New York Times*, October 17, 1905.

15. Philadelphia's .161 batting average in the 1905 World's Series remained the major league record-low for 60 years. The Los Angeles Dodgers broke that record when they batted .142 against the Baltimore Orioles in the 1966 World Series. Three years later, in 1969, the Orioles broke Philadelphia's American League record, by batting .146 against the New York Mets.

TWELVE: THE GIANTS FADE AND SO DOES DAHLEN

1. All betting at American racetracks was done with bookmakers until 1933, when the first pari-mutuel machines were introduced at Arlington Park in suburban Chicago.

2. The Cubs' 116 wins (116–36) came in a 154–game schedule. The only team to win 116 games since was the 2001 Seattle Mariners. Seattle was 116–46 in a 162-game schedule.

3. The June 23, 1906, *Sporting Life* article describing this event surmised that the Irish flags were there to honor those Giants of Irish descent. Among them, they believed, was Dahlen, who of course was German, not Irish.

4. Quoted by Joe Vila in the October 13, 1906, *Sporting News*.

5. It was the second time Dahlen had fallen for the hidden ball trick. Chicago's Charlie Dexter had victimized him on May 13, 1902, when he was with Brooklyn.

6. Dahlen was fourth in the league in walks and seventh in being hit by pitches.

7. Hynd, *The Giants of the Polo Grounds*, p. 142.

8. *New York Times*, April 12, 1907.

9. *Sporting News*, May 4, 1907.

10. *New York Times*, August 22, 1907.

THIRTEEN: BANISHED TO BOSTON

1. While the *New York Press* and *New York Times* reported the choice was between Dahlen and Hannifin, the Boston *Globe* said it was between Hannifin and pitcher Ferguson.

2. John Ganzel got the job as Reds manager.

3. *Sporting Life*, March 14, 1908.

4. *Boston Globe*, June 6, 1908.

5. *Sporting Life*, June 20, 1908.

6. *Sporting Life*, November 28, 1908.

7. *Ibid.*

8. *Sporting Life*, December 5, 1908.

9. *Sporting News*, December 10, 1908.

10. Sandy Cronkhite, a Fort Plain-Nelliston historian, says her mother told her stories of how Dahlen would return to the area at the end of each season with baseballs for the local children.

11. *New York World*, December 12, 1909.

FOURTEEN: MANAGING THE DODGERS

1. *Sporting Life*, June 18, 1910.
2. *Sporting Life*, June 11, 1910.
3. *Brooklyn Daily Eagle*, July 12, 1910.
4. *Leslie's Illustrated Weekly*, September 8, 1910.
5. *Sporting Life*, September 3, 1910.
6. *Sporting Life*, October 22, 1910.
7. *Sporting Life*, October 15, 1910.
8. *Sporting Life*, January 14, 1911.
9. *Ibid.*
10. *Sporting Life*, February 18, 1911.
11. *Ibid.*
12. The Dodgers scored a total of 10 runs in those six losses.
13. *Brooklyn Daily Eagle*, June 14, 1911.
14. This game also was the second and final major league appearance for Charles "Victory" Faust. John McGraw used the tragicomic Faust to pitch the ninth, the final inning of the season.

FIFTEEN: BUILDING A
CONTENDER—FOR SOMEONE ELSE

1. William "Doc" Scanlan took up the full-time practice of medicine and never played for Philadelphia.
2. In 1912, the Eastern League changed its name to the International League.
3. *Brooklyn Daily Eagle*, April 21, 1912.
4. *Ibid.*
5. *Ibid.*
6. *New York Times*, April 21, 1912.
7. *Brooklyn Daily Eagle*, April 24, 1912.
8. In Rube Marquard's next outing, he lost to the Cubs, 7–2, ending the streak at 19.
9. The Cardinals kept Miller Huggins and made him their player/manager in 1913, replacing Roger Bresnahan.
10. *Sporting Life*, November 9, 1912.
11. *Sporting Life*, January 11, 1913.
12. Stewart Wolpin, *Bums No More!* (New York: Harkavy Press and St. Martin's Press, 1995) p.8.
13. Lowry, *Green Cathedrals*, p. 11.
14. *Sporting Life*, January 11, 1913.

SIXTEEN: THE END OF THE LINE

1. *Brooklyn Daily Eagle*, November 17, 1913.
2. Toledo moved to Cleveland for the 1914 season.
3. *Brooklyn Daily Eagle*, March 21, 1914.
4. From a May 6, 1937, Philadelphia Phillies news release.
5. *Sporting News*, October 8, 1936.
6. *Ibid.*
7. *Sporting News*, January 14, 1943.

8. *Ibid.*
9. *Ibid.*

SEVENTEEN: FROM
NELLISTON TO COOPERSTOWN

1. *Brockton* (MA) *Times*, April 3, 1912.
2. Bob Carroll, "For The Hall of Fame: Twelve Good Men," in *The National Pastime*, 1985, pp. 14–27.

Selected Bibliography

Ahrens, Art. "The Daily Dahlen of 1894," *Baseball Research Journal* (1975), pp. 57–60.

Allen, Oliver E. *New York, New York*. New York: Macmillan, 1990.

Alexander, Charles C. *John McGraw*. New York: Penguin, 1988.

_____. *Our Game — An American Baseball History*. New York: Henry Holt, 1991.

Barth, Gunther. *City People*. New York: Oxford University Press, 1980.

Bjarkman, Peter, ed. *Encyclopedia of Major League Baseball Team Histories*. Westport, CT: Meckler Publishing, 1991.

Carroll, Bob. "For the Hall of Fame: Twelve Good Men," *The National Pastime* (1985), pp. 14–27

Charlton, James. *The Baseball Chronology*. New York: Macmillan, 1991.

Dewey, Donald, and Nicholas Acocella. *The Ball Clubs*. New York: HarperCollins, 1996.

DeValeria, Dennis, and Jeanne Burke DeValeria. *Honus Wagner: A Biography*. Pittsburgh: University of Pittsburgh Press, 1998.

Frommer, Harvey. *New York City Baseball*. New York: Macmillan, 1980

Gershman, Michael. *Diamonds*. New York: Houghton Mifflin Company, 1993.

Honig, Donald. *Baseball America*. New York: Macmillan, 1985.

Hynd, Noel. *The Giants of the Polo Grounds*. New York: Doubleday, 1988.

James, Bill. *The New Bill James Historical Baseball Abstract*. New York: Free Press, 2003.

_____. *The Politics of Glory*. New York: Macmillan, 1994.

James, Bill, and Jim Henzler. *Win Shares*. Morton Grove, IL: STATS Inc. Publishing, 2002.

Kermisch, Al. "Researcher's Notebook Unravels More Mysteries," *Baseball Research Journal* (1986), pp. 32–33.

Koppett, Leonard. *The Man in the Dugout*. Philadelphia: Temple University Press, 2000.

Leib, Fred. *Baseball As I Have Known It*. New York: Coward, McCann & Geoghegan, 1977.

Levine, Peter. *A. G. Spalding and the Rise of Baseball*. New York: Oxford University Press, 1985.

Light, Jonathan F. *The Cultural Encyclopedia of Baseball*. Jefferson, NC: McFarland, 1997.

Lowry, Philip J. *Green Cathedrals*. Manhattan, KS: Ag Press, 1986.

McGraw, John J. *My Thirty Years in Baseball*. New York: Boni and Livingston, 1923.

Neft, David S., Richard M. Cohen, and Michael L. Neft. *The Sports Encyclopedia: Baseball, 21st Edition*. New York: St. Martin's Press, 2001.

Nemec, David. *The Great Encyclopedia of 19th Century Major League Baseball*. New York: Donald I. Fine Books, 1997.

_____. *The Great Book of Baseball Knowledge*. Chicago: Masters, 1999.

Okkonen, Marc. *Baseball Uniforms of the 20th Century*. New York: Sterling, 1991.

Okrent, Daniel, and Harris Lewine, ed. *The Ultimate Baseball Book*. Boston: Houghton Mifflin, 1979.

Koppett, Leonard. *The Man in the Dugout*. Philadelphia: Temple University Press, 2000.

Rice, Damon. *Seasons Past*. New York: Praeger, 1976.

Ritter, Lawrence S. *The Glory of Their Times*. New York: Macmillan, 1966.

Robinson, Ray. *Matty: An American Hero*. New York: Oxford University Press, 1993.

Seymour, Harold. *Baseball: The Early Years*. New York: Oxford University Press, 1960.

_____. *Baseball: The Golden Age*. New York: Oxford University Press, 1971.

Shatzkin, Mike. *The Ballplayers*. New York: William Morrow, 1990.

Snyder-Grenier, Ellen M. *Brooklyn!: An Illustrated History (Critical Perspectives on the Past)*. Brooklyn: Brooklyn Historical Society, 1996.

Solomon, Burt. *Where They Ain't*. New York: Free Press, 1999

Sowell, Mike. *July 2, 1903*. New York: Macmillan, 1992.

Stark, Benton. *The Year They Called Off the World Series: A True Story*. Garden City Park, New York: Avery, 1991.

Tiemann, Robert L. *Dodger Classics*. St. Louis: Baseball Histories, Inc., 1983.

_____. "The Forgotten Winning Streak of 1891," *Baseball Research Journal* (1989), pp. 2–5.

_____. "The National League in 1893," *Baseball Research Journal* (1993), p. 18.

Tiemann, Robert L., and Mark Rucker, eds. *Nineteenth Century Stars*. Kansas City: The Society for American Baseball Research, 1989.

Thorn, John, Pete Palmer, and Michael Gershman, eds. *Total Baseball*. *7th ed.* Kingston, New York: Total Sports Publishing, 2001.

Voight, David. "1894!" *Baseball Research Journal* (1994), p. 82.

Ward, Geoffrey C., and Ken Burns. *Baseball: An Illustrated History*. New York: Alfred A. Knopf, 1994

Wolpin, Stewart. *Bums No More!: The Championship Season of the 1955 Brooklyn Dodgers*. New York: Harkavy and St. Martin's, 1995.

NEWSPAPERS

Boston Globe

Boston Herald

Boston Post

Chicago Inter Ocean

Chicago Tribune

New York American

New York Daily News

New York Herald

New York Herald Tribune

New York Journal American

New York Post

New York Press

New York Sun

New York Times

New York Tribune

New York World

New York World Telegram

Philadelphia Bulletin

Philadelphia Inquirer

Philadelphia Press

Sporting Life

Sporting News

Index

Abbey, Bert 34, 37
Abell, Ferdinand 60, 109
Aitchison, Raleigh 198
Allen, Frank 185, 195
Almada, Mel 223n
Ames, Leon "Red" 145, 151 157, 164
Anson, Adrian "Cap" 1, 6, 8–9, 12–16,
    18–20, 22, 24, 26–27, 29, 31, 33–35,
    37–48, 52–54, 58, 62, 71, 137, 141,
    155, 162, 170, 226n
Anson, Dorothy 137
Anson, Henry 54
Aparicio, Luis 2, 208, 212–216
Appling, Luke 212–16
Ashburn, Richie 1, 208

Babb, Charlie 119–20, 125–26
Bancroft, Dave 212–16
Banks, Ernie 212–16
Barclay, George 107
Barger, Cy 172–74, 177, 179, 181, 186
Barnie, Billy 51, 94, 224n
Barry, Shad 88
Bartels, Harriet 205
Barton, Clara 5
Bates, Johnny 168
Battin, Joe 6
Bausewine, George 143
Beaumont, Ginger 100, 140
Beckley, Jake 97, 209–11
Belanger, Mark 207
Bell, George 172–74, 177–78, 181
Bender, Albert "Chief" 145–47
Bernhard, Bill 79
Bergen, Bill 172, 182, 185
Boudreau, Lou 212–16

Bowerman, Frank 49, 127, 130–31, 136,
    154, 160–61, 164, 166, 168
Brain, Dave 161–62
Bransfield, Kitty 100
Brashear, Roy 107
Brennan, Ad 195
Brennan, Bill 180–81, 190–91
Bresnahan, Roger 125, 144, 147–48, 151,
    155, 157–58, 160, 167, 192–93, 200,
    230n
Bridwell, Al 160–62, 164
Briggs, Button 43–44, 48
Brodie, Steve 65
Bronkie, Herman 201
Brouthers, Dan 22
Brown, Buster 168
Brown, Mordecai "Three Finger" 127,
    129, 139, 151, 153, 164
Browne, George 108, 128, 154, 160–61,
    164
Brush, John T. 107, 132–34, 144–45,
    147, 152, 179
Burch, Al 172, 175, 179, 183
Burk, Sandy 183
Burkett, Jesse 65, 101, 103, 209–11
Burns, Tom 10, 14, 53–54, 57–59,
    61–64, 155, 224n
Byrne, Charles 52, 64, 66
Byrne, William G. 117

Callahan, Jimmy 48–50, 57, 88–89
Camnitz, Howie 177
Camp, Kid 38, 223n
Canavan, Jimmy 19–20
Carrick, Bill 74, 76–77
Carroll, Cliff 19, 155

Casey, Doc 67, 73
Cassidy, Pete 67
Cepeda, Orlando 1
Chance, Frank 53, 58, 99, 150–51, 180, 192–94, 224n, 228n
Chase, Hal 172, 176–77, 185
Chesbro, Jack 83, 100–1, 115–16, 132, 226n, 227n
Clark, G. W. 35–36
Clarke, Fred 68, 78, 83, 87, 99–100, 116, 119, 131, 143, 152, 177, 185, 209–11
Clarkson, John 14, 30, 156
Clemente, Roberto 207
Cleveland, Grover 5
Clymer, Otis 142
Coakley, Andy 145–46, 157
Cobb, Ty 26
Coffey, Jack 168
Cohan, George M. 146
Cole, Lewis "King" 173
Collins, Bill 198
Collins, Jimmy 66, 93
Comerford, Dan 177
Comiskey, Charles 94, 103, 188
Concepcion, Dave 207
Connolly, Tom 55–56, 76–77
Connor, Jim 49, 54, 58–59
Connor, Roger 7, 14
Conway, John 153
Cooney, Jimmy 11–12, 20, 155
Corbett, Jim 47, 69, 71, 146, 151
Corbett, Joe 47
Corcoran, Tommy 155
Corridon, Frank 157
Coulson, Bob 178, 181
Coveleski, Harry 164
Crane, Cannonball 7
Crane, Sam 7
Crawford, Sam 97
Cronin, Jack 119–20
Cronin, Joe 212–16
Cross, Lave 33, 76–77, 90, 93–94, 146–47, 193
Cross, Lem 32
Cross, Monte 146–47
Cunningham, Bert 50, 98–99
Cushman, Charlie 18
Cutshaw, George 191–92, 195, 197

Dahlen, Corrine 54, 106, 205
Dahlen, Daniel 3–5

Dahlen, Daniel, Jr. 4
Dahlen, Frank 4
Dahlen, Harry 4, 205
Dahlen, Jeanette (Hoglund) 123, 169, 177, 202, 205
Dahlen, William F. "Bill": American All-Stars 51, 52; American League offers 93, 102–4, 108, 112; baseball intelligence 15, 75–76, 95–96, 104, 115, 163, 170, 193; childhood 4–5; Chronicle Cup 81, 83–88, 93; at Clinton Liberal Institute 5–6; contracts and money 6, 18–19, 23, 43, 54, 57, 102–3, 108, 112, 114, 121, 155; in Cuba 88–90; death of 205; discovery of 6–7; education 5–6; evangelism 136; first marriage 106; Hall of Fame qualifications 1–2, 206–8; hitting streak 30–33; horse racing habit 12, 35, 44, 49, 53, 56–57, 103, 114, 116, 149–50, 159, 176; illnesses of 32–33, 56, 68, 97, 155; injuries to 34, 49–50, 57, 70, 104, 137; major league debut 9–10; mental attitude 11, 19–22, 27–28, 31, 33, 38–40, 43–48, 52–54, 56–58, 61–64, 82–83, 90, 96, 102, 108, 113, 115, 121, 139, 201, 207; in minor leagues 6–7; rumored trades 26–27, 40, 43–44, 46, 52, 57, 59, 71, 82, 165–67; second marriage 122–23; trades to Boston 160–61; trades to Brooklyn 61–62; trades to New York 118–21; umpire problems 55–56, 69–70, 75–76, 78–80, 98–99, 105–7, 117, 127, 130–31, 134, 141, 153, 159, 163, 175–76, 181–83, 186–91; World Series 147–48
Dahlen's season stats: *1891* 14–15; *1892* 22; *1893* 26; *1894* 29–30, 33; *1895* 37; *1896* 43; *1897* 51; *1898* 58; *1899* 70; *1900* 82; *1901* 97; *1902* 109; *1904* 135; *1905* 139; *1906* 146; *1907* 159; *1908* 165; *1909* 168
Dalton, Jack 172, 174, 178
Daly, Tom 70, 73, 75–76, 83, 88, 90–91, 99, 101
Daubert, Jake 172, 174–78, 181, 185, 188, 191–92, 195, 197–98, 200, 202
Davidson, Bill 171–72, 174, 179
Davis, George 2, 79, 82, 88, 101, 118, 121–22, 209–16, 227n
Davis, Harry 93, 144

Davis, Lefty 99–100
Day, John 7, 14, 222n
Decker, George 20, 31, 41, 43, 48, 50, 59, 68
Deery, Frankie 183
Delahanty, Ed 29, 33, 43, 59, 96, 101, 207, 209–11, 227n
DeMontreville, Gene 61–64, 72–73, 75, 83, 94–95
Dent, Eddie 186
Desseau, Rube 172
Deverey, Bill 111, 179
Devlin, Art 124, 126–28, 139–40, 142–43, 149–50, 153, 161, 228n
Devore, Josh 190
Dexter, Charlie 105–6, 229n
Dillon, Pop 131
DiMaggio, Joe 33, 204–5, 207
Dinneen, Bill 101
Doerr, Bobby 208
Doheny, Ed 100–1
Dolan, Albert "Cozy" 195
Dolan, Patrick "Cozy" 97, 107, 128
Donahue, Red 98, 101
Donahue, Tim 39, 43, 55, 59, 89, 141
Donlin, Mike 124, 138, 140–42, 144, 148–51, 154–56, 204
Donovan, Bill 83, 88, 97–98, 105, 109, 112, 121, 165, 193
Donovan, Patsy 117, 165, 167, 170
Dooin, Red 172
Dougherty, Patsy 131–32
Dovey, George 161–62, 164–68
Dovey, John 168
Doyle, Jack 52, 80, 88, 111–12, 114, 116, 161
Doyle, Larry 155
Dreyfuss, Barney 68, 78, 81–82, 84, 94, 101, 117, 119, 143
Drucke, Louis 183
Duffy, Hugh 9, 29–30, 209–11
Duggleby, Bill 101, 107–8, 129, 157, 226n
Dungan, Sam 21, 23
Dunn, Jack 68, 70, 72, 75–76, 83, 134
Duryea, Jesse 10
Dwyer, Frank 9, 31, 98, 103–4

Earp, Wyatt 47
Eason, Mal 153, 181

Ebbets, Charles 60, 64–66, 88, 91–92, 102–3, 109, 117, 121, 142, 165–70, 173–74, 176, 178–79, 184, 186, 188–89, 191–94, 197–203, 224n
Ebbets, Genevieve 193
Egan, Dick 175
Elberfeld, Kid 112, 122, 132, 227n
Ely, Fred 46, 99
Emslie, Bob 55, 70, 75, 105–6, 127, 139, 141, 143, 153
Erwin, Tex 172–74, 177, 183, 185, 188, 190, 198
Evans, Roy 114
Everitt, Bill 37–39, 43, 48, 55, 58, 64, 223n
Evers, Johnny 15, 58, 139, 150
Ewing, Buck 7, 88, 156
Ewing, John 14

Farrell, Duke 9, 16, 67–68, 73, 82–83, 86, 95
Farrell, Frank 111, 133–34, 152, 179
Farrell, John 106
Faust, Charles (Victory) 230n
Ferguson, Bob 8
Ferguson, Cecil 155, 160–61, 229n
Ferry, Jack 192
Finneran, Bill 182, 188
Fischer, Bill 185, 195, 197
Fisher, Chauncey 32
Fitzsimmons, Bob 47, 69
Flaherty, Patsy 157
Fletcher, Art 188, 190
Flick, Elmer 78, 101
Flood, Tim 101, 105, 115
Foster, Elmer 155
Foster, Pop 88
Fox, Nellie 1
Frary, Ralph 182–83
Fraser, Chick 42, 127, 129
Freedman, Andrew 35, 39, 111, 124
Freeman, Buck 93
Friend, Danny 42, 48
Frisbee, Charlie 75
Fullmer, Shorty 27
Fultz, Dave 131

Galvin, Jim 9–10, 16, 36
Ganzel, John 166, 169, 229n
Garvin, Ned 114
Gatins, Frank 94

Gaynor, William 186
Gehringer, Charlie 207
Gibson, George 143
Gilbert, Billy 125–26, 133–34, 142, 147,
    149–51, 153, 155, 203
Glasscock, Jack 22
Gleason, Kid 14, 59, 75, 88
Gochnauer, John 98, 112–13
Gore, George 7
Grady, Mike 80, 88–89
Graff, Louis 9
Griffin, Mike 56, 224n
Griffith, Clark 26, 29, 34, 36, 37, 39,
    43–44, 46–49, 55, 57, 93, 114, 131,
    158, 166
Groh, Heinie 187–89
Grout, Edward 71
Gumbert, Ad 9, 12, 16–17, 155

Hahn, Noodles 97, 108, 128
Hall, Russ 54
Hamilton, Billy 29, 33, 66, 209–11
Hanlon, Ned 9–10, 52, 57, 60–69,
    71–73, 75, 77, 81–84, 87–88, 91–92,
    94–97, 99–100, 102–109, 111–16,
    119–21, 125, 153, 161–62, 165, 170,
    226n
Hannifin, Jack 155, 161, 164, 229n
Harper, Jack 128
Harrison, Carter 28
Hart, James 13–16, 18–19, 26, 27, 32,
    34, 36, 40–41, 43, 44, 46, 53–57, 59,
    62–63, 103, 117, 207, 222n, 228n
Hartsel, Topsy 147
Hartzell, Albert 130
Hawley, Pink 79, 89
Hearne, Hughie 106
Hearst, William Randolph 7
Heenan, John C. 69, 225n
Hendrix, Claude 192,
Heydler, John 56, 224n
Herrmann, Garry 117, 151
Herzog, Buck 167, 187
Hess, Otto 196
Hickman, Charlie 88
Higgins, Bob 183
Hite, Mabel 155–56
Hoffer, Bill 49
Hoffman, Danny 147
Holliday, Bug 11, 15
Holmes, Ducky 65

Hopper, De Wolf 127, 151
Hopper, Mrs. De Wolf 127
Howell, Harry 65, 72, 86, 88–89, 94
Huggins, Miller 191, 230n
Hughes, Jim 64, 70, 72, 94, 98, 106–7,
    112
Hulbert, William 8, 208
Hull, Dr. Robert B. 123
Hulswitt, Rudy 108, 166, 201
Hummel, John 166–67, 172, 176, 178,
    180, 185, 191, 197, 201
Hunt, John 55
Hunter, George 171
Hunter, Newt 182
Hurst, Tim 49, 55, 79, 84
Hutchison, Bill 10, 12–13, 16, 21, 23–24,
    29, 37, 40–41, 155, 222n

Irwin, Charlie 31, 94, 103, 105, 109
Isbell, Frank 55

Jackson, Joe 26
Jackson, Reggie 207
Jackson, Travis 212–16
Jefferson, Thomas 130
Jeffries, Jim 69, 137, 228n
Jennings, Hugh 2, 52, 57, 59–62, 64,
    67–69, 73, 75–76, 79, 81, 83, 88,
    93–95, 99, 115, 126, 200, 207, 209–16
Johnson, Ban 63, 101, 111, 116, 131–33
Johnson, Jack 228n
Johnstone, Jim 134, 141, 153, 164
Jones, Fielder 73, 83, 93–94, 144, 152,
    193, 200
Jones, Oscar 114, 126
Jordan, Dutch 115
Jordan, Tim 172
Joyce, Bill 30

Keefe, Tim 7, 156, 190
Keeler, Willie 33, 52, 60, 64, 70, 72–73,
    75–76, 81, 83, 85–86, 88, 93, 95, 97,
    99, 102–4, 108–9, 111–12, 114–17, 121,
    123, 132–33, 149, 154–55, 169–71, 189,
    193, 204–5, 209–11, 224n
Kelley, Joe 42, 57, 59–61, 64, 70, 72–73,
    76, 79, 81, 83–86, 88, 91, 93, 95, 99,
    101–3, 117, 128, 154, 160–65, 193,
    209–11
Kennedy, Bill 66, 68, 70, 73–75, 91, 93,
    95, 97, 137

Kent, Maury 185, 190
Kitson, Frank 65, 72, 75, 85, 93, 98, 105, 112, 121, 193
Kittridge, Mal 16–18, 23, 34, 37, 39, 43, 68, 141, 155–56
Klem, Bill 141–42, 157, 159, 175–76, 186–87
Kling, Johnny 151, 169, 175
Knabe, Otto 195
Knell, Phil 36
Knetzer, Elmer 172, 181
Knowles, Fred 117, 147, 154

LaChance, Candy 65
Lajoie, Nap 78, 93, 208
Lake, Simon 5
Lange, Bill 25–26, 37–38, 40, 43, 47–49, 54–55, 57–59, 61–62
Latham, Arlie 189, 204
Lauder, Billy 126
Leach, Tommy 78, 82, 100, 141, 200, 228n
Leever, Sam 83, 85–86, 100–1
Leifield, Lefty 154, 162, 182
LeJeune, Larry 179
Lennox, Ed 172, 178
Lewis, Phil 165–66
Linares, Abel 89
Lindaman, Vive 148
Lobert, Hans 160, 195
Loftus, Tom 64, 112
Lombardi, Ernie 208
Long, Herman 30, 46–47, 51, 66
Lovett, Tom 30
Lowe, Bobby 30, 105
Luby, Pat 155–56
Lucid, Con 33
Lumley, Harry 140, 167–68, 170–71, 173
Lundgren, Carl 139, 151
Lynch, Thomas 181–82, 189

Mack, Connie 94, 100, 144–46, 154
Magee, Sherry 195
Magoon, George 65, 75
Maranville, Rabbit 2, 208, 212–16
Marquard, Rube 180, 186, 189–91, 197, 230n
Marshall, Doc 134, 153
Mason, George 91
Masterson, Bat 47
Mathewson, Christy 114, 124–29, 134,

138–39, 143–48, 150–51, 154–55, 157–59, 163–64, 203–4, 228n, 229n
Maul, Al 64
Maxwell, Bert 183
Mayer, Erskine 195
Mays, Willie 25
Mazeroski, Bill 1, 208
McAleer, Jimmy 154
McBride, Algie 41
McCann, Gene 96, 105
McCarthy, Tommy 206
McCarty, Lew 198
McClellan, George 137–38, 151
McCormick, Barry 43, 49–50
McCormick, Harry "Moose" 124
McCreery, Tom 42, 95, 100–1, 108, 111–12
McElveen, Pryor 176
McGann, Dan 64, 67, 101, 126, 130–31, 140–42, 144, 150–51, 154, 157, 160–61, 163, 165
McGill, Willie 24, 29
McGinnity, Joe 65, 72, 76, 79–80, 83, 85–86, 93–94, 103, 116, 124–26, 128–29, 134, 138, 145–47, 153–54, 157, 164, 167
McGraw, John 60–61, 64–66, 73, 77, 93–95, 102, 113–14, 116, 118–20, 124–27, 129–39, 142–47, 149–50, 152–55, 157–65, 167, 170, 179–80, 185, 188–89, 193, 196, 204, 207, 227n, 228n, 230n
McGuire, Deacon 67, 73, 83, 86, 93, 96, 98–99, 101
McGwire, Mark 223n
McIntire, Harry 162, 167, 171
McJames, Doc 64, 70, 72, 97
McKeever, Ed 184, 200
McKeever, Steve 184, 200
McKinley, William 42
McLaughlin, Warren 226n
McMillan, Tommy 171
McPhee, Bid 22, 208
McQuaid, Jack 14
McQuillan, George 172–73
Meekin, Jouett 30, 223n
Meneffe, Jock 105
Mercer, Win 75, 88
Merkle, Fred 164, 185–87, 203
Mertes, Sam 55, 58, 135, 140, 146, 150, 153

Meyer, Benny 195
Meyers, Chief 187–88
Miller, Otto 185, 191, 195, 198
Moran, Augie 117
Moran, Herbie 185
Moren, Lew 162
Moroney, Jim 162
Mowrey, Mike 166
Mullane, Tony 11, 14, 124–25
Murnane, Tim 26
Murphy, Charles 224n
Murphy, Danny 147
Murphy, Joe 10
Murray, Billy 157, 169, 172
Mutrie, Jim 7, 13

Nagle, Tom 155
Nahon, Abe 133
Needham, Tom 160–61
Newhouser, Hal 208
Newton, Doc 90, 97, 103, 105, 112
Nichols, Charles "Kid" 13, 17, 30, 66, 68, 98
Nops, Jerry 65, 72, 90
Northen, Hub 185, 191, 195

O'Brien, Tom 88
O'Connor, Jack 85–86
O'Day, Hank 50, 55, 69, 99, 146, 180–81
Odwell, Fred 130
O'Rourke, Jim 7, 30
Orth, Al 101
Overall, Orval 138

Parker, Harley "Doc" 97
Parrott, Jiggs 19–20, 23, 31, 38, 41
Parrott, Tom 32
Paskert, Dode 195
Peckinpaugh, Roger 2
Peitz, Heinie 27
Perez, Tony 1
Pfeffer, Fred 9, 12, 18–20, 31, 35, 41, 46, 59, 155, 223n
Pfiester, Jack 151
Phelps, Eddie 185
Phillippe, Deacon 78, 81, 83, 86, 100–1, 127
Plank, Eddie 145–46
Powell, Jack 101
Power, Charles 106

Powers, Pat 24
Pulliam, Harry 68, 99, 110, 117, 127, 130, 137, 143, 153, 159, 163, 168

Radbourn, Charley "Hoss" 14, 156
Ragan, Pat 183, 195
Raymond, Bugs 180–81
Reed, Walter 89
Reese, Dr. John "Bonesetter" 197
Reese, Pee Wee 118, 121, 212–16
Reilly, Josh 41
Reitz, Heinie 126
Reulbach, Ed 140, 151, 197–98, 202, 227n
Rhines, Billy 10
Rhoads, Bob 105
Richardson, Danny 7, 14
Rigler, Cy 163, 175, 187–90
Ritchey, Claude 68, 78, 100, 143
Ritchie, Lew 168
Rizzuto, Phil 121, 208, 212–16
Robinson, Wilbert 60, 64–65, 73, 188–89, 200–3
Robison, Frank 117
Rowan, Jack 173
Rucker, Nap 167, 172–74, 177–81, 185–87, 190–91, 193, 195, 197, 201
Rusie, Amos 11–12, 14, 223n
Russell, Lillian 19
Russell, W. Hepburn 179
Ryan, Jimmy 9, 21, 23, 28–30, 34, 37, 39, 43, 46, 48, 54–55, 58, 155, 223n
Ryan, Rosy 203

Scanlan, Doc 172, 180–82, 185, 230n
Schardt, Bill 178, 181–82, 186
Schmidt, Henry 114–15
Schriver, Pop 23, 82, 88–89
Schulte, Frank "Wildfire" 151
Seaton, Tom 195
Selbach, Kip 99
Selee, Frank 13, 66, 150
Seward, Ed 27
Sewell, Joe 212–16
Seybold, Socks 147
Seymour, Cy 69–70, 88, 128, 153–54, 157, 167
Shannon, Spike 153
Shay, Danny 134, 158
Shean, Dave 168
Sheckard, Jimmy 65, 72–73, 79, 81, 83,

88–89, 99, 101, 106, 108, 120, 122, 151
Shellhorne, Conrad 4–5
Shellhorne, John 4
Shellhorne, Rosina 4
Sheridan, Jack 62, 146
Shibe, Ben 154
Shindle, Billy 66
Simpson, Tommy 89, 95
Slagle, Jimmy 105, 151
Sloan, Tod 149
Smith, Billy 69
Smith, George 52
Smith, Happy 171
Smith, Harry 168, 198
Smith, James "Red" 185, 198
Smith, Ozzie 2, 207–8, 212–16
Smith, Tony 171–72, 174, 178
Smoot, Homer 107
Snodgrass, Fred 190
Snyder, Pop 78–79
Soden, Arthur 14
Spalding, Albert G. 8, 13, 15–16, 18, 25–26, 53, 222n
Spalding, J. Walter 26
Spink, Al 26
Stack, Eddie 185, 187, 197
Stahl, Jake 200
Stark, Dolly 188
Starr, Charlie 168
Stein, Ed 155
Steinfeldt, Harry 97, 150
Stengel, Casey 191–92, 195–98
Stevens, Harry 175
Stewart, Ace 38–39
Stivetts, Jack 30
Stovey, Harry 11
Strang, Sammy 99, 115–16, 131, 140, 154
Stratton, Scott 37
Sullivan, John L. 19, 69, 71
Sutthoff, Jack 128
Sutton, Larry 174
Swartwood, Ed 79–80, 187
Swartz, Christian 4
Swartz, Elizabeth 4
Sweeney, Bill 162

Taft, William Howard 171
Tannehill, Jesse 83, 88, 100–1, 116
Taylor, Jack B. 54
Taylor, Jack W. 108, 129

Taylor, John I. 133
Taylor, Luther "Dummy" 98, 127–29, 140, 145, 154
Tebeau, George 36
Tebeau, Patsy 36, 59
Tener, John 9
Tenney, Fred 66, 75, 160–61, 163
Terry, Adonis 29, 37
Tesreau, Jeff 189–90, 192, 197
Thomas, Roy 96, 228n
Thomas, Walt 165
Thompson, Sam 29
Thornton, Walter 39, 50
Tiernan, Mike 21
Tinker, Joe 58, 115, 150, 212–16
Tooley, Bert 178, 181, 183, 185
Truby, Harry 41
Turner, Tuck 29
Tuthill, Harry 149

Unglaub, Bob 131–32

Van Haltren, George 9, 42, 75, 77
Vaughan, Arky 212–16
Von der Ahe, Chris 18, 22, 35
Von der Horst, Harry 60, 109, 117

Waddell, Rube 78, 83–85, 145–46, 229n
Wagner, Honus 2, 67–68, 78, 83, 93–94, 99–100, 118–20, 135, 142–43, 153–54, 158, 182, 207, 212–16, 228n
Wagner, J. Earle 6
Wallace, Bobby 2, 65, 101, 209–16
Ward, John Montgomery 24, 26, 79, 118, 137, 212–16
Ward, Rube 106
Warner, Jack 130, 141
Washington, George 66
Watson, George H. 117
Weimer, Jake 151
Werden, Perry 50
Wheat, Zack 171–72, 174–75, 177–78, 181, 185, 191, 195, 198, 201
Wheeler, Ed 105–7
Wicker, Bob 106, 128
Wilhelm, Kaiser 172
Williams, Jimmy 85, 94, 132–33
Williams, Pop 105
Williamson, Ned 9
Willis, Vic 105
Wilmot, Walt 12, 37, 40–41, 155

Wiltse, George "Hooks" 124, 145, 155, 159, 164, 180
Wilson, Art 187–89
Woods, Walt 55, 68

Yastrzemski, Carl 207
Yeager, Joe 68, 75
Yerkes, Stan 108
Yingling, Earl 185

York, Tom 6
Young, Cy 10, 65, 93, 175, 223n
Young, Irv 163
Young, Nicholas 6, 35–36, 78, 84, 103, 106, 110
Yount, Robin 207, 212–16

Zimmer, Chief 85, 130–31, 154
Zimmerman, Eddie 178, 181–82, 185